DATE DUE

DEMCO 38-296

RICHARD RODNEY BENNETT

Richard Rodney Bennett. Photo courtesy of Richard Bennett.

RICHARD RODNEY BENNETT

A Bio-Bibliography

Compiled by
Stewart R. Craggs

Bio-Bibliographies in Music, Number 24
Donald L. Hixon, Series Adviser

Greenwood Press
New York • Westport, Connecticut • London

Library of Congress Cataloging-in-Publication Data

Craggs, Stewart R.
  Richard Rodney Bennett : a bio-bibliography / compiled by Stewart
R. Craggs.
    p. cm.—(Bio-bibliographies in music, ISSN 0742-6968 ; no.
24)
  Discography: p.
  Includes bibliographical references.
  ISBN 0-313-26179-2 (lib. bdg. : alk. paper)
  1. Bennett, Richard Rodney—Bibliography. I. Title. II. Series.
ML134.B4425C7   1990
  016.78′092—dc20   89-23674

British Library Cataloguing in Publication Data is available.

Library of Congress Catalog Card Number: 89-23674
ISBN: 0-313-26179-2
ISSN: 0742-6968

First published in 1990

Greenwood Press, Inc.
88 Post Road West, Westport, Connecticut 06881

Printed in the United States of America

The paper used in this book complies with the
Permanent Paper Standard issued by the National
Information Standards Organization (Z39.48-1984).

10 9 8 7 6 5 4 3 2 1

To Val,
with love

Contents

Preface

Richard Rodney Bennett is one of Britain's most
distinguished, versatile, and prolific twentieth century
composers, his music ranging across a wide spectrum of styles
from opera and ballet through orchestral and chamber music to
jazz. He is therefore a most appropriate subject for the
Greenwood Press composer bio-bibliography series.

The present volume, the first-ever to be published about
Bennett, attempts to document his vast and ever increasing
output. I am, however, aware that there are works missing
from the list, including juvenilia (Bennett has been writing
music since he was six), and I would be very grateful if any
readers could contact me through Greenwood Press should they
know of the existence of any of these works so that they can
be included in any future edition.

It consists of the following:

(1)   a short biography;

(2)   a list and details of works and performances, classified
      by genre and then arranged alphabetically by title of
      composition. Following each title are particulars of a
      work's first and other selected performances, with
      reference to commentaries from reviews listed in the
      "Bibliography".

      I have endeavoured to examine original manuscripts in
      order to obtain much of the information given. Some I
      have not seen, particularly the film and incidental
      music scores.

      Each work is prefaced by a mnemonic "W" and each
      performance of that work is identified by successive
      lower case letters. I seriously considered including a
      section on Bennett's many arrangements of music by other
      composers (Berlin, Coward, Gershwin, Kern to name but a
      very few) but, without the help of Mr. Bennett to
      provide the necessary documentation, this proved an
      impossible aim. One or two recordings of arrangements
      are however included in the appropriate section.

(3) a select <u>discography</u> of commercially produced
     long-playing records.   Each recording is listed
     alphabetically by title, and each work prefaced by a
     mnemonic "D".   Reference is made to reviews of the
     recordings cited in the "Bibliography" and,

(4) an annotated <u>bibliography</u> of writing by and about
     Richard Rodney Bennett, his style and his music, with
     annotations often taking the form of quotations taken
     from reviews.   Each citation is preceded by the mnemonic
     "B".   Entries in the Bibliography refer to "Works and
     Performances" and "Discography" sections.

In   addition,   appendices   provide   alphabetical   and
chronological listings of Bennett's works.   A complete
general <u>index</u> of names (personal and corporate) concludes the
volume.

Acknowledgments

Many people and institutions have contributed to the preparation of this volume. In particular, I should like to extend special thanks to the following individuals.

For providing specialised assistance:
Robin ANDERSON, Promotions Manager, Universal Edition, London; John BETHELL, founder of the International Double Bass Competition and Workshop; Susan BRADSHAW, colleague and friend of the composer; Anne BUNDOCK, for translating much material for me; Helen CHARLTON and colleagues, for obtaining copies of much material; Anne-Marie DABROWSKA, PA to the Cheltenham Festival Administrator; Tim DAY, Curator of Western Music at the National Sound Archive; Giles EASTERBROOK, of Novello & Co., Howard FERGUSON, former teacher of the composer; John MANDUELL, Programme Director of the Cheltenham Festival; Bryan MARSON-SMITH, of the City Music Society; Celia NEWMAN, PA to Richard Pulford of the South Bank Centre, London; Caroline OAKES, managing director of the Clarion Concert Agency Ltd., Richard POPPLEWELL, organist of the Chapel Royal, St. James's Palace; George RIZZA, Managing Director, Novello & Co.; Christopher ROBINSON, Assistant Keeper of the Theatre Collection, University of Bristol; Rowena SKELTON-WALLACE, of Lemon & Durbridge Ltd.; Fiona SOUTHEY, of Novello & Co for many kindnesses; Rosamund STRODE, Keeper of Manuscripts and Archivist, the Britten-Pears Library, Aldeburgh; Lawrence TAGG, of Newcastle City Libraries to whom I owe a great debt of gratitude; Jeremy TYNDALL, Cheltenham Festival Administrator; Judith VAN NOATE, Humanities Librarian, J. Murrey Atkins Library, UNC-Charlotte, North Carolina, Paul WILSON, former Librarian, the Britten-Pears Library, Aldeburgh and Andrew WYLLIE, of EMI Music Publishing Ltd.

For providing specialised bibliographical assistance:

Fiona ARMSTRONG, Head of Reference and Information Services, Edinburgh Public Library; Mrs. E.P. ARTHUR, Archive Office, Royal Opera House, Covent Garden; Paul BARRITT, leader of Divertimenti; Jim BERROW, executive producer, Central Independent Television; Miss E.A. BIRD, Music Librarian, University College of North Wales, Bangor; Mrs. M. BUTLER,

Fishguard Music Festival; Robin CARLOW, Harvard University Archives; Llyena F. BOYLAN, Executive Director, Lehigh Valley Chamber Orchestra; Christopher BUNTING; Teresa CARROLL, Area Librarian, Milton Keynes; Graham CHAMBERS, BBC TV Music Library; Sue CLARK, Manager - Music Services, Yorkshire TV; Yvonne COPE, Area Librarian, Slough; Malcolm COTTLE, London Concord Singers; Jacqueline COWDREY, Royal Albert Hall; Richard COWNDEN, BBC TV Music Library; PM Curtis, Assistant Senior Librarian, Maidenhead Library; Janet DORMER, Survival Anglia, Ltd; Richard DRAKEFORD, Little Missenden Festival; Richard EVANS, Chief Executive, Bath International Festival; FARNHAM FESTIVAL Director; Levi FOX, Director, the Shakespeare Birthplace Trust; Carole GARNER, Opera North; Renee C. GINGRAS, Denver Symphony Orchestra; Alan W. GODFREY, Consumer Relations Manager, Beecham Bovril Brands; Matthew GREENALL, British Music Information Centre Manager; GUILDHALL Library, London; Louis HALSEY; Simon HALSEY; Mike HAMBELTON, Shell-Film and Video Unit; Siri Fischer HANSEN, Secretary to Sam Wanamaker, Shakespeare Globe Centre; Miss J.M. HARPER, Chief Librarian, Birmingham Post and Mail; A.D. HARRIS, Hon. Secretary, Bromsgrove Festival; Mrs. Pat HARRISON, Little Missenden Festival;; Suzanne HARTIN, St. Louis Symphony Orchestra; Mrs. A. HEAP, Local History Librarian, Leeds City Libraries; Rt. Hon. Edward HEATH; Skip HUMPHRIES, Head of Music Services, LWT; Garry HUMPHREYS, Chairman, the English Song Award; Peter ISHERWOOD, Director, Coventry Centre for the Performing Arts; Mrs. J. JAMES, Area Librarian, Newbury; Philip JONES; A. JOYCE, Reference Library, Bath; Lina LALANDI, English Bach Festival Trust; Mary LONGLEY, Secretary, the Haddo House Choral & Operatic Society; Linda MARSDEN, Music Librarian, Cheltenham Library; Margaret MARTON, Cleveland Plain Dealer; Margaret MATICKA, Head of Reader Services, University of New English, Armidale, NSW; Gary W. MILLER, Music Director, New York City Gay Men's Chorus; Mrs. Jean MORRIS, Librarian, Worcester Evening News; Michael NICHOLAS, organist, Norwich Cathedral; Francesca NORBERG, Office Manager, 92 Y St. Performing Arts; Robert OLSON, Professor of Music, University of Colorado at Boulder; Simon ORBELL, Edinburgh International Festival, Glynn PERRIN; Jeanne PHILLIPS, WUNC, Chapel Hill, NC; Pauline PLEASANCE, Burgh House Trust; Thomas J. PNIEWSKI, Hunter College City, University of New York; Kaye S. PRENTICE, Librarian, Coventry Technical College; Gail REITANO, Archivist, ICA; Tim REYNISH; Michael J. ROGAN, Reference Librarian, Music Department, Boston Public Library; Elizabeth ROLT, Secretary, Seaton and District Music Club; St.JOHN'S, SMITH SQUARE; Margaret SANDERS, Librarian, Information Services, Worcester City Library; Dennis SAYER, Administrator, Portsmouth String Quartet Competition; Elizabeth SCHAAF, Archivist, Peabody Conservatory of Music; Wilhelm SCHLUTER, Internationales Musikinstitut, Darmstadt; Darrel SCHULTZ, Denver Post Library; Andrew SHENTON, Director of Music, St. Matthew's Church, Northampton; Rosemary L. SMITH, Concerts Secretary, University of York; Joan L. SORGER, Head of Main Library, Cleveland Public Library; George STEPHENSON, Director, Mid Northumberland Arts Group; Rosalind TATHAM, Leighton Park School; John THORN, Divisional Librarian, Portsmouth; Deidre TILLEY; Evelyn TROOP, Administrative Assistant, Newbury Spring Festival; Pierre VIDAL, Department of Music,

Bibliotheque Nationale; M. WALSHAW, Secretary, Keele Concerts Society; Alan WILKINSON, Director, King's Lynn Festival; Rosemary WILLIAMSON, Music Librarian, University of Nottingham; Clive WILSON, Festival Director, Harrogate International Festival; Christopher WILTSHIRE; WINDSOR FESTIVAL; D. WITHNEY, Finsbury Reference Librarian, Ruzena WOOD, Research Assistant, National Library of Scotland; J. WRIGHT, Dorian Wind Quintet; Elizabeth WYVALL, Secretary to the Director of Music, King's College, Cambridge, and the YORKSHIRE POST.

Finally I must thank the ERMULI Trust for assistance given towards my researches for this volume, Pauline LOMAX for typing most of my correspondence and Mrs. Helen CRUTE and the ladies of the The Secretariat for producing a magnificent script yet again from my illegible jottings.

Biography

Richard Rodney Bennett was born on 29 March 1936 (a birthday he shared with Sir William Walton) at Broadstairs in Kent. His father, Royden Barrie, was a writer of children's books and lyrics for songs, some of which were set by another English composer, Eric Coates (1886 - 1957).

Bennett's mother was a composer in her younger days. She knew Holst, whose student she was, John Ireland and Constant Lambert; her speciality was playing the works of Debussy and Ravel. Indeed Bennett told Elmer Bernstein that his mother '...wrote lyrical chamber music... influenced by Debussy quite a lot. This was around 1920 when that was quite an advanced thing to do. She performed in student circles but gave it up when she married my father. She went on to be a music reviewer and worked as an accompanist.'(1)

The war years were spent in Devon where Bennett recalls that '...my father believed that children shouldn't be given toys but that they should be given things to create things with so we were given paper and paints and manuscript paper.... I entertained myself by pretending to write music.'(2)

Bennett was also given records of contemporary music of the time including the Walton Viola Concerto, Constant Lambert's Rio Grande and Benjamin Britten's Serenade. However, it was Walton who remained a most important influence on him.(3)

From 1949 to 1953, Bennett was educated at Leighton Park School, Reading (Reckitt House) and then took a scholarship to the Royal Academy of Music in London where he studied with Lennox Berkeley and Howard Ferguson. It can be seen in the list of works that Bennett had already written a String Quartet (W75) and a Theme and Variations for Violin and Viola (W111), and was, by the age of 16, composing 12-note music when this technique was still hardly taken seriously. While still a schoolboy, he had piano lessons from Elizabeth Lutyens.

Of his student days, Bennett has said that '... apart from the fact that I had two marvellous composition teachers - Lennox Berkeley and Howard Ferguson - I learnt absolutely

nothing of any kind. The playing of works was not encouraged
in anyway.'(4) Bennett was lucky however in that he '... got
into film music quite early on and this enabled me to be
immediately in a professional environment for which I craved.
My teacher Howard Ferguson kindly introduced me to a man
named John Hollingsworth who was a very fine musical director
in the cinema and concert conductor, and he gave me a
documentary on insurance to do.'(5)

Bennett has also recalled that 'I fitted all my classes into
one day, because I had so few, and in any case this saved on
bus-fare. We cut most of the classes in theory and were not
obliged to take exams. At no time was I taught counterpoint,
except what I later taught myself, musical appreciation,
keyboard harmony, the standard repertoire, conducting (in
fact I endeavoured to take lessons in conducting but was
informed that this could wait until my fourth year, by which
time I had left) and there were no classes in contemporary
music of any description whatever. We soon realised that
the only way of finding out about all the exciting things
that were going on in the Continent was... to go there. From
about 1955 onwards I attended the Darmstadt Summer School and
for the first time came in contact with Stockhausen, Boulez,
Maderna, Nono, Pousseur and Berio.'(6)

In 1957, Bennett won a French government scholarship and went
to Paris, and for the next two years studied privately with
Pierre Boulez. 'He was the first musician I had ever met who
really took me apart, who questioned everything I did, who
demanded to know why I had used such and such a technique - I
had always assumed that any technical innovation was fair
game for my own uses. He taught me to find out what I was
really about, to examine what was mine and what I was merely
borrowing to find out how I "looked" in it. When I presented
him with an industrious piece of classroom analysis he would
ask me WHY the composer had found it necessary to write like
this - and I had no answer. I could not see beyond the bare
bones of the technique; I was thinking theory, not music. I
believe he helped me to begin to understand what kind of
musical personality I had - if any.'(7) Later Bennett (with
Susan Bradshaw, a fellow student), wrote analytical studies
of Boulez's music and translated his <u>Penser la musique
aujourd'hui</u> (as <u>Boulez on Music Today</u>).

Returning to London in 1959, Bennett soon established himself
as one of Britain's most brilliant prolific, successful and
versatile composers and performers. He made his home there
for the next twenty years, apart from a year spent as
composer-in-residence at the Peabody Institute, Baltimore.
He was made a CBE in 1977. Then in 1979 he moved to New York
in order to 'get away from the musical life in London', which
Bennett has called 'seductive'.(8) Another reason was 'to
get away from the various musical committees', a reason,
incidentally, which also made Sir William Walton leave London
in the early 1950s for Ischia. Bennett has obviously found
America a better place to work and as with Thea Musgrave and
Peter Racine Fricker it has not disturbed the flow of
creativity.

Bennett had first met Thea Musgrave at Dartington Summer School in 1953 when he was 17; she had just returned from Paris and her studies with Nadia Boulanger. Since then they have not only been linked by friendship and collaboration (for instance Bennett helped Miss Musgrave to prepare the tapes used in her opera, The Voice of Ariadne) but also by shared attitudes and approaches to certain types of compositions. Both have been preoccupied with the combination of electronic sound and live performer, and both with the introduction of dramatic elements into abstract music.

In a recent interview, Bennett revealed that he and Miss Musgrave had shown new compositions to each other for many years, and described how he had come to trust her assessment and views about them which he called 'fair and objective'. Bennett also revealed how he had 'got stuck at the end of a cadenza in my Oboe Concerto for up to six to eight weeks, not knowing which way to go' and had finally consulted Thea Musgrave. 'There are very few people to whom I would do that!'(9)

Most of Bennett's concert works, major or minor, have been listed and commented upon; but Bennett's lighter (so-called) achievements - his film scores, his extended jazz works, his popular song and arrangements - have received much less attention from the critics. Yet it is probably in these areas of endeavour that he has reached his greatest public. Although his more popular public image is that of a composer and performer of serious music, he is in private an expert jazz pianist - jazz is Bennett's hobby and his passion. This led in August 1975 (at the 3-Choirs Festival in Worcester) to the formation of a duo, the collaboration with the Mississippi-born jazz and blues singer, Marian Montgomery. Together they have built up a large repertoire of popular songs from the 1920s to the present including American classics, blues, Gershwin, Porter, Sondheim, all arranged by Bennett, and many of his own songs, ingeniously integrated into their very popular and sophisticated show 'Just Friends'. This unique duo has since been in heavy demand at theatres and festivals all over the world.

Other arrangements include some further Gershwin transcriptions for the King's Singers; Rodgers, Porter and Weill arrangements for Eartha Kitt (and the Nash Ensemble), one of a number of singers for whom he has acted as accompanist - others include the Norwegian jazz singer Karin Krog and the American popular singer Chris Connor; Kern arrangements for the horn player Barry Tuckwell; and a Noel Coward anthology for the 1970 Aldeburgh Festival.

Arlen, Barnes, Berlin, Clarke, Loesser, Newman, Novello and Romberg are another batch of composers whose songs and other works have received similar treatment. An early interview with Bennett underlines this passion for jazz:

'...I joined an audience... in a small, bare hall almost beyond the fringe of the Edinburgh Festival. Already

under way was one of those bright little shoe string
revues....

Through the cigarette smoke I could see a jazz group –
guitars, bass and drums – on the platform, and below
them a young pianist was conjuring from a modest upright
a cool jazz arrangement of Softly as in a morning
sunrise [Romberg]. Then I looked at the pianist again.
Could it be? Yes, beyond a doubt it was composer
Richard Rodney Bennett forsaking Boulez for Beat.

'When I was a student, I earned my living by playing
jazz,' he explained.... 'My serious work doesn't leave
much time for it now, but these people are friends of
mine, and this is fun.'

The show, for which he had also written the musical
arrangements, was a late night relaxation for Bennett
....'(10)

What of the future? Bennett has admitted that he is a better
composer then he used to be. He does not however wish to
compose any more opera, but would rather write more vocal
music.(11)
'I hope I am a composer who provides music which is beautiful
to listen to and which people can use, because one without
the other is to me only a half way stage.
My only ambition is to go on being wanted... I want to feel
that my music will go on being wanted. I want the
commissions to go on coming in because it suggests that I'm
actually there for some purpose. I don't like the idea of
composition as a sort of self indulgence and if nobody asked
me to write music anymore it would be tragic for me because
I'd think I didn't have a function anymore....'(12)

1.   Elmer Bernstein. 'A Conversation with Richard Rodney
     Bennett' Film Music Notebook, 2(1) 1976, p.16
2.   Interview with RRB in Crossover: Richard Rodney Bennett.
     Televised on ITV Network, 17 May 1987
3.   In a letter to the present author [dated 26 July 1976],
     Bennett wrote: "He was my first childhood influence – I
     had the Primrose 78s of the Viola Concerto when I was
     very young, and I still feel that this work is a
     masterpiece".
4.   Interview with RRB and Michael Oliver, marking Bennett's
     50th birthday. BBC Radio 3, 23 March 1986
5.   Interview with RRB in Crossover: Richard Rodney Bennett.
     Televised on ITV Network, 17 May 1987
6.   Richard Rodney Bennett, 'A Changing Musical World or The
     Circus Moves On' Peabody Notes, XXIV(2) November 1970,
     p.1
7.   ibid.
8.   Interview with RRB and Michael Oliver, marking Bennett's
     50th birthday. BBC Radio 3, 23 March 1986
9.   Interview with RRB and Michael Oliver, marking Thea
     Musgrave's 60th birthday. BBC Radio 3, 22 May 1988
10. Eric Mason. 'Night Beat'
     Music and Musicians, 12 (October) 1963, p.42

11. Interview with RRB and Michael Oliver, marking Bennett's
     50th birthday. BBC Radio 3, 23 March 1986
12. Interview with RRB in Crossover: Richard Rodney Bennett.
     Televised on ITV Network, 17 May 1987

Works and Performances

"See" references, e.g. See: B133, identify citations in the "Bibliography" section.

I.   OPERAS

   W1.   THE LEDGE (Mills Music Ⓒ 1963; c. 28 mins.)

         Opera in one act. Libretto by Adrian Mitchell
         Commissioned by Rostrum Ltd. See: B50

         3 singers/1+1.1.1+Eb and bc.1/2.1. tenor and
         bass trombones.1/timp. and perc.(3)/piano and
         celesta/hp/strings

         Dedicated to Anthony Wright

         The action takes place in a big city. On a
         ledge projecting from a large office building
         stands a young man...
         Introduction   (Molto animato)
         Scene 1:Afternoon   (Tempo rubato)
         Interlude   (Molto animato)
         Scene II:Night   (Lento esitando)
         Epilogue:Dawn   (Molto adagio e calmo)

         The score is dated: London xii 60 - iii 61

         Premiere

   W1a   1961 (12 September): London; Sadler's Wells
         Theatre;
         Joe   Gerald English
         The Other Man   John Cameron
         Joe's wife   Dorothy Dorow
         The English Chamber Orchestra (leader, Emanuel
         Hurwitz), conducted by Alexander Gibson
         Producer : John Blatchley
         Designer : Timothy O'Brien
         Lighting : Charles Bristow
         See: B12,B101,B104,B213,B327,B352

Other selected performances

W1b   A German translation of the libretto, by Walter
       Bergmann, is included in the published vocal
       score. The translation of the title in the
       vocal score is Am Abgrund, whilst in the
       manuscript it appears as Am Rande.

       The first performance in Germany took place in
       Krefeld. See: B5, B247

W2.   THE MINES OF SULPHUR (Universal Edition ©1966; 104
       mins.)

       Opera in three acts. Libretto by Beverley Cross
       German translation by Kurt Herrmann
       Commissioned by the Sadler's Wells Opera Trust.
       See: B55,B85,B161,B303,B340

       9 singers/2+1.2.2+bc.2/4+1(behind).2.3.1./timp./
       perc.(3)/piano and celesta/hp/strings

       Dedicated to Benjamin Britten

       The action takes place in the hall of a manor
       house in the West Country, the home of Braxton.
       Time: A winter's night, some 200 years ago.

       Act I
       No.1 : Introduction   (Moderato ma agitato)
          2   (Doppio movimento)
          3   (Allegro)
          4   (Presto)
          5   (Poco lento e libero)
          6   (Allegretto grazioso)
          7   (Lento)
          8   (Poco allegro)
          9   (Allegretto grazioso)
         10   (Lento e molto espr.)

       Act II
       No.11 : Overture   (Molto vivace)
         12   (Alla marcia)
         13   (Recitativo)
         14   (Duetto : Allegretto)
         15   (Aria : Lento e dolce)
         16   (Agitato)
         17   (Rubato)
         18 : Interlude   (Molto vivace)
         19   (Alla marcia)
         20 : Nocturne I   (Allegretto lirico)
         21   (Vivace)
         22   (Tempo libero)
         23 : Nocturne II   (Appassionato)
         24   (Allegro)
         25 : Nocturne III   (Molto lento)
         26   (Presto)
         27   (Liberamente, ma con moto)
         28   (Lento ma non troppo)

```
            29                      (Moderato quasi recit.)
        Act III
        No.30                       (Molto agitato)
            31                      (Allegro)
            32
            33                      (Poco lento)
            34                      (Piu mosso, liberamente)
            35                      (Poco allegro)
            36                      (Moderato ma agitato)
            37                      (Poco lento)
            38                      (Recit)
            39                      (Poco lento, semplice)
            40                      (Senza misura)
```
The score is dated: London, Aldeburgh, Penn, Edinburgh. April-Nov 1963

Premiere

W2a   1965 (24 February): London; Sadler's Wells Theatre;

Braxton, a landowner   Frank Olegario
Rosalind, a gypsy   Joyce Blackham
Boconnion, a deserter   Gregory Dempsey
Tovey, a tramp   Gwyn Griffiths
Sherrin, a manager (in the play: the Count)
                        Harold Blackburn
Jenny, an actress (in the play: Haidee)
                        Catherine Wilson
Leda, an actress   (in the play: Mrs Traxel)
                        Ann Howard
Fenney, an actor   (in the play: Hugo)
                        David Hillman
Tooley, an actor   (in the play: a Flunkey)
                        David Bowman
Trim, a mute   John Fryatt

The Sadler's Wells Theatre Orchestra, conducted by Colin Davis.
Producer: Colin Graham
See:B33,B108,B131,B166,B216,B272,B294,B322,B328, B356,B375,B383

Other selected performances:

After the premiere, the Sadler's Wells Company took The Mines of Sulphur to Zagreb and Paris in May 1965, and it was again included in their London repertoire in November 1965.

W2b   1966 (25 February): Milan; La Scala; cast included Gloria Lane (Rosalind): Floriana Cavalli (Jenny); Giovanni Gibin (Boconnion); Alvinio Misciano (Fenney) and Armanda Bonato (Leda). Theatre Orchestra conducted by Nino Sanzogno Scenery: Corrado Cagli
Producer: John Huston. See: B185, B345

W2c   1967 (17 March): Cologne; the Opera House - under the title of Ballade im Moor.

Cast included Barbara Scherler (Rosalind); Patricia Cullen (Jenny); Maura Moreira (Leda) and Gregory Dempsey (Boconnion).
Opera Orchestra conducted by Christoph von Dohnanyi
Scenery: Max Bignens
Producer: Hans Neugebauer. See: B219,B228,B290

W2d   1967 (September): Stockholm; the Drottningholm Court Theatre - under the title of The Uninvited Guest.
Cast included Elisabeth Söderström (Jenny); Edith Thallaugh (Rosalind) and Arne Tyren (Braxton/Sherrin).
Glyndebourne Opera Orchestra conducted by Bryden Thomson
Scenery: C.J. Ström
Producer: Göran Gentele. See: B95

W2e   1968 (17 January): New York; Juilliard School of Music Concert Hall, 130 Claremont Avenue, New York City;

Braxton	Alan Ord
Rosalind	Barbara Shuttleworth
Boconnion	Robert Jones
Tovey	Muneo Okawa
Sherrin	Robert Shiesley
Jenny	Evelyn Mandac
Leda	Janet Wagner
Fenney	Michael Best
Tooley	Arthur Thompson
Trim	Hal Walters

Juilliard Opera Theatre Orchestra, conducted by Jean Morel
Scenery: Douglas Schmidt
Costumes: Hal George
Lighting: Sidney Bennett
Producer: John Houseman. See: B3,B129,B230, B248,B350

W2f   1973 (27 September): London; the London Coliseum;

Braxton	Bryan Drake
Rosalind	Shirley Chapman
Boconnion	Gregory Dempsey
Tovey	Norman Welsby
Sherrin	Dennis Wicks
Leda	Ann Howard
Fenney	Terry Jenkins
Tooley	David Bowman
Jenny	Lois McDonall
Trim	John Fryatt

Sadler's Wells Opera Orchestra, conducted by David Lloyd-Jones
Scenery: Alix Stone
Lighting: Charles Bristow
Producer: Colin Graham. See: B106,B174,B276,B329

W2g   1980 (27 March): Leeds; the Grand Theatre;

Braxton	Philip Summerscales

Rosalind	Fiona Kimm
Boconnion	Robert Ferguson
Tovey	Thomas Lawlor
Sherrin	Eric Garrett
Leda	Ann Howard
Fenney	Mark Hamilton
Tooley	Michael Lewis
Jenny	Sally Burgess
Trim	John Fryatt

English National Opera North Orchestra,
conducted by Clive Timms
Scenery: Alix Stone
Lighting: Charles Bristow
Producer: Colin Graham
See: B79,B81,B122,B215,B226,B264

W3. A PENNY FOR A SONG (Universal Edition © 1967; 110
mins.)
Opera in two acts. Libretto by Colin Graham,
adapted from the play by John Whiting (1917-1963).
German translation by Kurt Herrmann. Commissioned
by Sadler's Wells Opera Trust with the help of the
Calouste Gulbenkian Foundation.

11 singers/2.2.2.2/2.2.2.0/timp./perc.(3)/piano and
celesta/hp/strings. Stage ensemble: harpsichord,
trumpet and drum

The scene is the garden of Sir Timothy Bellboys'
house in Dorset. The time is early morning of a
day in the summer of the year 1804. See: B60, B70,
B165

ACT I
Morning
Introduction : orchestra (Molto moderato e
                         tranquillo)
Scene I   (Allegretto)
      II   (Poco lento)
      III   (Andante tranquillo)
      IV   (Agitato)
      V   (Allegretto amabile)
      VI   (Moderato recitando)
      VII   (Lento e libero)
      VIII   (Molto moderato)
      IX   (Allegretto)
      X   (Alla marcia)
      XI   (Andante)
      XII   (Vivace)

ACT II
Later in the day
Introduction : orchestra (Molto vivace)
      XIII   (Poco meno mosso)
      XIV   (Poco allegro)
      XV   (Agitato)
      XVI   (Alla marcia)
      XVII   (Tranquillo)
      XVIII   (Andante comodo)
      XIX   (Poco allegro)

```
XX                  (Molto vivace)
XXI                 (Contenerezza)
XXII                (Adagio)
Act I is dated  : 20. viii.66
Act II is dated : Islington 4.xi.66
```

Premiere

W3a   1967 (31 October): London; Sadler's Wells Theatre;

William Humpage	Harold Blackburn
Pippin (a maid)	Iris Saunders
Sir Timothy Bellboys	John Fryatt
Lamprett Bellboys	
(Timothy's brother)	Eric Shilling
Hester Bellboys	
(his wife)	Joan Davies
Dorcas Bellboys	
(their daughter)	Margaret Neville
Edward Sterne	Alan Charles
A Little Boy	Anthony Westall
Hallam Matthews	Emile Belcourt
Samuel Breeze	
(Hallam's man)	Stafford Dean
George Selincourt	Denis Dowling
The Reverend	
Joseph Brotherhood	Leigh Maurice
James Giddy	Allen Chapman
Rufus Piggott	Neville Griffiths

The Sadler's Wells Orchestra (leader: Barry Collins), conducted by Bryan Balkwill
Designer : Alix Stone
Lighting : Charles Bristow
Producer : Colin Graham
See: B39,B42,B109,B132,B162,B204,B268

Other selected performance:

W3b   1968 (26 January): Munich; the National Theatre – under the title of Napoleon Kommt.

Humpage	Raimund Grumbach
Pippin	Gertrud Freedman
Sir Timothy Bellboys	Gerhard Stolze
Lamprett	Max Proebstl
Hester	Martha Mödl
Dorcas	Ingeborg Hallstein
Edward Sterne	Hans Wilbrink
A Little Boy	Georg Gross
Hallam Matthews	Richard Holm
Samuel Breeze	Albrecht Peter
George Selincourt	Kieth Engen
The Reverend	
Joseph Brotherhood	Carl Hoppe
James Giddy	Karl Ostertag
Rufus Piggott	Willibald Schwister

The National Theatre Orchestra, conducted by Christoph von Dohnanyi
Designer : Leni Bauer-Ecsy
Producer : Günther Rennert
See: B210,B238,B349

W4. <u>VICTORY</u> (Universal Edition © 1970; 112 mins.)

Opera in three acts. Libretto by Beverley Cross, based on the novel by Joseph Conrad (1857-1924). Commissioned by The Friends of Covent Garden. <u>See</u>: B89,B127,B134,B135,B223, B288

13 Singers/3.2.2+bc.2+db/4.3.3.1/timp./perc.(3) /piano(doubling celesta)/hp/strings
Act I only:
<u>Ladies Orchestra</u> (on stage):flute, violin, cello, mandoline, guitar and accordion.

Dedicated to Hans Werner Henze

Act I : The courtyard of Schomberg's hotel in
          Surabaya
          1895 : Dutch East Indies.
          (Moderato)
Act II : Scene 1 - The Island of Samburan -
                    before Heyst's bungalow in a
                    clearing above the beach.
                    (Molto moderato)
          Scene 2 - The Card room at Schomberg's
                    hotel. (Stesso tempo)
Act III : The Island of Samburan. (Molto
          moderato)

Act I is dated   : 26.xi.68
Act II is dated : 23.iv.69
Act III is dated : Islington. August 68 - July
                   8. '69

Premiere

W4a   1970 (13 April): London; the Royal Opera House, Covent Garden;

Schomberg, (a hotel-keeper)	Inia te Wiata
Frau Schomberg (his wife)	Avia June
Zangiacomo (Manager of a Ladies' Orchestra)	Kenneth Macdonald
Lena (an English girl)	Anne Howells
First Sailor	David Lennox
Mr. Jones (a professional gambler)	John Lanigan
Martin Ricardo (Jones' "secretary")	Michael Maurel
Pedro (Jones' bodyguard)	Anthony Chinn
Axel Heyst (an intellectual recluse)	Donald McIntyre
Captain Davidson	Edgar Evans
Two Singing-girls	Susan Maisey Celia Penney
Koen	Eric Garrett

(a dutch planter)
First mate   David Whelan
First clerk   Clifford Starr
Second clerk   William Clothier
A Customs Officer   Brian Holmes

The Royal Opera House Orchestra (leader: Charles Taylor) and Chorus (chorus master: Douglas Robinson), conducted by Edward Downes
Designer : Alix Stone
Lighting : William Bundy
Producer : Colin Graham
See: B133,B155,B347,B351

Other selected performances:

W4b   The first performance in Germany took place in June 1970 when the Royal Opera performed Victory in Berlin.
       See: B229,B257

II. BALLETS

W5. <u>ISADORA</u> (Unpublished but handled by Novello; 120 mins.)

Ballet in two acts with choreography by Kenneth Macmillan. Scenario by Gillian Freeman.
Commissioned by the Royal Ballet Company.
<u>See</u>:B124,B128,B232,B372,B373

2+1. 2+1 .2+bc+Eflat cl.alto sax.+ten.sax.2/
4.3.2+1.1/timp./perc.(3)/piano   (doubling
celesta)/hp/strings; on stage: 1+1.0.2.sax.1
/0.1.1.1/perc.(2)/piano/str.1.0.0.0.1; chorus on
tape.

Dedicated to Fred Sadoff
(Macmillan dedicated the ballet to Miss Phyllis Adams)

ACT I
Scene 1 - The seashore at Nordwyck (Senza
           misura)
      2 - Liverpool Street Station (Vivo)
      3 - The New Gallery, Regent Street
           (Inquieto)
      4 - Berlin (Andante affetuoso)
      5 - Budapest (Drammatice)
      6 - Craig's Studio (Adagio)
      7 - Nordwyck (Con moto appass.)
      8 - Isadora's School (Inquieto)
      9 - St. Petersburg Station   (Vivo)
     10 - Nordwyck (Sostenuto appass.)

ACT II
Scene 1 - Nice (Senza misura/Vivace)
      2 - Singer's House (Allegretto grazioso)
      3 - Russian Station (Vivo)
      4 - Singer's House (Quasi cadenza/con
                           moto)
      5 - Isadora's School (Allegro giusto)
      6 - Paris: Singer's House (Mesto)
      7 - The Funeral Procession (Marcia
                              funebre)
      8 - Seashore at Vicireggio (Lento e dolce)
      9 - Singer's House: August 1914 (Lento)
     10 - Montage (Adagio)
     11 - Russian Station (Poco lento)
     12 - 1st Party in Russia (Molto vivo)
     13 - The Maryinsky Theatre (Allegro
                              maestoso)
     14 - 2nd Party in Russia (Allegretto
                              ritmico)
     15 - Transition to America -
           (Interlude) (Alla marcia, ritmico)
     16 - Boston Theatre (Alla marcia)
     17 - Nice   (Vivace)
     18 - Epilogue   (Vivace)

Act I is dated : New York City - September 27
'80

Act II is dated : Los Angeles - December 17 '80

Premiere

W5a   1981 (30 April): London; the Royal Opera House,
       Covent Garden;
       ACT I
       Isadora   Merle Park
       Her Mother   Julie Wood
       Her Brother   Robert Jude
       Her Sister   Rosalind Eyre
       Her Favourite Pupil   Jennifer Jackson
       Her Children
       Deidre and Patrick   Alison Coburn
                                Brian Godfrey
       A Sailor   Graham Fletcher
       Ballet Dancers   Rosalyn Whitten
                                Judith Howe
                                Genesia Rosato
                                Bryony Brind
                                Deirdre Eyden
                                Wendy Groombridge
                                Pippa Wylde
       Spanish Dancers   Sally Inkin
                                Graham Fletcher
       Loie Fuller   Laura Connor
       Nursey   Monica Mason
       Oskar Beregi   Derek Deane
       Edward Gordon Craig   Julian Hosking
       Russian Station   Genesia Rosato
                                Judith Howe
                                Michael Batchelor
                                Anthony Dowson
                                with artists of the Royal
                                Ballet

       ACT II

       Paris Singer   Derek Rencher
       Isadora's Rival   Sally Inkin
       Tango Boy   Ashley Page
       Andre Caplet   Garry Grant
       Max Merz   David Drew
       Her Pupils   Madonna Benjamin
                                Jennifer Jackson
                                Gillian Kingsley
                                Julie Lincoln
                                Karen Paisey
                                Julie Rose
       Man on the Beach   Ross MacGibbon
       Sergei Esenin   Stephen Jefferies
                                with artists of the Royal
                                Ballet
       The Royal Opera House Orchestra (leader:
       Santiago Bravo), conducted by Barry Wordsworth
       Pianists: Anthony Twiner/Henry Roche

Recorded voices by the ROH Male Chorus, conducted by John McCarthy
Scenery and costumes : Barry Kay
Lighting : John B. Read
See: B16,B119,B370

W6.   NOCTUARY

(Unpublished, but handled by Novello; 27 mins.)
(Variations on a theme of Scott Joplin for piano solo)
Ballet in one act with choreography by Kenneth Macmillan

Dedicated to Franklin Underwood

Noctuary: A diary of the events of night. This piece is based on three sections of Scott Joplin's Solace - A Mexican Serenade (1909) for piano.

Tema I :	Andante Variation I	-
Tema II:	— Variation II	Appass.
Tema III:	— Variation III	A tempo, con calore
	Variation IV	Grazioso
	Variation V	Con tristezza
	Variation VI	Animando
	Variation VII	Scherzando
	Variation VIII	Grotesco
	Variation IX	Arioso (Doppio valore)
	Variation X	Inquieto
	Variation XI	Minaccianado
	Variation XII	Alla toccato
	Variation XIII	Sospeso
	Variation XIV	Presto (tempo molto giusto)
	Finale -	Lento e lontano.

The score is dated: New York City, July 1 - 28 1981

Premiere

The first performance, planned for Tuesday, 2 March 1982, by Sadler's Wells Ballet at its home theatre in London was postponed.

Other selected performances:

W6a   1985 (3 June) : Armidale, New South Wales, Australia; University Hall, University of New England; John McCabe (piano). See: B26

W6b   1985 (3 August) : Harrogate; Lounge Hall; John McCabe (piano) (First English performance)

W6c   1985 (5 August) : Ripon; the Cathedral Church of
       St. Peter and St. Wilfred; John McCabe (piano).
       See: B225

III. ORCHESTRAL MUSIC

W7. ACTAEON (Novello ⓒ 1980; 20 mins.)
(Metamorphosis I) for horn and orchestra. See:
B224, B344

> 2+1.2+1.2+2.2/3.3.3.1/timp./perc.(3)/piano
> (doubling celesta)/hp/strings
>
> Dedicated to Barry Tuckwell, for whom it was
> written
>
> Adagio – Allegro ritmico – Pastorale – Presto –
> Adagio
>
> The score is dated : Barnsbury Sept–Oct '76,
>   March–April '77

Premiere

W7a 1977 (12 August): London; the Royal Albert Hall;
Barry Tuckwell (horn); BBC Symphony Orchestra;
Walter Susskind, conductor. See: B179,B357,
B368

W8. ANNIVERSARIES (Novello ⓒ 1986; 17 mins.) for
orchestra
Commissioned by the British Broadcasting
Corporation to celebrate its sixtieth Anniversary

> 2+1.2+1.2+1.2+1/4.3.3.1/timp./perc.(3)/piano
> (doubling celesta)/hp/strings.
>
> Dedicated to my friend Bud Bazelon for his
> sixtieth birthday
>
> 1. Vivo e declamato
> 2. Episode 1 (Woodwind): Leggiero e fantastico
> 3. Con fuoco
> 4. Episode 2 (Tuned Percussion, Piano,Harp):
>   Drammatico
> 5. Arioso
> 6. Episode 3 (Strings): Appassionato
> 7. Tranquillo
> 8. Episode 4 (Percussion): Con brio
> 9. Brilliante
> 10. Episode 5 (Brass): Strepitoso
> 11. Finale: Vivo e declamato
>
> [The score is dated: New York City May 1982]

Premiere

W8a 1982 (9 September): London; the Royal Albert Hall;
BBC Symphony Orchestra; James Loughran,
conductor. See: B297

W9. AUBADE (Universal Edition ⓒ 1965; 10½ mins.) for
orchestra

Commissioned by the British Broadcasting Corporation for the 1964 season of Promenade Concerts.
See: B168

2+1.2.2.2/4.2.3.1/timp./perc.(3)/celesta/hp/
strings

Dedicated to the memory of John Hollingsworth

'Aubade' (morning song), in one movement, is
built in a simple arch-form "... around an
atmospheric and cadenza-like central section."
The score is headed by a quotation for John
Donne's Sermon LXXIII.

The score is dated : Islington 24.iv.64

Premiere

W9a   1964 (11 September): London; the Royal Albert
       Hall; BBC Symphony Orchestra; John Carewe,
       conductor. See: B11,B13,B110,B311,B320

W10.   CONCERTO FOR CLARINET (B-flat) and STRING ORCHESTRA
       (Unpublished, but handled by Novello; 18 mins.)
       Commissioned by Keele Concerts Society with funds
       from West Midlands Arts

       0.0.0.0/0.0.0.0/str: 8 6 4 4 2
       Dedicated to Michael Collins, for whom it was
       written.

       1. Aria (Andante molto)
       2. Capriccio (Con brio)

       The score is dated: New York City Nov-Dec '87

Premiere

W10a   1988 (15 February): Keele; University Chapel;
       Michael Collins (clarinet); Orchestra da Camera;
       Philip Jones, conductor

W11.   CONCERTO FOR DOUBLE-BASS AND CHAMBER ORCHESTRA
       (Novello ©1978; 20 mins.)
       Commissioned by the Secretariat of the 1978 Isle of
       Man International Double-Bass Competition (in
       August 1978) with funds provided by the Calouste
       Gulbenkian Foundation of Lisbon

       0.2+1.0.0/2.0.0.0/str: 6 5 4 3 2

       Declamato
       Quasi cadenza, drammatico
       Elegiaco
       Quasi cadenza, liberamente con fantasia
       Energico

The score is dated: London 22.vi.78

Premiere

W11a 1978 (15 October): London; Queen Elizabeth Hall;
      Jiri Hudec (double bass) – the winner of the
      1978 Isle of Man International Double Bass
      Competition –; the English Chamber Orchestra;
      Michael Tilson Thomas, conductor. See: B333

W12. CONCERTO FOR GUITAR AND CHAMBER ENSEMBLE (Universal
     Edition ©1971; 20 mins.) See: B231

     1+1.1+1.1.0/1.1.0.0/perc.(2)/celesta/violin/
     viola/cello
     The composer acknowledges the help of Michael
     Blake Watkins, in the score, for his valuable
     advice on guitar technique

     Dedicated to Julian Bream

     Lento e rubato – Vivo – Con brio

     [The score was completed in September 1970]

     Premieres

W12a 1970 (18 November): London; Queen Elizabeth Hall;
      Julian Bream (guitar); the Melos Ensemble of
      London; Andre Previn, conductor. See: B259,B300

W12b 1971 (25 October): New York; Alice Tully Hall;
      Julian Bream (guitar); instrumental ensemble;
      Christopher Keene, conductor

W13. CONCERTO FOR HARPSICHORD AND ORCHESTRA (Novello ©
     1982; 22 mins.)
     Commissioned by the St. Louis Symphony Orchestra in
     celebration of it centenary

     2+1.2+1.2+2.2/2.2.2.1/timp./perc.(3)/piano
     (doubling celesta)/hp/strings

     I.   Con moto, tranquillo
     II. Adagio maestoso
     (segue)
     III. Presto; Tranquillo; Molto vivo

     The score is dated: New York – Los Angeles
     May–July '80

     Premieres

W13a 1980 (4 December): St. Louis; Powell Symphony
      Hall; Richard Rodney Bennett (harpsichord); St.
      Louis Symphony Orchestra; Leonard Slatkin,
      conductor

W13b 1982 (27 October): Liverpool; Philharmonic Hall;
      Richard Rodney Bennett (harpsichord); Royal
      Liverpool Philharmonic Orchestra; Charles
      Groves, conductor

W14. CONCERTO FOR HORN AND ORCHESTRA
     (Unpublished, but handled by Universal Edition; 9
     mins.)

     Unable to trace instrumentation

     1. Allegro Maestoso
     2. Adagio sostenuto
     3. Allegro con brio

     This concerto was written in 1955-6, when
     Bennett was 19. It was inspired by Dennis Brain
     who at 36 in 1957 was killed in a car crash.

     Premiere

W14a 1967 (18 February): London; Royal Festival Hall;
      Ifor James (horn); London Philharmonic Orche-
      stra; Trevor Harvey, conductor

W15. CONCERTO FOR MARIMBA AND CHAMBER ORCHESTRA
     (Unpublished, but handled by Novello; 16 mins.)
     Commissioned by William Moersch

     2+1.1+1.1+1.1/2.2.0.0/perc.(1)/hp/strings : 7 6
     4 4 2

     I.   Con moto
     II.   Con brio

     The score is dated: New York City January 17 '88

     Premieres

W15a 1988 (11 March): Allentown; Muhlenberg College
      Center for the Arts; William Moersch (marimba);
      Lehigh Valley Chamber Orchestra; Donald Spieth,
      conductor

W15b 1988 (17 March): New York; Alice Tully Hall,
      Lincoln Center; William Moersch (marimba);
      Lehigh Valley Chamber Orchestra; Donald Spieth,
      conductor. See:B233

W16. CONCERTO FOR OBOE AND STRING ORCHESTRA
     (Universal Edition © 1973; 16 mins.)
     Commissioned by the English Chamber Orchestra and
     Music Society

     0.0.0.0/0.0.0.0/str : 8 6 4 4 2

     Dedicated to Heinz Holliger, for whom it was
     written

I.   Vivo
II.   Adagio
The score is dated: London/Berlin
                    Dec 13th '69-May 6th '70

Premieres

W16a 1971 (6 June):Snape; the Maltings; Heinz Holliger
      (oboe); the English Chamber Orchestra; Paul
      Sacher, conductor. See: B153, B256

W16b 1972 (11 February): London, Queen Elizabeth Hall;
      Heinz Holliger (oboe); the English Chamber
      Orchestra; Raymond Leppard, conductor. See:
      B138,B381

W17. CONCERTO FOR ORCHESTRA
      (Novello ©1974; 23 mins.)
      Commissioned by the Denver Branch of the English
      Speaking Union.
      In homage to Benjamin Britten on his 60th birthday,
      Bennett took, as the abstract musical starting-
      point of this work, the twelve-note series used by
      Britten in one movement of his Cantata Academica.
      See: B44

          2+1.2+1.2.2+1/4.3.3.1/timp./perc.(3)/piano
          (doubling celesta)/hp/strings

          I.   Aubade   (Vivo)
          II.   Adagio - Presto spettrale - Adagio
          III. Variations - Tema (Presto)
                Var I   (Leggero) woodwind and high
                                     strings
                Var II   (Molto agitato) horns
                Var III   (Misterioso) tremolo strings
                Var IV   (Strepitoso) brass
                Var V   (Quasi campane) 'like bells'
                Var VI   (Appassionato) upper strings
                Var VII   (Scherzando) percussion
                Var VIII   (Brillante) woodwind and brass
                Finale   (Molto ritmico-Maestoso)

          The score is dated:
          End of movement I   - 11.viii.73
          End of movement II   - 23.x.73
          End of movement III - 15.viii.73
          Barnsbury, June - October '73

Premieres

W17a 1974 (25 February): Denver; Auditorium Theatre;
      Denver Symphony Orchestra; Brian Priestman,
      conductor. See:B151

W17b 1974 (28 June): London; the Royal Festival Hall;
      Royal Liverpool Philharmonic Orchestra; Charles
      Groves, conductor. See:B46

W18. CONCERTO No.1 FOR PIANO AND ORCHESTRA
(Universal Edition © 1969; 25 mins.)
Commissioned by the Feeney Trust for the City of
Birmingham Symphony Orchestra. See:B221, B361

2.2.2.2/4.3.3.1/timp./perc.(3)/celesta/strings

Dedicated to Stephen Bishop

1.   Moderato
2.   Presto
3.   Lento
4.   Vivo
(The fourth movement follows the third without a
break)

The score is dated : Penn   Easter Day 1968

Premiere

W18a 1968 (19 September): Birmingham; the Town Hall;
Stephen Bishop (piano); City of Birmingham
Symphony Orchestra; Hugo Rignold, conductor.
See: B258, B274

W19. CONCERTO No.2 FOR PIANO AND CHAMBER ORCHESTRA(1976)
Despite intensive research, and this work being
included in some lists of compositions, I have been
unable to trace any details

W20. CONCERTO FOR [ALTO] SAXOPHONE AND STRING ORCHESTRA
(Unpublished but handled by Novello; 16 mins.)
Commissioned by Leslie Bishop for John Harle and
London Musici

Str 6 4 3 2 1

Dedicated to John Harle

I.   Molto vivo
II.   Interlude : Andante
III.   Allegro - lento

The score is dated: New York City
                    July-September '88

Premiere

W20a 1988 (14 October): London; St. John's, Smith
Square; John Harle (saxophone); London Musici;
Mark Stephenson, conductor.

W21. CONCERTO FOR VIOLA AND CHAMBER ORCHESTRA
(Novello © 1975; 16 mins.)
Commissioned by the Northern Sinfonia for Roger
Best

1.1+1.1+1.1/2.0.0.0/str : 6 5 3 3 2

Con fuoco

The score is dated: March-May 28th '73
Malibu-Santa Barbara-
St.Louis-New York-London

Premieres

W21a   1973 (3 July): York; Central Hall of the
University; Roger Best (viola); Northern
Sinfonia; David Atherton conductor. See:B82,
B83,B235

W21b   1974 (15 March): London; Queen Elizabeth Hall;
Roger Best (viola); Northern Sinfonia; Rudolf
Schwarz, conductor. See:B74

W22.   CONCERTO FOR VIOLIN AND ORCHESTRA
(Novello © 1977; 22mins.)
Commissioned by the Feeney Trust and the West
Midlands Arts Association for the City of
Birmingham Symphony Orchestra

2+1.2+1.1.2/4.2.2+1.1/timp.(3)/perc.(3)/piano
(doubling celesta)/hp/strings

Dedicated to Ralph Holmes

I.   Allegro
'So look the mornings when the Sun
Paints them with fresh Vermilion...'
Robert Herrick (1591-1674): The Maiden
blush

II.   Andante lento
'...Time
Throned in a saffron evening, seems to
chime
All in...' idem : Epithalamion

The score is dated:
End of movement I - N.Y.C. May '75
End of movement II - New York City - Long Island
- London May 1-September 4
'75

Premieres

W22a   1976 (25 March): Birmingham; the Town Hall; Ralph
Holmes (violin); City of Birmingham Symphony
Orchestra; Louis Fremaux, conductor. See: B41,
B125

W22b   1976 (31 March): London, the Royal Festival Hall;
Ralph Holmes (violin); City of Birmingham
Symphony Orchestra; Louis Fremaux, conductor.
See: B36, B169,B176,B260

W23.   FIVE PIECES FOR ORCHESTRA
(Unpublished, but handled by Universal Edition; 9½
mins.)

2+1.2+1.2+1.2/3.2.3.1/timp./perc.(3)/strings

Dedicated to Howard Ferguson [fellow composer, and one of Bennett's teachers at the RAM]

1 : Maestoso - Molto moderato
2 : Molto agitato
3 : Poco adagio, elegiaco
4 : Scherzando
5 : Declamato - Lento e dolce

The score is dated: Devon-London, Sept-Oct 1956

Premieres

W23a 1956 (13 July): Darmstadt; Seminar Marienhöhe; Chamber Orchestra of the Cologne Academy of Music; Maurits Frank, conductor (Four pieces were played).
According to a programme note, written by the composer, the first of these pieces is based on one rhythmic figure, the second on 12 durations, the third on two rhythmic groups and the fourth consists of an introduction, based on four durations, and five variations based on their superposition in the introduction.

W23b 1960 (4 July): Cheltenham; the Town Hall; London Symphony Orchestra; Colin Davis, conductor See: B156

W24. FREDA'S FANDANGO FOR ORCHESTRA
A contribution to A Bouquet for Lennox [Berkeley] : 15 Variations on the "Reapers' Chorus" from "Ruth". Commissioned by the Cheltenham Festival (Unpublished, but handled by Novello; 1 min.)

As an 80th birthday tribute to Sir Lennox Berkeley, President of the Cheltenham Festival, John Manduell, the Programme Director of the Festival and himself a former pupil of Berkeley's , asked 15 other composers, all of whom had also studied composition under Sir Lennox Berkeley, each to contribute to this 'Bouquet'. The rules of entry were that each should write a variation on the Reapers' Chorus theme taken from the opening of Scene 2 of Berkeley's one-act opera Ruth. The maximum duration permitted was one minute, and the maximum orchestration was that of the full symphony orchestra as used by Webern in his Passacaglia Op.1.

John Manduell received all the contributions and put them in order as well as providing an orchestration of the introduction and statement of the theme. [Cheltenham Festival Programme, 1983]. Bennett's variation appeared as no. 13 (no. 12 in the score) and also embraced Freda, the wife of Sir Lennox Berkeley.

1+1.1+1.2.2/2.2.1+1.0/timp.(3)/perc.(2)/hp/
strings

Dedication: for Lennox's 80th birthday

Con eleganza

The score is dated: New York City Nov 16 '82

Premiere

W24a 1983 (2 July): Cheltenham; the Town Hall; Philhar-
      monia Orchestra; Brian Priestman, conductor.
      See: B241

W25. INTRADA FOR ORCHESTRA
      A contribution, with five other composers (Malcolm
      Arnold, Peter Maxwell Davies, Nicholas Maw, Thea
      Musgrave and Robert Simpson) on Happy Birthday to
      You, written to celebrate the 70th birthday of Sir
      William Walton. (Unpublished, but handled by
      Universal Edition; 50 secs.)

          2+1.2+1.2.2/4.3.2+1.1/timp.(4)/perc.(3)./ piano/
          hp/strings

          Dedication: for Sir William Walton on his
          seventieth birthday, [followed by the first 6
          notes of Happy Birthday to You]

          Molto vivo

          The score is dated: Baltimore 3 Dec '70

      Premiere

W25a 1972 (29 March): London; Royal Festival Hall;
      Richard Rodney Bennett (piano); London Symphony
      Orchestra; Andre Previn, conductor

W26. JOURNAL FOR ORCHESTRA
      (Mills Music ©) 1970; 13½ mins.)

          2+1.1.1+1.1/2.1.1.1/timp./perc.(3)/celesta/hp/
          strings

          Dedicated to Richard Narozny

          I.   Andante
          II.   Con moto
          III.   Poco allegro
          IV.   Molto vivace
          V.   Lento

          [This work was written during the spring of
          1960]

      Premiere

W26a 1961 (13 July): Cheltenham; the Town Hall; BBC
      Symphony Orchestra; Norman del Mar, conductor.
      <u>See</u>: B318

W27. <u>MOVING INTO AQUARIUS</u> FOR ORCHESTRA
      (Unpublished, but handled by Novello; 14 mins.)
      Written in collaboration with Thea Musgrave.
      Commissioned by the Royal Philharmonic Society in
      association with the Arts Council of Great Britain

          2+1.2+1.2.2/4.3.2+1.1/timp./perc.(3)/piano/hp/
          strings

          Dedicated 'to Michael'

      This work was written in honour of Sir Michael
      Tippett's 80th birthday. It consists of six
      contrasted sections, played without a break:

  (i) Dreamy - marked in the score as Misterioso   (TM)
 (ii) Scherzo -   "   "   "   "   " Molto vivo (RRB)
(iii) Lyrical -   "   "   "   "   " Lento e lirico(RRB)
 (iv) Giocoso -   "   "   "   "   " Giocoso   (TM)
  (v) Sombre -   "   "   "   "   " Tristamente (TM)
 (vi) Rumbustious" "   "   "   "   " Finale: Allegro con
                                               brio (RRB)

      These sections are framed and linked by 4 chords,
      each contained within a minor seventh based on C
      natural.
      <u>Moving into Aquarius</u> is based on a small group of
      thematic fragments taken from Tippett's music - and
      used by kind permission of Messrs. Schott & Co Ltd.
      The fragments came from the following works:

(1)   The passage for three horns which opens the <u>Ritual
      Dances</u> from <u>The Midsummer Marriage</u>.
(2)   The four repeated Cs from the first movement of the
      <u>Second Symphony</u>.
(3)   The chromatic viola theme which opens the second of
      the <u>Ritual Dances</u>.
(4)   The negro spiritual <u>Go Down Moses</u> which Tippett
      uses in <u>A Child of Our Time</u> and which Thea Musgrave
      uses in her opera <u>Harriet, the Woman Called Moses</u>.
(5)   The short polyphonic passage for four horns which
      concludes the slow movement of Tippett's <u>Second
      Symphony</u>.
(6)   The cello theme from the 3rd movement of the
      <u>Concerto for Double String Orchestra</u>

      There are also certain "hidden" quotes from other
      works by Tippett.

      According to Bennett, it was decided that the piece
      should not be a series of variations on a theme of
      Tippett nor merely a festive Divertissement, and
      secondly that both composers wanted to preserve a
      strict anonymity. So, for example, the person who
      copied the full score of a section (see above for

details) was not necessarily the person who wrote
it.

The score is dated: Norfolk, Va., New York City
Nov-Dec 1984

Premiere

W27a 1985 (23 January): London; the Royal Festival
       Hall; London Symphony Orchestra; Richard Hickox,
       conductor (Tippett's 80th birthday concert).
       See: B275

W28. MUSIC FOR AN OCCASION
     (Unpublished, but handled by Mills Music; 13 mins.)
     Commissioned by Associated Television

     Unable to trace the instrumentation

     According to the programme note the work was
     composed of three sections, each in Rondo form:
     Allegro-Molto; Moderato-Allegro; Deciso. The 'b'
     section of the first rondo was developed into
     the 'a' section of the second, and the third
     rondo contained elements of the first two. Thus
     the whole work was in a chainlike form.

Premiere

W28a 1959 (4 June): London; the Royal Festival Hall;
       London   Philharmonic   Orchestra;   William
       Steinberg, conductor. (A NATO International
       Celebrity Concert). See: B22

W29. MUSIC FOR STRINGS
     (Novello © 1981; 16 mins.)
     Commissioned jointly by the Cheltenham Festival and
     the Academy of St. Martin-in-the-Fields with funds
     provided by the Arts Council of Great Britain

     Str. 6 4 2 2 1 or 8 6 4 4 2

     Dedicated to Elizabeth Maconchy

     I.   Arioso
     II.   Vivo
     III.   Elegiaco
     IV.   Presto

     The score is dated: Barnsbury, Oct-Dec. '77

Premieres

W29a 1978 (7 July): Cheltenham; the Town Hall; The
       Academy of St. Martin-in-the-Fields; Neville
       Marriner, conductor. See: B113

W29b 1984 (5 February): London; Shaw Theatre; Divertimenti String Orchestra; Steuart Bedford, conductor

W30. NOCTURNES FOR CHAMBER ORCHESTRA
(Unpublished, but handled by Mills Music; 13 mins.)
Commissioned by the 1963 Cheltenham Festival

1.1.1.1/1.0.0.0/hp/strings

Dedicated to Meredith Davies

I. Appassionata - prefaced by a quote from Elegie XVI on his Mistris - "O my love is slaine" : John Donne

II. Dolce amabile - prefaced by an anonymous 14th century quote - "All night by the rose I lay"

III. Dolente - prefaced by a quote from Urn Burial: Sir Thomas Browne

[The work was written between 1962 and 1963]

Premieres

W30a 1963 (March): Vancouver; the BBC Chamber Orchestra; Meredith Davies, conductor

W30b 1963 (9 July): Cheltenham; the Town Hall; English Chamber Orchestra; Meredith Davies, conductor. See: B19,B157,B158,B378

W31. SERENADE FOR SMALL ORCHESTRA
(Novello © 1977; 14 mins.)
Commissioned by the London Celebrations Committee for the Queen's Silver Jubilee, 1977

2+1.2.2.1/2.2.1.0/timp.(3)/perc.(3)/piano/stings

Dedicated to my Mother

I.   Aubade   (Allegro)
II.   Siesta   (Lento)
III. Nocturne (Molto vivace)

The score is dated : London, Copenhagen, Nov-Dec'76

Premiere

W31a 1977 (24 April): London; the Royal Albert Hall; Orchestra of the Royal College of Music; David Willcocks, conductor (the 5th National Festival of the Schools Music Association)

W32. SINFONIETTA FOR ORCHESTRA
(Unpublished, but handled by Novello; 10 mins.)
Commissioned by the National Federation of Music

Societies for their 50th Anniversary with funds
provided by the Arts Council of Great Britain

2+1.2.2.2/2.2.0.0/timp.(3)/perc.(1)/piano/
strings

Vivo-Lento e dolce - Con brio

The score is dated: New York City March 10 -
April 10 '84

Premiere

W32a 1985 (16 February): St. Ives; the Free Church
      Centre; the Huntingdonshire Philharmonic
      Orchestra; Christopher Brown, conductor

W33. SONNETS TO ORPHEUS FOR CELLO AND ORCHESTRA
     (Novello ⓒ 1985; 30 mins.)
     Commissioned for the Edinburgh Festival (1979) with
     funds provided by the Arts Council of Great Britain

     2+1.2+1.2+2.2+1/2.2.2.1/timp./perc.(3)/piano
     doubling celesta/2 hps/strings

     Dedicated to Dan Klein

     Each of the five movements of this work was
     suggested by lines taken from the Sonnets to
     Orpheus by Rainer Maria Rilke, translated by A.
     Poulin, Jr.

     I. Allegro
         "A tree sprang up. O sheet transcendance!
         O Orpheus sings!..."   [1,1]

        II. Capriccioso
             "And with tiny steps the clocks
             walk beside our primal day."   [1,12]

       III. Arioso
             "Erect no memorial store. Let the rose
             bloom every year to remind us of him" [1,5]

        IV. Molto animato
             "Only the Song above the land
             blesses and celebrates."   [1,19]

         V. Adagio
             "But the echo of your music lingered
             in rocks and lions, trees and birds. You
             still sing there."   [1,26]

     The score is dated: London - New York City Dec
     21 '78 - May 9 '79

Premiere

W33a 1979 (3 September): Edinburgh; Usher Hall;
      Heinrich Schiff (cello); Halle Orchestra; James
      Loughran, conductor. See: B186, B286

W34. STANZAS FOR ORCHESTRA (1959)
     Despite intensive research and this work being
     included in several lists of compositions, I have
     been unable to trace any details

W35. SUITE FOR SMALL ORCHESTRA
     (Universal Edition © 1966; 9 mins.)
     This suite has been adapted from two books of songs
     for children, The Aviary (W176) and The Insect
     World (W182), both published by Universal Edition.
     The vocal part may be sung in combination with the
     orchestral version.

         1.1.1.1/2.1.1.0/perc.(1)/harp (or piano)/strings

      I.   The Bird's Lament (Con moto)
           Origin : 'The Aviary', No.1
           Text : John Clare (1793-1864)

      II. The Widow Bird (Con tristezza)
           Origin : 'The Aviary', No.4
           Text : Percy Bysshe Shelley (1792-1822)

      III. The Ladybird (Alla valse, leggiero e
                             ritmico)
           Origin : 'The Insect World', No.4 (under
                     the title 'Clock-a-clay')
           Text : John Clare (1793-1864)

      IV. Glow worms   (Andante espressivo)
           Origin : 'The Insect World', No.3
           Text : Andrew Marvell (1621-1678)

      V.   The Lark   (Vivace)
           Origin : 'The Aviary', No.5
           Text : Samuel Taylor Coleridge (1772-1834)

     [This work was composed in 1965]

     Premiere

     Unable to trace

W36. SUITE FRANCAISE FOR SMALL ORCHESTRA
     (Mills Music © 1970; 7½mins.)

         1+1.1.2.1/2.1.1.0/timp./perc.(2)/hp/strings

     Dedicated to Thea [Musgrave]

         1. A l'ombre d'un buissonet (Andante)
         2. Triste est le ciel (Poco lento)
         3. Allons gay (Molto vivace)
         (French popular songs of the 15th and 16th
         centuries)

This suite was originally conceived as a setting for voices.

The score is dated: June 12th 1961

Premiere

W36a 1961 (27 October): Cardiff; BBC Studies; BBC Welsh Orchestra; Meredith Davies, conductor. This recording was subsequently played in the BBC Home Service on 6 November at 1200 hours

W37. SYMPHONY No.1 FOR ORCHESTRA
      (Universal Edition © 1966; 21 mins.)
      Commissioned by the Peter Stuyvesant Foundation for the London Symphony Orchestra. See: B63

      2+1.2+1.2+1.2/4.2.3.1/timp./perc.(3)/hp/strings

      The second movement (only) bears the inscription "to D.K."

      I.   Allegro
      II.   Andante
      III.   Molto vivace

      The score is dated:
      End of movement I   - 12.IX.65
      End of movement II   -   -
      End of movement III - Islington, Aug - Nov 1965

Premieres

W37a 1966 (10 February): London, the Royal Festival Hall; London Symphony Orchestra; Istvan Kertesz, conductor. See: B6,B163,B358,B382

W37b 1966 (3 April): New York; Philharmonic Hall; London Symphony Orchestra; Istvan Kertesz, conductor

W38. SYMPHONY No.2 (in one movement) FOR ORCHESTRA
      (Universal Edition © 1968; 19-20 mins.)
      Commissioned by the New York Philharmonic Orchestra in celebration of its 125th Anniversary. See: B87

      2+1.2+1.1.2+1/4.3.2+1.1/timp.(3)/perc.(3)/ piano (doubling celesta)/hp/strings

      Allegro - Moderato - Vivace

      The score is dated: London - Tuscany
                          June - Sept 1967

Premieres

W38a 1968 (18 January): New York; Philharmonic Hall; New York Philharmonic Orchestra; Leonard Bernstein, conductor. See: B365

W38b 1969 (20 February): London; the Royal Festival
      Hall; London Symphony Orchestra; Andre Previn,
      conductor. See: B102, B205,B323,B339,B360,B362

W39. SYMPHONY No.3 FOR ORCHESTRA
     (Unpublished, but handled by Novello; 22 mins.)
     Commissioned for the 1987 Three Choirs Festival by
     the Elgar Foundation with additional funds from
     West Midlands Arts. See: B184

     2.1+1.2.1/2.0.0.0/timp./perc.(2)/piano/hp/
     strings

     Dedicated to Edward Downes

     1.   Andante - Vivo
     2.   Allegretto
     3.   Adagio

     The score is dated: New York City - London
                                April - July '87

Premiere

W39a 1987 (24 August): Worcester; Cathedral Church of
      Christ and St. Mary; BBC Philharmonic Orchestra;
      Edward Downes, conductor. See: B227, B246,B389

W40. ZODIAC FOR ORCHESTRA
     (Novello ©1977; 17 mins.)
     Commissioned by the National Symphony Orchestra,
     Washington D.C., on the occasion of the USA
     Bicentennial celebrations

     3+1.2+1.3+1.2+1/4.3.2+1.1/timp.(3)/ perc.(3)/
     piano (doubling celesta)/hp/strings

     Dedicated to Elisabeth Lutyens for her 70th
     birthday, with love and admiration

     According to the composer, this work consists of
     twelve sections, each representing a sign of the
     Zodiac, framed by five ritornelli. Each
     section features a particular instrumental
     group, as follows:

     Ritornello 1 (Con fuoco) : brass

     THE SPRING SIGNS
     Aries (Stesso tempo): trumpets, trombones
     Taurus (Appassionato): violas, cellos, double
            basses
     Gemini (Scherzando): piccolo, flutes, clarinets,
            bass clarinet

     Ritornello 2 (Vivo): tuned percussion, piano,
                                harp
     THE SUMMER SIGNS
     Cancer (Adagio) : muted strings

Leo (Agitato) : horns, trombones, tuba
Virgo (Calmo) : flutes, oboes, clarinets

Ritornello 3 (Vivo) : strings

THE AUTUMN SIGNS
Libra   (Maestoso) : horns, tuba
Scorpio (Con malizia): oboes, cor anglais,
         bassoon, double bassoon
Sagittarius (Appassionato) : violins

Ritornello 4 (Vivo) : woodwind

THE WINTER SIGNS
Capricorn (Grotesco): cor anglais, bass
          clarinet, bassoons, double bassoon
Aquarius (Declamato): horns, trumpets
Pisces (Presto): strings

Ritornello 5 (Con fuoco) : full orchestra

The score is dated: London. Dec'75–June '76

Premieres

W40a 1976 (30 March): Washington D.C.; John F. Kennedy
      Center   for   the   Performing   Arts;   National
      Symphony Orchestra; Antal Dorati, conductor

W40b 1976 (27 August): London; the Royal Albert Hall;
      Royal   Philharmonic   Orchestra,   Antal   Dorati,
      conductor. See: B37, B178

IV. CHAMBER AND SOLO INSTRUMENTAL MUSIC

W41. AFTER ARIADNE FOR VIOLA AND PIANO
(Unpublished, but handled by Novello; 12 mins.)
Along with 'Lamento d'Arianna (1986) for string
quartet, After Ariadne is based on Monteverdi's
madrigal 'Lasciate Mi Morire'
Commissioned by Paul Silverthorne

Dedicated to Paul Silverthorne

Commoto - Lento - Mosso - Maestoso

The score is dated: New York City Oct. 23 '86

Premiere

W41a 1987 (7 July): Cheltenham; the Pittville Pump
Room; Paul Silverthorne (viola) and Richard
Rodney Bennett (piano). See: W388

W42. AFTER SYRINX I FOR OBOE AND PIANO
(Unpublished, but handled by Novello; 12 mins.)
'After Syrinx' is the first of a series of
compositions based on Claude Debussy's 'Syrinx' for
solo flute (1913).
Commissioned by the Seaton and District Music Club
with support from South West Arts

Dedicated to Malcolm Messiter

Adagio flessibile - Presto e leggiero -
(Scherzo I) - Cadenza I (Feroce) - Ballabile,
grazioso (Scherzo II) - Cadenza II (con fuoco) -
Adagio

The score is dated: New York City April 5 '82

Premieres

W42a 1983 (13 October): Seaton (Devon); the Town Hall;
Malcolm Messiter (oboe) and Clifford Benson
(piano). See: B14

W42b 1984 (1 April): London; Purcell Room; Robin Canter
(oboe) and Francis Routh (piano)

W43. AFTER SYRINX II FOR SOLO MARIMBA
(Unpublished, but handled by Novello; 10 mins.)
This piece is the second of a series of pieces
based on 'Syrinx' for solo flute (1913) by Debussy.
In the manuscript, the composer suggests that After
Syrinx II could be preceded by a performance (by a
flautist) of Debussy's 'Syrinx'

Dedicated to William Moersch

Molto moderato (capriccioso e poco rubato) –
Allegro – Lento con fantasia – Alla marcia,
grotesco – Tranquillo

The score is dated: New York City
February 11 '84
Revised March /85

Premieres

W43a 1984 (21 May): New York; Merkin Concert Hall;
William Moersch (marimba)

W43b 1985(3 December): Bury; Derby Hall Arts Centre;
Simon Limbrick (marimba)

W43c 1987 (12 April): London; Purcell Room; William
Moersch (marimba)

W44. ALBA FOR ORGAN
(Novello © 1978; 7 mins.)
Commissioned by the West Riding Cathedrals
Festival, with funds provided by the Arts Council
for Great Britain.
This work is based on the Tema Seriale from
Benjamin Britten's Cantata Academica; it also
exists in an orchestral version as the first
movement (Aubade) of Concerto for Orchestra (W17).
There is a note in the printed score which says
that the composer is indebted to Christopher Bowers
-Broadbent for his advice on organ registration.

Dedicated to Benjamin Britten on his sixtieth
birthday – 22 November 1973

Vivo

The score is dated: York – London
28 June – 10 July 1973

Premiere

W44a 1973 (3 November): Bradford, Cathedral and Parish
Church of St. Peter; Jonathan Bielby (organ)

W45. ANAGRAM (1970-71)
(Unpublished)

This is said to have been composed in the Peabody
Conservatoire Electronic Music Studio during the
composer's stay there. Other than that I have been
unable to trace any further details

W46. CALENDAR FOR CHAMBER ENSEMBLE
(Mills Music © 1970; 12 mins.)
According to the composer, this work represents "an
orderly arrangement of diversions in time"

1+1.0.1.1/0.1.1.0/timp./perc.(2)/piano/violin/
viola/cello

Dedicated to John Carewe

I.   Allegro
II.   Lento espressivo
III.   Molto animato

The score is dated:
End of movement I   : 16.IX.60
End of movement II   : 28.IX.60
End of movement III : London, Warsaw
                        IX - X, 1960

Premiere

W46a 1960 (24 November): London; BBC Studio 1, Maida
      Vale; the Melos Ensemble, the Goldsbrough
      Ensemble and members of the English Chamber
      Orchestra; John Carewe, conductor (A BBC
      Thursday Invitation Concert). See: B214

W47. A CANON FOR STRAVINSKY: FOR STRING TRIO
     (Unpublished, but handled by Universal Edition; 1½
     mins.)
     This is one of 12 compositions, written to
     celebrate Stravinsky's 85th birthday, which
     appeared in the Summer 1967 edition of TEMPO. The
     others were written by Birtwistle, Crosse, Davies,
     Dennis, Finnissy, Maw, Ogdon, Smalley, Souster,
     Tavener and Williamson

     Molto lento e dolce

     The score is dated: 28.3.67

Premiere

W47a 1967 (15 July): Cheltenham; Town Hall; Leonardo
      Ensemble (A Society for the Promotion of New
      Music Concert). See:B310, B390

W48. CAPRICCIO FOR PIANO (4 Hands)
     (Universal Edition ©1968; 6 mins.)

     Dedicated to Bob and Ben

     Vivo

Premiere

W48a 1969 (25 February): London; Purcell Room; Richard
      Rodney Bennett and Susan Bradshaw (piano). See:
      B116

W49. COMMEDIA I FOR SIX PLAYERS
     (Universal Edition © 1973; 15-16 mins.)

Commissioned by the 1972 English Bach Festival with funds made available by the Arts Council of Great Britain. See: B171

> Commedia I was suggested by the characters of traditional Italian and French comedy : though there is no 'plot', the instruments represent those characters (except in the Ensemble) as follows:
> Flute - Columbine
> Bass Clarinet (in B-flat) - Pantaloon
> Alto Saxophone (in E flat) - Harlequin
> Trumpet (in B-flat) - Punchinello
> Cello - Pierrot
> (plus percussion - 1 player)

> Dedicated to Sir William Walton [in honour of his 70th birthday]

1.   ENSEMBLE 1 : Con fuoco
2.   Solo 1 : Affetuoso. Cello
3.   Duo 1 : Stesso tempo. Bass Clarinet and Cello
4.   ENSEMBLE 2 : Grazioso
5.   Trio 1 : Sostenuto. Flute, Bass Clarinet and Trumpet
6.   Solo 2 : Improvisando. Alto Saxophone and Percussion
7.   Duo 2 : Stesso tempo. Alto Saxophone, Cello and Percussion
8.   ENSEMBLE 3 : Vivo
9.   Solo 3: Stesso tempo. Trumpet and Ensemble
10. ENSEMBLE 4 : Stesso tempo
11. Duo 3 : Liberamente. Flute and Bass Clarinet
12. Solo 4 : Improvisando. Bass Clarinet
13. Trio 2 : Drammatico. Alto Saxophone, Trumpet and Cello
14. ENSEMBLE 5 : Grazioso
15. Duo 4 : Amoroso. Flute and Alto Saxophone
16. Solo 5 : Elegiaco. Flute
17. ENSEMBLE 6 : Con fuoco

The score is dated: Barnsbury February - March
                                                    1972

Premieres

W49a 1972 (16 April): Oxford, the Town Hall; London Sinfonietta; William Walton, conductor. (A Walton 70th birthday concert). See: B114

W49b 1976 (9 February): Washington, D.C.; Folger Library; Twentieth Century Consort; Christopher Kendall, conductor

W50. COMMEDIA II FOR FLUTE, CELLO AND PIANO (Novello © 1975; 9 mins.)
Commissioned by the New York Camerata. See: B171

A note by the composer in the score says the
form of the four works entitled Commedia
(1972-3) is mosaic-like, composed of a number of
short, inter-related sections. The instruments
are thought of as actors in a play, meeting in
ensemble 'scenes' but also having monologues and
duologues. In this work, four closely-related
ensembles frame three groups of solos and duets.

```
ENSEMBLE:   Vivo
Solo  :  poco rubato      Flute
Duo   :  Molto tranquillo   Cello and Piano
ENSEMBLE:   Vivo
Solo  :  Drammatico      Piano
Duo   :  Lento           Flute and Cello
ENSEMBLE:   Vivo
Solo  :  Poco meno, sempre rubato   Cello
Duo   :  Adagio          Flute and Piano
ENSEMBLE:   Vivo
```

The score is dated: Barnsbury, 20 October 1972

Premieres

W50a 1973 (5 April): New York; Alice Tully Hall; New
      York Camerata

W50b 1978 (23 April): Boston; Museum of Fine Arts;
      Collage

W51. COMMEDIA III FOR 10 INSTRUMENTS
      (Novello ©1975; 17 mins.)
      Commissioned by the Nash Ensemble Society with
      funds provided by the Arts Council of Great Britain
      See: B171

      1+1.1+1.1.0/1.1.0.0/perc.(2)/piano+celesta/ vio-
      lin/cello (A suggested layout of instruments
      appears in the score)

      Dedicated, in admiration, to Leonard Rosenman

      According to the composer, the work consists of
      four main sections framing three cadenza-like
      passages, the first for woodwind, the second for
      the strings, and the third for the brass. The
      last section refers back increasingly to
      material used earlier, until finally the work
      come full circle and quotes from the opening.

      Con fuoco
        Quasi cadenza scherzando
      Vivo
        Quasi cadenza appassionato
      Elegiaco
        Quasi cadenza drammatico
      Con slancio

      The score is dated: London - Norway

10.i.73 - 6.ii.73

Premiere

W51a 1973 (25 February): London; Queen Elizabeth Hall;
        Nash Ensemble; Elgar Howarth, conductor. See:
        B117

W52. COMMEDIA IV FOR BRASS QUINTET
        (Novello © 1975; 13 mins.)
        Commissioned by the Malcolm Sargent Cancer Fund for
        the Philip Jones Brass Ensemble. See: B171, B206

            Trumpet 1 in C, Trumpet 2 in C, Horn in F; Tenor
            Trombone and Tuba (A suggested layout of
            instruments is provided in the score)

            In a note, the composer says that in this work,
            six brief ensembles frame five groups of solos,
            duets and trios; the form is symmetrically built
            around a central passage for solo horn

            Declamato
                Poco mosso (tr + horn)
            Ballabile
                Declamato - Drammatico (tr + trb + tuba)
            Notturno
                Ballabile (horn + tuba)
            Capriccioso
                - - -   (trb)
            Drammatico
                Capriccioso (tr - 2)
            Finale

        Premiere

W52a 1974 (27 April): London; Queen Elizabeth Hall;
        Philip Jones Brass Ensemble (Malcolm Sargent
        Birthday Concert)

W53. CONCERTO FOR WIND QUINTET
        (Novello © 1984; 17 mins.)
        Commissioned by the National Flute Association, the
        International Double Reed Society, the Interna-
        tional Clarinet Society and the International Horn
        Society

            Flute/piccolo, oboe, clarinet in B-flat, horn in
            F and bassoon

            I.   Poco allegro
            II.   Little elegy (Andante)
            III. Capriccio (Vivo e ritmico)

            The score is dated: New York City
                                Sept 6 - Oct 16 1983

Premieres

W53a 1984 (15 August): Roehampton; the Froebel
Institute; 'Fodor Quintet' (the 1984 International Clarinet Congress)

W53b 1984 (16 October); Washington D.C.; John F.
Kennedy Center for the Performing Arts; Dorian
Wind Quintet

W53c 1985 (11 August): Boulder, Colorado; College of
Music, University of Colorado; Colorado Wind
Quintet (14th Annual Conference of the
International Double Reed Society)

W53d 1986 (10 March): London; The Place; Phoenix Wind
Quintet

W54. CYCLE OF PIECES FOR PIANO : I - IX (1956-7)
(Unpublished)

No. IX is dedicated to Susan [Bradshaw]

The score is dated:
Nos. I - IV viii 56 - iii 57 London-Paris. A note
appears about No IV: the tempo of this piece is
as fast as possible determined by the smallest
note value.

No.	V	Paris 31.III.57
No.	VI	Paris 24.VI.57
No.	VII	Unable to trace
No.	VIII	14.IX.57
No.	IX(Tempo ad lib.)	n.d.

Premiere

W54a 1958 (25 January): Paris; Salle Gaveau; Paul
Jacobs (piano). (Nos. I,V,VI and VII) (Les
Concerts du Domaine Musical)

A note in the programme describes the pieces
thus:

No.I is based on sonorous, harmonising
complexes, limited in number; their mood varies
according to the modifications imposed on their
register, their length and their dynamics.

No.V is composed of three section, the third
being a kind of synthesis of the two others.

No.VI comprises firstly an introduction with
extemely varied elements, then a development
where these differences are reduced, and a final
section where the original elements tend to
blend together in a close simplification.

No.VII is a sequence of short sections, each one
suggesting an area defined by variations on the
initial themes.

W55. CYCLE II FOR PAUL JACOBS FOR PIANO (1958)
(Unpublished)

Cycle II was written in 1957 and 1958 when Bennett was studying with Pierre Boulez, and it is the only work written at that time which the composer considers to be of any value. The work is said to represent a reaction against abstract schemes of total serialisation.

The score is dated: Paris January – April 1958

Premiere

W55a 1958 (April): Paris; Galerie Claude Bernard; Paul Jacobs, (piano)

Other selected performances

W55b 1960 (June) : Cologne – ISCM Festival; Paul Jacobs (piano)

W55c 1960 (10 August): Tanglewood; Berkshire Music Centre; Paul Jacobs (piano)

W55d 1960 (16 October): Cornell University; Paul Jacobs (piano)

W55e 1960 (24 October): Harvard; Paine Hall, Harvard University; Paul Jacobs (piano)

W56. DUO CONCERTANTE FOR CLARINET (IN B-FLAT) AND PIANO
(Unpublished, but handled by Novello; 10 mins.)
Commissioned by the 1985 Cheltenham Festival, with additional funds from South West Arts and the Royal Overseas League, for Nicholas Cox and Vanessa Latarche

Presto con fuoco – Andante – Vivo

The score is dated: New York City
September 7 '85

Premieres

W56a 1986 (17 July): Cheltenham; Pittville Pump Room; Nicholas Cox (clarinet) and Vanessa Latarche (piano). See: B242

W56b 1986 (18 September): London; Royal Overseas League; Nicholas Cox (clarinet) and Vanessa Latarche (piano)

W57. DREAM DANCING FOR 13 PLAYERS
(Unpublished, but handled by Novello; 16 mins.)
Commissioned by the London Sinfonietta to celebrate the composer's 50th birthday [29.3.86]

In a note in the manuscript, Bennett writes that 'Dream Dancing' is scored for the instrumentation which Claude Debussy had planned to use for the last of his six late sonatas, of which only three were written. It is the 5th in a series of pieces based on Debussy's 'Syrinx' (1912) for solo flute.

1.1+1.1+1.1/1.1.0.0/harpsichord (lightly ampli-fied if necessary)/piano and celesta/hp/str: 1 0 1 1 1

Dedicated to Deborah and Kenneth [Macmillan], with love

I. Adagio tranquillo
    This movement is prefaced by lines from A Winter's Tale by Dylan Thomas:
                    "And the dancers move
    On the departed, snow bushed green,
                    wanton in moonlight
    As a dust of pigeons".

II. Molto vivo
    This movement takes lines from John Keats' The Eve of Saint Agnes:
                    "... the argent revelry
    with plume, tiara and all rich array,
    Numerous as shadows......"

In a programme note, Bennett adds that both movements contain interludes for the small chamber groups from Debussy's written and unwritten sonatas. The second movement, a fantastic scherzo, is based on the rhythmic structure of Debussy's 'Masques' (1904) for solo piano.
There are incidentially songs by both Cole Porter and Jerome Kern entitled Dream Dancing.

The score is dated:
End of movement I : January 7 [1986]
[it having been started in December 1985]

End of movement II : New York City
                      February 10 '86

Premieres

W57a 1986 (23 May): London; Queen Elizabeth Hall; London Sinfonietta; David Atherton, conductor. See: B392

W57b 1987 (10 May): New York; State University of New York at Purchase; members of the Purchase Symphony Orchestra; David Milnes, conductor

W58. FANFARE FOR BRASS QUINTET (1962)

(Unpublished, but handled by Mills Music; 2 mins.)
Written for Philip Jones, a gift from the composer

2 trumpets, horn, trombone and tuba

The score is dated: Islington, November 1962

Premiere

W58a   1963   (24   November):   Devizes   (Wiltshire);
       Dauntsey's School; Philip Jones Brass Ensemble:
       Philip Jones and Elgar Howarth (trumpets), Ifor
       James (horn), John Iveson (trombone) and John
       Fletcher (tuba)

W59. FANTASY FOR PIANO
     (Mills Music © 1963; 11 mins.)
     Commissioned   by   the   British   Broadcasting
     Corporation. See: B30, B53, B270

       Dedicated to John Brown

       I.   Poco allegro
       II. Molto lento
       III. Vivace

       [The Fantasy was completed in April 1962]

Premiere

W59a   1962 (7 June): Coventry; Central Hall; Liza
       Fuchsova (piano)
       (A Thursday Invitation Concert broadcast from
       the Coventry Festival). See: B27

W60. FIVE STUDIES FOR PIANO
     (Universal Edition © 1965; 15 mins.)
     See: B270

       Dedicated to Paul Jacobs and Yonty Solomon

       I.   Flessible, poco rubato
       II.   Presto e leggiero, mano destra
             (a study for the right hand only)
       III. Agitato
       IV.   Recitando, mano sinistra
             (a study for the left hand only)
       V.   Appassionato

       Numbers I,III and IV were written in 1962
       Numbers II and V were written in 1964
       The score is dated: Islington May 2/64

Premiere

W60a   1964 (27 October): London, Wigmore Hall; Yonty
       Solomon (piano)
       (The first public performance). See: B218

W61. FOUR IMPROVISATIONS FOR SOLO VIOLIN (1955)
     (Unpublished, but handled by Mills Music)

          I.   Molto moderato
          II.   Allegretto poco capriccioso spettrale
          III.   Appassionato
          IV.   Dolce

     Premiere

W61a 1956 (4 December): London; Wigmore Hall; Yfrah
     Neaman (violin)
     (A Society for the Promotion of New Music
     Concert) See: B283

W62. FOUR PIECE SUITE : DIVERTIMENTO FOR TWO PIANOS
     (Novello © 1984; 15 mins.)

          Dedicated to Andre Previn

          1. Samba triste (gentle and rhythmic)
          2. Country blues (Slow and lazy)
          3. Ragtime waltz : Homage to Scott Joplin
             (Moderate waltz time)
          4. Finale (Tempo di hard rock)

          (The individual movements may be performed
          separately)

          The score is dated:
          End of movement 1 : 6.V.74
          End of movement 2 : 12.V.74
          End of movement 3 : 17.V.74
          End of movement 4 : Barnsbury 21.V.74

     Premieres

W62a 1974 (31 August): London; BBC Studios; Richard
     Rodney Bennett and Susan Bradshaw (pianos).
     This recording was subsequently played in the
     BBC's Radio 3 on 3 October 1974

W62b 1975 (December): Sydney (Australia); Anthony
     Lindsay and Simon Young (pianos). The first
     public performance

W62c 1976 (8 June): London; Collegiate Theatre; Dance
     Prism – choreography by Jane Elizabeth Roberts
     and Gideon Avrahami (A ballet using the Four
     Piece Suite)

W63. IMPROMPTU FOR SOLO FLUTE
     (Unpublished, but handled by Universal Edition; 2½
     mins.)
     This is one of 11 compositions ('A Garland for Dr.
     K.), written to celebrate the 80th birthday of Dr.
     Alfred Kalmus (1889-1972) who was head of the
     publishing firm which bears his name and a director
     of Universal Edition.

The others were written by Bedford, Berio,
Birtwistle, Boulez, Halffter, Haubenstock-Ramati,
Pousseur, Rands, Stockhausen and Wood.

Comodo, espressivo e poco rubato

The score is dated: Islington. 31.3.69

Premiere

W63a 1969 (22 April): London; Queen Elizabeth Hall;
      Judith Pearce (flute)
      (The Boulez item, however, did not arrive in
      time for the concert and a section of Boulez's
      'Domaines' (in the version for solo clarinet)
      was substituted. The Boulez item was later
      performed privately at Dr. Kalmus' house and
      according to the composer no longer exists,
      except on the gramophone record - see
      discography (D20). See: B103, B265

W64. IMPROMPTU ON THE NAME OF HAYDN: FOR SOLO PIANO
      (Unpublished, but handled by Novello; 3 mins.)
      Commissioned by the BBC to celebrate Haydn's 250th
      birthday, this is one of 6 compositions ('Homage to
      Haydn'), the others written by George Benjamin,
      Lennox Berkeley, Robert Sherlaw Johnson, John
      McCabe and Edmund Rubbra

      Dedicated to John McCabe

      Andante flessibile

      The score is dated: New York City December 17
      '81

Premieres

W64a 1982 (18 March): London; BBC Studios; John McCabe
      (piano)
      This recording was subsequently played in the
      BBC's Radio 3 on 31 March 1982

W64b 1983 (4 January): New York; Merkin Concert Hall;
      Dorothy Lewis-Griffith (piano)

W65. IMPROMPTUS FOR GUITAR
      (Universal Edition © 1971; 8 mins.) See: B72,
      B231

      Dedicated to Julian [Bream]

      I.   Recitativo
      II.   Agitato
      III. Elegiaco
      IV.   Con fuoco
      V.   Arioso

      [The Impromptus were written in 1968]

The published score contains the notice: The composer is very grateful to Julian Bream for his valuable advice and encouragement

Premiere

W65a   1969 (11 June): Blythburgh; Parish Church of the Holy Trinity; Julian Bream (guitar)

W66.   A JAZZ CALENDAR: SEVEN PIECES (BASED ON THE TRADITIONAL RHYME) FOR TWELVE PLAYERS (Unpublished, but handled by Universal Edition; 31 mins.)
Commissioned by the BBC Third Programme. See: B52, B217

Flute, alto saxophone, tenor saxophone, baritone saxophone, 2 trumpets, horn, trombone (or bass trumpet), tuba, piano, bass and drums

Dedicated to Jean Hart

I.   "Monday's child is fair of face (fairly slow)
II.   Tuesday's child is full of grace (Medium up tempo, lightly)
III.   Wednesday's child is full of woe (Slow)
IV.   Thursday's child has far to go (Jazz waltz)
V.   Friday's child is loving and giving, (Slow and lazy)
VI.   Saturday's child works hard for its living (Medium tempo)
VII.   The child that is born on the Sabbath day is bonny and blithe and good and gay" (Up tempo)

The score is dated: Islington 28.3.64

Premieres

W66a   1964 (9 May): London; BBC Studios; John Scott (flute), John Dankworth (alto sax), Duncan Lamont (tenor sax), Ronnie Ross (baritone sax), Stan Roderick and Leon Calvert (trumpets), Alan Civil (horn), Ray Premru (bass trumpet), Ron Snyder (tuba), Alan Branscombe (piano), Kenny Napper (bass) and Alan Ganley (drums); Marcus Dods, conductor
This recording was subsequently played in the BBC's Third Programme on 5 June 1964. See:B371

W66b   1968 (9 January): London; the Royal Opera House, Covent Garden.
Arranged as a ballet and choreographed by Frederick Ashton, with scenery and costumes by Derek Jarman and lighting by William Bundy

Bennett had to add a tiny prelude to the
original suite in the form of three rising
arpeggio scales. See: B314, B377

Monday	Vergie Derman
Tuesday	Merle Park, Anthony Dowell, Robert Mead
Wednesday	Vyvyan Lorraine

Monday	Vergie Derman	
Tuesday	Merle Park, Anthony Dowell, Robert Mead	
Wednesday	Vyvyan Lorraine	
	Paul Brown,	David Drew
	Ian Hamilton	Derek Rencher
Thursday	Alexander Grant	Diana Vere
	Lesley Collier	Carole Hill
	Patrica Linton	Geraldine Morris
	Suzanna Raymond	
Friday	Antoinette Sibley	Rudolf Nureyev
Saturday	Desmond Doyle	
	Michael Coleman	Lambert Cox
	Frank Freeman	Jonathan Kelly
	Keith Martin	Kenneth Mason
	Peter O'Brien	Wayne Sleep
Sunday	Marilyn Trounson and entire cast	

Flute	Tony Roberts
Alto saxophone	Duncan Lamont
Tenor saxophone	Tony Coe
Baritone saxophone	Ronnie Ross
Trumpets	Leon Calvert
	Ken Wheeler
Trombone	Bobby Lamb
Tuba	Alfie Reece
French Horn	Maurice Miller
Piano	Pat Smythe
Bass	Dave Holland
Drums	Jack Dougan
Conductor	John Lanchbery

See: B96, B136, B159, B321, B395

W67. KANDINSKY VARIATIONS FOR TWO PIANOS
(Novello ©1983; 16 mins.)

The movement titles of this work were suggested by
paintings and graphic pieces by Wassily Kandinsky
(1866-1944)

Dedicated to Susan Bradshaw

1 Wechselseitiger Gleichklang (Alternating chord) - Maestoso
2 Kleine Welten (Tiny Worlds) - Presto
3 Grüner Duft (Green fragrance) - Tranquillo
4 Scherzklänge (Comic Sounds) - Molto vivo
5 Durchgehend (Piercing) - Lento, poco liberamente
6 Himmelblau (Sky-blue) - Giocoso

[The work was written during 1977]

Premiere

W67a 1977 (1 December): London; Wigmore Hall; Richard
      Rodney Bennett and Susan Bradshaw (pianos).
      See: B112

W68. LAMENTO D'ARIANNA FOR STRING QUARTET
      (Unpublished, but handled by Novello; 10½ mins.)
      Commissioned by the Bromsgrove Festival with funds
      provided by West Midlands Arts. It is based on
      Monteverdi's madrigal 'Lasciate Mi Morire' (Lamento
      d'Arianna, part 1)

      Dedicated to the Medici Quartet

      Poco adagio - Con moto - Drammatico - Allegro
      inquieto - Maestoso

      The score is dated: New York City - London
                          March 28 '86

      Premiere

W68a 1986 (7 May): Bromsgrove; North Worcestershire
      College; Medici String Quartet: Paul Robertson
      (violin), David Matthews (violin), Ivo-Jan van
      der Werff (viola) and Anthony Lewis (cello).
      See: B126

W69. MADCRICALS FOR TWO PIANOS
      (Unpublished, but handled by Universal Edition)

      Written in 1970-71 whilst Bennett was composer-in-
      residence at the Peabody Conservatory of Music,
      Baltimore

      Premiere

W69a 1971 (4 February): Baltimore; Peabody Conservatory
      of Music; Richard Rodney Bennett and William
      Bland (pianos)

W70. MEMENTO FOR FLUTE AND STRINGS
      (Unpublished, but handled by Novello; 18 mins.)
      Commissioned by Susan Milan with funds provided by
      the Arts Council of Great Britain

      Str. 3.3.3.2.1. or 6.5.4.3.2

      Dedicated to Susan Milan, and inscribed to the
      memory of Pat Smythe, 7 May 1983

      1. Canto   (Molto moderato)
      2. Intermezzo   (Allegretto)
      3. Elegiac Blues   (Lento con tristezza)

      The score is dated: New York City May 28 '83

      Premieres

W70a 1983 (28 September): Windsor; Waterloo Chamber, Windsor Castle; Susan Milan (flute); strings of the London Philharmonic Orchestra; Christopher Robinson, conductor. See: B10

W70b 1983 (10 November): London; St John's Smith Square; Susan Milan (flute); London Concertante Ensemble; Nicholas Kraemer, conductor. See: B202

W71. METAMORPHOSES FOR STRING OCTET
(Unpublished, but handled by Novello; 13 mins.)
Commissioned by the Academy of St. Martin-in-the-Fields Chamber Ensemble.
The work is based on a theme from the Adagio from Thea Musgrave's String Quartet of 1958

Str. 4.2.2.0

Dedicated to Thea [Musgrave]

Adagio-Molto vivo-Drammatico-Lirico-Scherzando-Notturno-Capriccio-Maestoso-Molto mosso

The score is dated: New York City April 16 '80

Premieres

W71a 1980 (21 July): Fishguard; Fishguard School Concert Hall; Academy of St. Martin-in-the-Fields Chamber Ensemble. See: B243, B244

W71b 1980 (29 July): London; Church of St. Martin-in-the-Fields; Academy of St. Martin-in-the-Fields Chamber Ensemble

W72. MUSIC FOR STRING QUARTET
(Novello © 1982; 9 mins.)
Commissioned as a test piece for the (1982) City of Portsmouth International String Quartet Competition

Vivo-Arioso-Vivo-Arioso-Vivo-Arioso-Scherzando-Arioso-Scherzando-Arioso,maestoso-Scherzando-Molto agitato-Vivo, come prima-Scherzando-Vivo

The score is dated: New York City Aug 31 '81

Premiere

W72a 1982 (29 March): Portsmouth; Central Library Concert Hall (semi-finals of the competition). Unable to trace who first placed the quartet, although the piece had to be played at the second stage by all quartets who had reached that part of the contest. The first three prizes for the 1982 Competition were awarded to:

1st Hagen String Quartet (Austria)
2nd Havlak String Quartet (Czechoslovakia)
3rd Auryn String Quartet (West Germany)

W73. <u>MUSIC FOR TWO PIANOS: I-IV</u> (1957-8)
(Unpublished)
Commissioned by Susan Bradshaw and John Streets

Dedicated to Susan Bradshaw and John Streets

The score is dated:
I.   Paris iv 57
II.   Richmond May 1957
III.   Richmond May 1957
IV.   vii - 58

<u>Premieres</u>

W73a 1957 (6 June): London; Wigmore Hall; Susan
Bradshaw and John Streets (pianos) (Numbers I
and II)

W73b 1958 (25 August): Dartington; Great Hall,
(Dartington Summer School); Richard Rodney
Bennett and Susan Bradshaw (pianos) (Numbers I
to III)

W73c 1958 (7 September); Darmstadt; the Orangery, State
Theatre; Richard Rodney Bennett and Susan
Bradshaw (pianos)

W74. <u>QUARTET FOR OBOE AND STRING TRIO</u>
(Novello © 1976; 16½ mins.)
Commissioned by the 1975 King's Lynn Festival for
the Melos Ensemble

Dedicated to Tessa and Michael, 8 February 1975
[Tessa Fryer and Michael Blake Watkins on the
occasion of their marriage]

I.   Con fuoco
Cadenza I : cello (viola)
II.   Elegiaco
Cadenza II : viola (oboe, violin)
III.   Scherzando
Cadenza III : violin (cello, oboe)
IV.   Arioso
Cadenza IV : oboe (cello)
V.   Con fuoco

This score is dated : Barnsbury
                      Dec 8 '74 - Jan 1 '75

<u>Premieres</u>

W74a 1975 (28 July): King's Lynn; St. Nicholas' Chapel;
Peter Graeme (oboe), Jürgen Hess (violin), Cecil
Aronowitz (viola) and Terence Weil (cello)

W74b 1976 (7 March): London; Wigmore Hall; Members of
the Nash Ensemble. <u>See</u>: B176

W75. <u>QUARTET No.1. FOR STRINGS</u> (1951)

(Unpublished)

Unable to trace any details of this work written
when the composer was 15 years of age

W76. QUARTET No.2. FOR STRINGS (1953)
(Unpublished)

    I.   Allegro moderato
    II.   Allegro vivo - Poco lento - Allegro vivo
    III.   Lento
    IV.   Adagio - Allegro deciso

Premiere

W76a 1954 (5 October): London; Arts Council; Macnaghten
        String Quartet: Anne   Macnaghten (violin),
        Elizabeth Rajna (violin), Margaret Major (viola)
        and Arnold Ashby (cello). (A Society for the
        Promotion of New Music Concert). See: B279

W77. QUARTET No.3. FOR STRINGS (1953)
(Unpublished)

    I.   Lento appassionato
    II.   Allegretto scherzando
    III.   Lento espressivo
    IV.   Vivo

Premiere

W77a 1955 (1 February): London;   Arts   Council;
        Macnaghten String Quartet: Anne Macnaghten
        (violin), Elizabeth Rajna (violin), Margaret
        Major (viola) and Arnold Ashby (cello). (A
        Society for the Promotion of New Music Concert).
        See: B277

Other selected performances

W77b 1955 (2 December): London; Royal Academy of Music;
        Meyer Stolow (violin), John Willison (violin)
        Rodney McLeod (viola) and Christopher Gough
        (cello)
        (A concert arranged by the RAM New Music Club)

W78. QUARTET No.4. FOR STRINGS
(Universal Edition © 1966; 14 mins.)
Commissioned by the City Music Society, for its
21st Anniversary concert

    Dedicated to James Phillips

    I.   Molto vivace - lento espressive
    II.   Allegro - Andante - Adagio

    The score is dated: London 22.vi.64

Premiere

W78a 1965 (6 May): London; Goldsmith's Hall; Allegri
      String Quartet: Eli Goren (violin), Peter Thomas
      (violin), Patrick Ireland (viola) and William
      Pleeth (cello). See: B23, B266

W79. QUINTET   FOR CLARINET,   STRING   TRIO   AND   PIANO
      (1961-2) (Unpublished)
      Unable to trace any details about this work.

      Premiere

W79a 1962 (March): London; 4 St. James Square; Fine Arts
     Chamber Ensemble. See: B107

W80. QUINTET FOR FLUTE, OBOE, CLARINET, HORN AND BASSOON
      (1957)
      (Unpublished)

      Unable to trace any details about this work which
      was written in Paris whilst Bennett was studying
      with Boulez in 1957.

W81. QUINTET FOR FLUTE, OBOE, CLARINET (IN B-FLAT) HORN
      (IN F) AND BASSOON
      (Universal Edition ©1968; 15 mins.)
      Commissioned by the Serge Koussevitzky Music
      Foundation in the Library of Congress, Washington
      D.C., on 15 November 1965

          Dedicated to the memory of Serge and Natalie
          Koussevitzky

          I.   Notturno 1   (Molto lento)
          II.   (Molto vivace)
          III.   Notturno 2   (Lento)
          IV.   Variations - Tema (Presto)
                    Var I
                        II
                        III
                        IV (tempo giusto)
                        V (Scherzando)
                        VI
                        VII
                        VIII
                        XI
          This score is dated: Islington Dec. 67 - Jun 68

      Premiere

W81a 1968 (17 March): London; Queen Elizabeth Hall;
     Leonardo Ensemble. See: B267

W82. REFLECTIONS ON A THEME OF WILLIAM WALTON FOR ELEVEN
      SOLO STRINGS.
      (Unpublished, but handled by Novello; 15 mins.)
      Commissioned by the Guildhall String Ensemble with
      assistance from Legal and General Assurance.

The theme of this work is the 12-note series which appears in the last movement of Walton's <u>Symphony No.2.</u> (used with permission from OUP)

Str. 6.2.2.1

Dedicated to the memory of Sir William Walton [1902-1983]

Prelude   :   Sostenuto
3 Variations :   Pochiss. piu mosso
                 Vivo
                 Dolce elegiaco
Interlude : Capriccioso
2 Variations :   Presto scherzando
                 Adagio
Postlude   :   Sostenuto

The score is dated: New York City March 13 '85

Premiere

W82a 1985 (20 May): London; Queen Elizabeth Hall; Guildhall String Ensemble: Robert Salter, Gillian Kent, Benjamin Buckton, Jane Carwardine, Karen James, Leo Payne (violins), Clare Finnimore, Clive Howard (violas), Jane Fenton, Michael Stirling and Mary Scully (double bass). See: B73

W83. ROMANCES FOR HORN AND PIANO
(Unpublished, but handled by Novello; 12 mins.)

Written for Barry Tuckwell and dedicated to his wife, Hilary

1. Adagio
2. Allegretto
3. Presto
4. Adagio

The score is dated: New York City March 23 '85

Premieres

W83a 1986 (25 February): New York; Theresa L. Kaufmann Concert Hall (celebrating the 50th Anniversary of Performing Arts at the 92nd Street Y); Barry Tuckwell (horn), and Richard Rodney Bennett (piano)

W83b 1986 (31 May): London; Wigmore Hall; Barry Tuckwell (horn) and Richard Rodney Bennett (piano)

W84. RONDO FOR FLUTE, BASSOON, VIOLA AND HARP
(Unpublished, but handled by Universal Edition)
This is first movement of a composite work, "Reflections on a theme of Benjamin Britten",

written in honour of Britten's fiftieth birthday
(November 1963). The other two movements were
written by Nicholas Maw (Intermezzo) and Malcolm
Williamson (Tarantella). The theme used was the
Teme Seriale from 'Cantata Academica'. See: B312

Premiere

W84a 1963 (25 October): London; Mahatma Ghandi Hall,
      Fitzroy Square; Melos Ensemble (A Macnaghten
      Concert). See: B309

W85. SCENA I FOR PIANO
      (Novello © 1975; 7½ mins.)
      Commissioned by the BBC for the 1974 BBC Piano
      Competition

      Dedicated to John Philips

      Con fuoco

      This score is dated: Barnsbury, 14 November 1973

Premiere

W85a 1974 (3 April): Lancaster; Great Hall of the
      University. Played by all contestants.
      First Stage : 3rd-5th April given before an
                    invited audience;
      Semi-Final : 6th April
      Final   : 7th April - Public concert
      (The three finalists were Elizabeth Altman,
      Philip Fowke and Yitkin Seow who came first).
      See: B334

W86. SCENA II FOR CELLO SOLO
      (Novello © 1976; 10 mins.)
      Commissioned by the Music Department of the
      University College of North Wales, Bangor, with
      funds provided by the Welsh Arts Council

      Dedicated to Cecile and Bud Bazelon

      Vivo

      The score is dated: Oslo-London
                          November 20-29, 1973

Premieres

W86a 1974 (25 April): Bangor, Powis Hall (University
      College of North Wales); Judith Mitchell (cello)

W86b 1974 (13 August): London, Queen Elizabeth Hall; Ko
      Iwasaki (cello)

W87. SCENA III FOR CLARINET (IN B-FLAT) SOLO
      (Novello © 1979; 8 mins.)

Written for the Park Lane Group's 'Young Artists and 20th Century Music' Series.
The score is prefaced by a quotation from e.e. cummings:
"Then shall I turn my face, and hear
One bird sing terribly afar in the lost lands."

Appassionato

The score is dated: Barnsbury, August 12 1977

Premiere

W87a   1978 (13 January): London; Purcell Room; Philip Edwards (clarinet)

W88.   SERENADE No.2. FOR ONDES MARTINOT AND PIANO (1984)
(Unpublished, but handled by Novello; 10 mins.)
Written for Cynthia Millar and dedicated to her.

I.   Allegretto
II.   Arioso
III. Scherzando

The score is dated:
End of movement I   : New York City Sept 27
End of movement II   : New York City Sept 22
End of movement III : New York City Sept 24

Premiere

W88a   1984   (11   October):   Little   Missenden (Buckinghamshire); Parish Church of St. John the Baptist; Cynthia Millar (ondes martenot) and Elmer Bernstein (piano)

W89.   SIX TUNES FOR THE INSTRUCTION OF SINGING BIRDS-FOR SOLO FLUTE
(Unpublished, but handled by Novello; 8 mins.)
Commissioned by Lady Margaret Douglas Home

Dedicated to Margaret

1. For the starling   (Molto vivo)
2. For the woodlark   (Flessibile)
3. For the canary-bird   (Giocoso)
4. For the garden bull-finch (Agitato)
5. For the East India nightingale (Lento
                                    cantabile)
6. For the starling   (Molto vivo)

The score is prefaced with the following:
'... choice observations and Directions Concerning ye Teaching of all sorts of Singing birds after ye flageolot and flute, if rightly made as to size and tone... with Lessons properly composed, within ye compass and faculty of each bird.'
The Bird Fancyer's Delight (1717)

[Six tunes were written in 1981]

Premieres

W89a   1981 (15 August): Burnham Market; Parish Church of St. Mary; Susan Milan (flute). <u>See</u>: B182

W89b   1981 (24 September): London; Purcell Room; Susan Milan (flute)

W90.   <u>SONATA AFTER SYRINX</u> FOR FLUTE, VIOLA AND HARP
(Unpublished, but handled by Novello; 13 mins.)
'Sonata after Syrinx' is the third of a series of compositions based on Claude Debussy's 'Syrinx' for solo flute (1912). In the score, Bennett suggests that is should be preceded by a performance of 'Syrinx' which it should follow without a break. There is also a note indicating that the harpist plays from the score, and that the composer is indebted to Skaila Kanga for her invaluable assistance with the harp part.
Commissioned by the Nash Ensemble for their concert to mark the composer's 50th birthday in 1986

Dedicated to Amelia Freedman

Molto moderato - Presto (Scherzo 1) - Alla habanera - Cadenza (for viola and harp: lento rubato) - Vivo (Scherzo 2) - Poco adagio (solo harp) - Adagio

The score is dated: New York City August 28 '85

Premiere

W90a   1986 (20 May): London; Wigmore Hall; Nash Ensemble

W91.   <u>SONATA FOR CELLO</u> (1955)
(Unpublished)
Written for Christopher Bunting and dedicated to him.
Lento - Allegro - Appena meno mosso - Allegro - Lento come prima - Adagio espressivo - Allegro agitato - Adagio espressivo

Premiere

Unable to trace

W92.   <u>SONATA FOR GUITAR</u>
(Unpublished, but handled by Novello; 18 mins.)
Edited by David Leisner. <u>See</u>: B71

Dedicated to Julian Bream

1.   Allegro
2.   Lento
3.   Vivo
4.   Fantasia : Allegro

The score is dated: New York City Nov 23 - Dec 10 '83

Premieres

W92a   1985 (17 July): Cheltenham; the Town Hall; Julian Bream (guitar)

W92b   1986 (23 January) : London; Wigmore Hall; Julian Bream (guitar)

W93.   SONATA FOR HORN AND PIANO
(Unpublished, but handled by Novello; 13 mins.)
Written for Barry Tuckwell

Dedicated to Barry and Hilary Tuckwell

Declamato - Molto vivo - Lento e lirico - Molto vivo - Lento e ritmico - Con brio - Cadenza (misterioso) - Agitato - Declamato

The score is dated: New York City - London
Jan 3 - Feb 3 '78

Premieres

W93a   1979 (8 September): Edinburgh; Freemason's Hall; Barry Tuckwell (horn) and Richard Rodney Bennett (piano)

W93b   1981 (28 April): London; Queen Elizabeth Hall; Barry Tuckwell (horn) and Richard Rodney Bennett (piano)   (Barry Tuckwell's 50th birthday concert)

W93c   1982 (5 December): New York; Alice Tully Hall (Lincoln Centre for the Performing Arts); Barry Tuckwell (horn) and Richard Rodney Bennett (piano)

W94.   SONATA FOR OBOE AND PIANO
(Mills Music © 1967; 15 mins.)

Dedicated to Philip Jones and Susan Bradshaw

I.   Vivace
II.   Lento espressivo
III.   Leggiero e ritmico
IV.   Agitato

The score is dated: London, New York, xi-xii,'61

Premiere

W94a   1962 (8 January): London; Wigmore Hall; Philip Jones (oboe) and Susan Bradshaw (piano). See: B20

W95.   SONATA FOR PIANO SOLO

(Universal Edition ©1956; 8 mins.)
See: B270

    I.   Allegro vivo
    II. Grave
    III. Allegro [with central Allegretto]

[The Sonata was written in 1954, at the time of
his entry into the Royal Academy of Music]. See:
B369

Premiere

W95a 1954 : London; Royal Academy of Music; Richard
      Rodney Bennett (piano)

W96. SONATA FOR SOPRANO SAXOPHONE [IN B-FLAT] AND PIANO
     (Unpublished, but handled by Novello; 19 mins.)
     Commissioned by John Harle, with funds from Greater
     London Arts

     Dedicated to John Harle

     1.   Poco allegro
     2.   Scherzando
     3.   Andante ('in memory of Harold Arlen')
     4.   Vivo

     The score is dated: New York City
                       Oct 25 - Dec 9 '86

Premiere

W96a 1988 (23 November): London; Purcell Room; John
      Harle (saxophone) and John Lenehan (piano)

W97. SONATA No.1. FOR SOLO VIOLIN
     (Unpublished, but handled by Universal Edition; 10
     mins.) Composed 1955 and revised 1961

     Lento - Allegro - Lento - Adagio - Cadenza -
     Adagio

Premiere

W97a 1963 (10 March): London; Broadcasting House;
      Manoug Parikian (violin) (A 3rd Programme
      broadcast)

W98. SONATA No.2. FOR SOLO VIOLIN
     (Universal Edition © 1965; 14 mins.)
     Commissioned by the Macnaghten Concerts

     Dedicated to Ralph Holmes

     I.   Allegro appassionato
     II. Dolce scherzando
     III. Variations : I - Sostenuto
                     II - Poco piu mosso

                        III - Tempo 1
                        IV - Con moto
                         V - Molto calmo

    [The sonata was written in October 1964]

Premieres

W98a 1965 (29 January): London; Arts Council; Ralph
      Holmes
      (A Macnaghten Concert). See: B338

W98b 1981 (25 January): New York; Alice Tully Hall
      (Lincoln Centre for the Performing Arts);
      Sylvia Rosenberg (violin)

W99. SONATA FOR VIOLIN AND PIANO
      (Unpublished, but handled by Novello; 18 mins.)
      Commissioned by Erich Gruenberg and John McCabe, to
      whom the Sonata is dedicated

        1.   Lirico
        2.   Mesto
        3.   Con brio

    The score is dated: New York City March 30 - May 8
                        London,   May 9 1978

Premiere

W99a 1979 (17 January): London; Wigmore Hall; Erich
      Gruenberg (violin) and John McCabe (piano)

W100. SONATA FOR WIND QUINTET AND PIANO
      (Unpublished, but handled by Novello; 15 mins.)
      Commisioned by the Dorian Quintet, partially funded
      by New York State Council on the Arts, and
      dedicated to them

    The sonata is in one continuous movement (Andante)

    The score is dated: New York City 11 Jan [1987]
    [composition having started in 1986]

Premieres

W100a 1987 (21 April): New York; Hunter College Play-
      house; Dorian Wind Quintet of New York:
      Elizabeth Mann (flute), Gerard Reuter (oboe),
      Jeremy Kirkbride (clarinet in B-flat), David
      Jolley (horn in F), Jane Taylor (bassoon) and
      Richard Rodney Bennett (piano)

W100b 1987 (15 May): Theale (Berkshire); Englefield
      House - the Long Gallery; Dorian Wind Quintet of
      New York.
      (European premier: Newbury Spring Festival).
      See: B220

W101. SONATINA FOR SOLO CLARINET IN B-FLAT
(Novello ©1982; 7 mins).
Commissioned by MidNAG (Mid Northumberland Arts
Group) for their National Clarinet Competition for
Young People, March 1983

Dedicated to Angela Morley

I.   Con fuoco
II.   Night thoughts (Lento)
III.   Scherzando

[The Sonatina was written in 1981]

Premieres

W101a 1983 (31 March): Newcastle upon Tyne; Northern
     Sinfonia Centre. All contestants were required
     to play two of the three movements.
     Alexander Allen was finally placed first, Richard
     Hosford came second, and John Yuill was awarded
     third place

W101b 1984 (27 March): London; British Music Information
     Centre; Marc Naylor (clarinet)

W102. SONATINA FOR SOLO FLUTE
(Universal Edition ©1955; 8 mins.)

I.   Poco lento - Allegro con grazia
II.   Lento - Allegro

[This Sonatina was written in April 1954, when the
composer was a student at the Royal Academy of
Music in London]

Premiere

W102a 1955 (1 March): London; Arts Council; Andrew
     Solomon (flute)
     (A Society for the Promotion of New Music
     Concert). See: B281

W103. SOUNDS AND SWEET AIRES FOR FLUTE, OBOE AND PIANO
(Unpublished, but handled by Novello; 13 mins.)
Commissioned by WUNC Radio, based at the University
of North Carolina, Chapel Hill, to commemorate its
tenth anniversary. It is based on a passage from
Shakespeare's The Tempest:
"Be not affeard, the Isle is full of noyses,
Sounds and sweet Aires, that give delight and hurt
not."

I.   Allegretto lirico - vivo
II.   Capriccioso
III.   Lento - con brio

The score is dated: New York - Chicago - St. Louis
                    October 9 - November 2 '85

Premieres

W103a 1986 (26 April): Chapel Hill (University of North
         Carolina); Hill Hall; Rebecca Troxler (flute),
         Ronald Weddle (oboe) and Richard Rodney Bennett
         (piano)

W103b 1987 (5 May): London; British Music Information
         Centre; Ensemble Australis: Alison Mitchell
         (flute), Lawrence Frankel (oboe) and Tony Gray
         (piano)

W104.STANZAS FOR FLUTE (1959)
      (Unpublished)

      Unable to trace any details of this work.

W105.STANZAS FOR ORGAN
      (Unpublished)

      Molto moderato - Allegretto - Lento - Allegro -
      Lente e dolce

      [This work was written in August 1960]

      Premiere

W105a 1960 (13 December): London; All Saints' Church,
         Margaret Street; Richard Popplewell (organ)

W106.STUDIES FOR FIVE INSTRUMENTS (FLUTE, VIOLIN,
      CLARINET AND ALTO SAXOPHONE)
      (Unpublished)
      Written in Paris in July 1957, especially for a
      Dartington Summer School concert

      In the programme, Bennett wrote that this composi-
      tion was a set of variations divided by cadenzas
      for solo instruments and percussion. The six
      variations are arranged in a symmetrical form, the
      first similar to the last, and the second - a
      scherzo - similar to the fifth. The third varia-
      tion and its retrograde - the fourth - are
      separated by a percussion cadenza, the centre point
      of the work.
      The violin part was originally written for oboe.

      Premiere

W106a 1957 (15 August): Dartington; Great Hall,
         (Dartington Summer School); New Music Ensemble:
         Rainer Schuelein (flute), Alfred Ljungren
         (violin), Colin Bradbury (clarinet), Leslie
         Walklin (bass clarinet), Gillian Marples (alto
         saxophone), Margaret Cotton and Cornelius Cardew
         (percussion); John Carewe, conductor

A piece by Susan Bradshaw was also included in the concert, in which Bennett played the percussion.

W107. STUDY FOR TRUMPET AND PIANO
(Unpublished)
Written in Paris, in March 1957, especially for an Aldeburgh Festival concert featuring Young Composers and Performances

A note describes the study and says that the point of departure of the construction is a limited group of material which is constantly varied within itself. The writing is not contrapuntal, but consists of a continual superposition of varying timbres, complexes of sounds (vertical and horizontal) and different speeds of movement.

Premiere

W107a 1957 (21 June): Aldeburgh (Suffolk); Jubilee Hall; Howard Snell (trumpet) and Cornelius Cardew (piano)

W108. SUITE FOR SKIP AND SADIE FOR PIANO DUET
(Unpublished, but handled by Novello; 8 mins.)

Skip and Sadie live in New York.
They are the composer's cats

1.	Good morning	(Alla marcia)
2.	Sadie's Waltz	(Con eleganza)
3.	Skip's Dance	(Molto vivo)
4.	Good Night	(Andante tranquillo)

The score is dated:
End of movement 1 - June 14
End of movement 2 - June 12
End of movement 3 - June 16
End of movement 4 - London June 15 '86

Premiere

W108a Sadie's Waltz - 1987 (17 May): played by Susan Bradshaw and the composer who appeared in "Crossing Over", Barry Gavin's film on Richard Rodney Bennett, made for Central Television.

W109. TANGO AFTER SYRINX FOR SOLO PIANO
(Unpublished, but handled by Novello; 3 mins.)
"Tango after Syrinx" is the fourth of a series of compositions based on Claude Debussy's 'Syrinx' for solo flute (1912).
Written for and dedicated to Yvar Mikhashoff

Languido e ritmico

The score is dated: New York City
December 16 '85

W110.<u>TELEGRAM</u> FOR SOLO PIANO
(Unpublished, but handled by Novello; 40 sec.)
Written for Elizabeth Lutyens' 70th birthday
concert

Dedicated to Liz, with love

Vivo

The score is dated: I.vi.76

<u>Premiere</u>

W110a 1976 (9 July): London; Purcell Room; Richard
Deering (piano)

W111.<u>THEME AND VARIATIONS FOR VIOLIN AND VIOLA</u> (1952)
(Unpublished)

Unable to trace any details of this work, written
when the composer was 16 years of age.

W112.<u>THREE ROMANTIC PIECES</u> FOR SOLO PIANO
(Unpublished, but handled by Novello; 17-18 mins.)
Commissioned by the BBC for Howard Ferguson's 80th
birthday concert

Dedicated to Howard Ferguson on his 80th
birthday, with love and gratitutde

1. Andante con moto
2. Allegro
3. Andante semplice

The first piece is dated June 8, and at the end
of the third piece is New York, Fairharbor,
York, London, June 22 '88

<u>Premiere</u>

W112a 1988 (28 October): Birmingham; Studio 1 (BBC),
Pebble Mill; Clifford Benson (piano)

W113.<u>TRAVEL NOTES 1</u> FOR STRING QUARTET
(Novello ©1982; 6 mins.)

Violins 1 and 2, Viola and Cello

Dedicated to Ann Macnaghten

1. A walking tune (Amabile)
2. In a hearse   (Dolente)
3. On horse back   (Stepitoso)
4. In a pram   (Teneramente)
5. Express train   (Energico)

The score is dated: Barnsbury Nov 27-29 '75

W114.<u>TRAVEL NOTES 2</u> FOR WOODWIND QUARTET (FLUTE, OBOE,

CLARINET IN B-FLAT, BASSOON) OR FOUR SAXOPHONES
(Novello © 1976; 6 mins.)

1. In an air-balloon   (Peaceful and flowing)
2. In a helicopter   (Lively)
3. In a bath-chair   (Very gently)
4. Car-chase   (As fast as possible)

W115. TRIO FOR FLUTE, OBOE AND CLARINET
(Universal Edition © 1966; 11 mins.)
Commissioned by the Muzicki Biennale Zagreb 1965
for Richard Adeney, Peter Graeme and Gervase de
Peyer

I.   Sostenuto
II.   Vivace
III.   Sostenuto
IV.   Scherzando
V.   Sostenuto
VI.   Flessibile

The score is dated Earl Soham, Suffolk.
Jan. 17 1965

Premiere

W115a 1965 : Zagreb; Festival of Contemporary Music;
Richard Adeney (flute), Peter Graeme (oboe) and
Gervase de Peyer (clarinet)

W116. TRIO FOR 3 VIOLINS OR 2 VIOLINS AND VIOLA
(Mills Music; © 1964)

Unable to trace any details about this work.

W117. VARIATIONS FOR OBOE (1953)
(Unpublished)

Unable to trace any details about this work.

Premiere

W117a 1953 (23 February): London, St. James Square (Arts
Council Headquarters); Joy Boughton (oboe).
See: B18, B263

W118. WINTER MUSIC FOR FLUTE AND PIANO
(Mills Music © 1960; 10 mins.)

Dedicated to William Bennett and Susan Bradshaw

I.   Recitativo - Allegro- Meno mosso, quasi
       recitativo
II.   Spettrale
III.   Lento e mesto - Andante - Piu lento -
       Andante - Tempo 1, lento

[Winter Music was written in 1960]

Premiere

W118a 1961 (8 January): London; Arts Council; William
        Bennett (flute) and Susan Bradshaw (piano).
        See: B31

V.   CHORAL MUSIC

W119. AND DEATH SHALL HAVE NO DOMINION - MOTET FOR MENS'
      VOICES (TTBB) AND SOLO FRENCH HORN.
      Text by Dylan Thomas
      (Unpublished, but handled by Novello; 8 mins.)
      Commissioned by the New York City Gay Men's Chorus
      and their conductor, Gary Miller.
      The poem is used with permission from David Higham
      Associates on behalf of the estate of Dylan Thomas

          Inscribed to the memory of Paul Jacobs

          Molto moderato

          The score is dated: New York City
                               February 16 '86

     Premieres

W119a 1986 (June). The planned premiere in New York did
          not take place owing to the level of difficulty
          for the singers and the unavailability of the
          French horn player for whom it was written.

W119b 1988 (7 July): London (Islington); Parish Church
          of St Mary; London Concord Singers; Patrick
          Clements   (French   horn);   Malcolm   Cottle,
          conductor.

W120. THE APPROACHES OF SLEEP - CANTATA FOR FOUR SOLO
      VOICES (SOPRANO, ALTO, TENOR AND BASS) AND TEN
      INSTRUMENTS
      Text by Sir Thomas Browne from "The Garden of
      Cyrus" (1658).
      (Mills Music © 1960; 12 mins.) See: B59

          1.1.1.1/1.1.0.0/hp/violin,viola,cello

          Dedicated to Liz

          I.   Lento
          II.   Agitato
          III. Adagio

          The score is dated:
          End of movement I   - 4.xi.59
          End of movement II   - 20.xi.59
          End of movement III   - 2.i.60

     Premiere

W120a 1961 (15 January): London; Royal Court Theatre;
          Dorothy Dorow (soprano), Rosemary Phillips
          (alto), Leslie Fryson (tenor) and John Frost
          (bass);   New   Music   Ensemble;   John   Carew,
          conductor

W121. EPITHALAMION - CANTATA FOR MIXED CHORUS (SATB) AND

ORCHESTRA
Text by Robert Herrick from 'A Nuptiall Song, or
Epithalamie on Sir Clipseby Crew and his Lady' –
Hesperides (1648). German translation by Ernst
Hartmann
(Universal Edition ©1966; 23 mins.)
Commissioned by the 1967 Leeds Triennial Musical
Festival

> 2+1.2+1.2+1.2/4.3.2+1.1/timp.//perc.(3)/piano
> (doubling celesta)/hp/strings

> Vivace

> The score is dated: Islington, Easter Day 1966

Premiere

W121a 1967 (15 April): Leeds; Town Hall; Festival Chorus
    (chorus master: Donald Hunt); London Symphony
    Orchestra; Istvan Kertesz conductor. See: B29,
    B78,B80,B234,B271,B380

W122. FAREWELL TO ARMS – MOTET FOR UNACCOMPANIED DOUBLE
    MIXED CHORUS (SSAATTBB)
    Text by George Peele from 'Polyhymnia'
    (Unpublished)
    Written for Graham Treacher and the New Music
    Singers

> The score is dated: London, September '59

Premiere

> Unable to trace

W123. FIVE CAROLS (1967)
    FOR UNACCOMPANIED MIXED CHORUS (SATB)
    (Universal Edition ©1967; 10 mins.)

> Dedicated to Michael Nicholas and the Choir of
> St, Matthew's Church, Northampton

> 1. There is no rose (Andante) text:Anonymous
> 2. Out of your sleep (Allegro fluente) text:
>   15th century
> 3. That younge child (Moderato) text: Anonymous
> 4. Sweet was the song (Poco lento) text:
>   William Ballett (17th century)
> 5. Susanni (Vivace) text: 14th century

Premieres

W123a 1967 (23 September): Northampton; Parish Church of
    St. Matthew; Church Choir; Michael Nicholas,
    conductor

W123b 1967 (24 September): London; Wigmore Hall; John
    Alldis choir; John Alldis, conductor. See:B337

W124. FOUR DEVOTIONS
FOR UNACCOMPANIED MIXED CHORUS (SATB)
Text by John Donne
(Universal Edition ©1975;   ? mins.)

    1. A Stature of Snowe   (Molto ritmico)
    2. A Flowre at Sun-rising   (Lento e dolce)
    3. Poor Intricated Soule   (Molto allegro)
    4. The Seasons of His Mercies   (Adagio)

    The score is dated:
    End of No.1. - Baltimore - March 28 '71
    End of No.2. - Baltimore - March 29 '71
    End of No.3. - New York - April 4 '71
    End of No.4. - Baltimore - March 19 '71

Premiere

    Unable to trace

W125. THE HOUSE OF SLEEPE
FOR SIX MALE VOICES (2 COUNTER TENORS, TENOR, 2
BARITONES, BASS)
Text by Ovid from Metamorphoses, in the 16th
century translation by Arthur Golding. The lines
on p.14 of the manuscript, beginning 'Thus came
Iris...' and ending '...with sleepe she spoke' are
taken from the translation by John Gower
(1370-1408).
(Unpublished, but handled by Universal Edition; 12
mins.)
Commissioned by the King's Singers with funds
provided by the Arts Council of Great Britain

    Dedicated to the King's Singers

    Most of this piece uses 'time-space' notation,
    in which the duration of a sound is shown by the
    space it takes up on the page. In general the
    layout of the score should indicate the freedom
    or strictness of the notation which, except in
    certain areas of precise ensemble, may be freely
    interpreted.

    The score is dated: Barnsbury
                        Sept 2 - 20, 1971

Premiere

W125a 1972 (18 January): London; Queen Elizabeth Hall;
      The King's Singers: Nigel Perrin (counter
      tenor), Alastair Hume (counter tenor), Alastair
      Thompson (tenor), Anthony Holt (baritone), Simon
      Carrington (baritone) and Brian Kay (bass)

W126. LETTERS TO LINDBERGH - CANTATA
FOR HIGH VOICES (SA) AND PIANO, FOUR HANDS
Text by Martin Hall: a partial selection from the
many letters received by Charles Lindbergh during

his non-stop solo flight from New York to Paris in 1927.
(Novello/Mercury Music Co. ©1984; 13 mins.)
Commissioned by Walthamstow Hall School, Sevenoaks, Kent, for their centenary year

Dedicated to Margaret and George Rizza

1. Prelude (piano duet only) Molto animato
2. From Scott of the Antartic Con moto
3. From the Titanic Scherzando
4. From Pluto Allegro con brio

The score is dated: November-December 1981
New York City

Premiere

W126a 1982 (16 May): London; Purcell Room; Walthamstow Hall School Choir; Yvonne Harris and Susanne Lloyd-Jones (piano); Margaret Lensky Rizza, conductor

W127.LONDON PASTORAL - CANTATA
FOR TENOR AND CHAMBER ORCHESTRA
Texts selected by Jonathan Griffin
(Belwin Mills Music ©1976; 14 mins.)
Commissioned by the Lord Mayor of London for the Festival of the City of London, July 1962

2+1.1.1.1/1.1.1.0/perc.(3)/hp/2 violins, viola, cello

Dedicated to Joan [Ingpen] and Sebastian [Shaw]

I.   Introduction - Sonnet (William Wordsworth): Lento e dolciss
II. Interlude (Vivace e leggiero) - Scherzo (John Lydgate): Poco piu moderato - Interlude
III. Soliloquy (Laurence Binyon): Lento con tristezza - Epilogue

The score is dated: Islington March-May '62

Premiere

W127a 1962 (13 July): London; Guildhall; Alexander Young (tenor); English Chamber Orchestra; Colin Davis, conductor: See: B17, B160, B222, B287, B391

W128.LULLABY BABY - CAROL
FOR UNACCOMPANIED MIXED CHORUS (SATB)
Text by John Phillip (1565)
(Unpublished, but handled by Novello; 3 mins.)

Written for and dedicated to the choir of King's College, Cambridge

Allegretto flessibile

The score is dated: New York City
                          August 26 '86

Premiere

Unable to trace

W129. LULLAY MINE LIKING - CAROL
      FOR   UNACCOMPANIED   MIXED   CHORUS   (SATB),   WITH
      OPTIONAL SATB SOLI (1984)
      Text: Anonymous
      (Novello ©1985; 3 mins.)

      Written for and dedicated to the Rt. Hon. Edward
      Heath

      Allegretto comodo

Premiere

W129a 1984 (23 December): Broadstairs, Kent; Grand Hotel
      Ballroom;   Broadstairs   Choir;   Edward   Heath,
      conductor
      (The 40th Broadstairs Town Carol Concert)

W130. NOCTURNALL UPON ST. LUCIE'S DAY - CANTATA
      FOR MEZZO SOPRANO AND PIANO (1954)
      Text by John Donne
      (Unpublished)

      Unable to trace any details

Premiere

W130a 1954 (19   October):   London;   Institute   of
      Contemporary   Arts;   Monica   Sinclair   (mezzo
      soprano);   unable to trace the pianist.   See:
      B280

W131. NONSENSE
      FOR MIXED CHORUS (SATB) AND PIANO DUET
      Text by Mervyn Peake from The Book of Nonsense,
      published by Peter Owen Ltd., London and reproduced
      by permission.
      (Unpublished, but handled by Novello; 20 mins.)

      Nonsense was written in 1979 in response to a
      commission from the County of Bedfordshire for a
      work for youth and orchestra. It was rejected
      because of "its unsuitability as a companion
      piece to Beethoven's Symphony No.9" (a condition
      of programming not revealed at the time). Hence
      the revisions made in 1984.

      Dedicated to Sheila MacCrindle

      1. Of pygmies, palms and pirates (Allegro con
                                        brio)

    2. Aunts and uncles (Presto con fuoco)
    3. Lean sideways on the wind (Molto
                               appassionato)
    4. O here it is! and there it is! (Allegro
                               leggiero)
    5. How fly the birds of Heaven? (Lento
                               religioso)
    6. The men in bowler hats (Alla valse, giocoso)
    7. The Dwarf of Battersea (Allegro agitato)

W131a 1984 (18 July): Chester; Gateway Theatre; National
      Youth Choir of Great Britain; Richard Rodney
      Bennett and Susan Bradshaw (pianos); Michael
      Brewer, conductor (A Chester Summer Music
      Festival concert). See: B68

W132.NOWEL - CAROL
    FOR UNACCOMPANIED MIXED CHORUS (SATB)
    Text by Walter de la Mare, reproduced by permission
    of the Literary Trustees of Walter de la Mare and
    The Society of Authors as their representative.
    (Novello ©1987; 2 mins.)

      Written for and dedicated to the Choir of King's
      College, Cambridge

      Moderato giocoso

      The score is dated: New York City
                      August 27 '86

    Premiere

W132a 1986 (24 December); Cambridge; King's College
      Chapel; Choir of King's College; Stephen
      Cleobury, conductor
      (The Festival of Nine Lessons and Carols)

W133.NOWELL, NOWELL, TIDINGS TRUE -
    'THE SALUTATION CAROL' ARRANGED FOR UNACCOMPANIED
    MIXED CHORUS (SATB) (1962)
    Text: 15th Century anon.
    (Novello © 1963; 3 mins.)
    Commissioned by Novello for its carol collection
    Sing Nowell, edited by Louis Halsey and Basil
    Ramsey.

      Poco allegro

    Premiere

      Unable to trace

W134.PUER NOBIS - CAROL
    FOR UNACCOMPANIED MIXED CHORUS (SATB)
    Text by Alice Meynell
    (Novello © 1983; 2 mins.)

Written at the request of and dedicated to the
Marchioness of Aberdeen

Andante

<u>Premiere</u>

W134a 1980 (21 December): Aberdeen; Haddo House Chapel;
      Haddo House Choral and Operatic Society; June
      Gordon (Marchioness of Aberdeen), conductor

W135.<u>PUT AWAY THE FLUTES</u> (1952)
     FOR SOPRANO, MIXED CHORUS (SATB) AND ORCHESTRA
     Text by W.R. Rodgers
     (Unpublished)

     Unable to trace any details about this very
     early (and Bennett's first serial) work.

W136.<u>RICERCAR</u> (1956)
     FOR UNACCOMPANIED MIXED CHORUS (SATB)
     (Unpublished)

     Unable to trace any details

<u>Premiere</u>

W136a 1956 (1 May): London; Wigmore Hall; Cappella
      Singers; Anthony Milner, conductor (A Society
      for the Promotion of New Music Concert). <u>See</u>:
      B278

W137.<u>SEACHANGE</u>
     FOR UNACCOMPANIED MIXED CHORUS (SATB) - MINIMUM 24
     VOICES (TENOR AND BARITONE SOLI IN 2ND MOVEMENT)
     (Unpublished, but handled by Novello; 15 mins.)
     Commissioned by the 1984 Three Choirs Festival with
     funds from West Midlands Arts

     Dedicated to Donald Hunt

     1. 'The isle is full of noyses ...'
          from <u>The Tempest</u> (Shakespeare) Tranquillo
     2. The Bermudas (Marvell) Lento
     3. 'The waves come rolling ...'
          from <u>The Faerie Queene</u> (Spencer) Allegro con
          bravura
     4. Full Fathom Five - <u>The Tempest</u> Lento

     The following notes also appear in the original
     manuscript:
          3 tubular bells should be placed out of sight of
          the audience and sounded before movements 1, 2
          and 4, as directed.
          The pitches in the 3rd movement are only very
          approximately suggested; however the movement is
          to be <u>sung</u> rather than spoken.

The widest vocal and dynamic range is to be used
and the maximum (melo) dramatic effect aimed
for; rhythmic precision is essential.
Unisons of pitch should be avoided, also any
suggestion of diatonic 'melody.'

The score is dated: New York City, Oct 31 – Nov 19
'83

Premieres

W137a 1984 (23 August): Worcester; Cathedral Church of
       Christ and St. Mary; Donald Hunt Singers;
       Donald Hunt, conductor. See: B32

W137b 1984 (28 October): London; Purcell Room; Pegasus;
       Richard Crossland, conductor. See: B75, B315

W138. THE SORROWS OF MARY – CAROL
      FOR UNACCOMPANIED MIXED CHORUS (SSATB) (1964)
      Text: 15th Century anon.
      (Oxford University Press © 1965; 3 mins.)
      Commissioned by Oxford University Press for its
      carol collection Carols of Today

      Molto moderato

Premiere

W138a 1964 (December): London; Wigmore Hall; Chamber
       Choir of the Guildhall School of Music; John
       Alldis, conductor. See: B105

W139. SPELLS: SIX POEMS
      FOR SOPRANO SOLO, MIXED CHORUS (SATB) AND ORCHESTRA
      Text by Kathleen Raine
      (Novello © 1975; 38 mins.)
      Commissioned by the Royal Philharmonic Orchestra
      with funds from the Calouste Gulbenkian Foundation
      for the 1975 Three Choirs Festival. See: B298

      2 + 1.2 + 1.2 + 1.2 + 1/4.3.3.1/timp/perc.(3)/
      piano (doubling celesta)/hp/strings

      Dedicated to Jane Manning and the choirs of the
      Three Choirs Festival

      1. Spell against sorrow (chorus and orchestra)
                              Con Moto
      2. Spell of safekeeping (soprano solo and
         orchestra)   Adagio
      3. Spell to bring lost creatures homes (chorus
         and orchestra)   Presto
      4. Spell of sleep (chorus unaccompanied)
                              Molto tranquillo
      5. Love Spell (soprano solo and orchestra)
                              Declamato
      6. Spell of creation (soprano solo, chorus and
         orchestra)   Solenne

Movements 2 and 5 (in that order) may be performed as a 13-minute work for soprano solo and orchestra, entitled <u>Love Spells</u>. Movement 4 may be performed alone. Both are published separately by Novello.

The score is dated:
End of Movement 1 - 4.vi.74
End of Movement 2 - 18.vi.74
End of Movement 3 - 1.vii.74
End of Movement 4 - 31.v.74
End of Movement 5 - 26.x.74
End of Movement 6 - London,Aldeburgh,New York
                      May 23 '74 - Jan 16 '75

<u>Premiere</u>

W139a 1975 (28 August): Worcester; Cathedral Church of Christ and St. Mary; Jane Manning (soprano); Three Choirs Festival Chorus; Royal Philharmonic Orchestra; Donald Hunt, conductor. <u>See</u>: B245, B355

W139b 1978 (15 May): London; Royal Festival Hall; Jane Manning (soprano); Bach Choir; Philharmonia Orchestra; David Willcocks, conductor

W140. <u>THREE ELEGIES</u>
FOR UNACCOMPANIED MIXED CHORUS (SSAATTBB) (1962)
Text by John Webster, respectively from 'The White Devil' (1612), 'The Duchess of Malfi' (circa 1613) and 'The Devil's Law Case' (1616)
(Mills Music ©1962; ? mins.)

Dedicated to Roger Clynes and The Regent Singers

1. Call for the robin redbreast   Lento
2. Hark! now everything is still   Allegro con
                                   morbidezza
3. All the flowers of the Spring   Dolce e
                                   solenne

<u>Premiere</u>

Unable to trace

W141. <u>THREE MADRIGALS</u>
FOR UNACCOMPANIED MIXED CHORUS (SATB) (1961)
Text: nos. 1 and 2 - Ben Johnson; no.3 - anonymous
(Mills Music nos. 1 and 2/Novello no. 3. © 1962; 10 mins.)

1. Still to be neat   Vivace
2. The Hour Glass   Poco lento, expressivo
3. And can the physician
   make sick men well? (Madrigal)   Poco allegro

No. 3 bears the only dedication: To Margaret

Premiere

W141a 1962 (6 March): London; Bishopsgate Insititute;
        Regent Singers; Roger Clynes, conductor

W142.THE TILLAQUILS - PARTSONG
     FOR UNACCOMPANIED MIXED CHORUS (SATB) (1955)
     Text by Laura Riding
     (Unpublished)
     Written for the Elizabethan Singers

     Premiere

W142a 1956 (11   March):   London;   Morley   College;
        Elizabethan Singers; Louis Halsey, conductor.
        See: B284

W143.TWO CAROLS
     FOR SOLI (SATB) AND UNACCOMPANIED MIXED CHORUS
     (SATB) (1968)
     Text: 15th anonymous and Robert Herrick (1647)
     (Universal Edition ©1968; 8 mins.)
     No.1. commissioned by The Louis Halsey Singers
     No.2. commissioned by the Rt. Hon. Edward Heath

          Dedicated to Louis Halsey (No.1.)
                    to The Rt. Hon Edward Heath (No.2.)

          1. Flower Carol   Moderato con moto/Poco piu
                               mosso
          2. What Sweeter Music   Con moto

     Premiere

W143a Flower Carol. 1968 12 (December): London; Church
        of   St.   Clement   Danes;   Christina   Clarke
        (soprano), Paul Esswood (counter-tenor) Martyn
        Hill (tenor) and Geoffrey Shaw (bass); Louis
        Halsey Singers; Louis Halsey, conductor

          What   Sweeter   Music.   1968   (22   December):
          Broadstairs,   Kent;   Grand   Hotel   Ballroom;
          Broadstairs Choir; Edward Heath, conductor (The
          25th Broadstairs Town Carol Concert)

W144.TWO LULLABIES
     FOR UNACCOMPANIED 3-PART WOMEN'S CHOIRS (SSA)(1963)
     Texts: Traditional [Latin] and James, John and
     Robert Wedderburn
     (Universal Edition ©1963; ? mins.)

          Dedicated to Margaret   (No.1.)
                    to Sheila   (No.2.)

          1. Dormi Jesu   Allegretto
          2. Balulalow   Piacevole

     Premiere

W144a 1963: London; Wigmore Hall; London Recital Group;
        Richard Sinton, conductor

W145.VERSES
    FOR UNACCOMPANIED MIXED CHORUS (SATB) (1964)
    Text by John Donne from The Litanie (1608)
    (Universal Edition ©1965; ? mins.)

            Dedicated to Richard Sinton and the London
                    Recital Group Nos. 1 and 3
                    The Choir of Coventry Cathedral
                            No. 2

        1. From needing danger to be good   Andante
        2. Through thy submitting all   Poco adagio
        3. Heare us, O heare us Lord   Maestoso

    Premiere

W145a 1964: London; Wigmore Hall; London Recital Group;
        Richard Sinton; conductor

VI. VOCAL MUSIC

W146.CRAZY JANE - CANTATA
FOR SOPRANO, CLARINET IN B-FLAT, CELLO AND PIANO
Text by W.B. Yeats from Words for Music Perhaps
(1932)
(Unpublished, but handled by Novello, 9 mins.)
Commissioned by BBC Television

Dedicated to Jane Manning and the Vesuvius
Ensemble

I.   Crazy Jane reproved Allegro declamato
II. Crazy Jane and Jack the Journeyman Lento
III.Crazy Jane on God   Molto animato

The score is dated: Islington December 12 '68

Premiere

W146a 1969 (17 June): London; Queen Elizabeth Hall; Jane
Manning (soprano); Vesuvius Ensemble.
(A public concert promoted by Youth and Music.
This was the first complete performance of the
cycle, two songs having been previously
performed in the programme Music Now on BBC TV)

W147.DREAM SONGS
FOR MEZZO - SOPRANO (OR UNISON HIGH VOICES) AND
PIANO
Text by Walter de la Mare from 'Collected Rhymes
and Verses,' published by Faber and Faber.   These
songs may be performed separately or as a cycle
(Unpublished, but handled by Novello; 9 mins.)

Written for and dedicated to Sasha [Alexander],
with love

1. The Song of the Wanderer Allegro giocoso
2. The Song of Shadows   Lento
3. Dream-song   Allegretto molto moderato
4. The Song of the Mad Prince Lento expressivo

The score is dated: New York City August 30 '86

W148.FIRST THING ABOUT ME
FOR SOPRANO AND PIANO (1970s)
(Unpublished, but handled by Novello)

Written for performance by Marian Montgomery and
featured at the Bath Festival in May 1978 with
the composer at the piano

W149.FIVE SONNETS OF LOUISE LABÉ
FOR SOPRANO AND ELEVEN PLAYERS (1984)
(Unpublished, but handled by Novello; 19 mins.)
Commissioned by the Chester Festival, 1984

1+1.1.1.1/1.0.0.0/hp/str.1.1.1.1.1

Dedicated to Teresa Cahill

1. O beaux yeux bruns   Andante molto
2. Je vis, je meurs   Allegro inquieto
3. Tout aussitot que je
   commence   Lento e dolce
4. Baise m'encore   Molto vivo
5. Tant que mes yeux   Lento

Premiere

W149a 1984 (24 July): Chester; Cathedral Church of.
      Christ and the Blessed Virgin Mary; Teresa
      Cahill (soprano); London Sinfonietta; Oliver
      Knussen, conductor. See: B68,B379

W149b 1986 (20 May): London; Wigmore Hall; Teresa Cahill
      (soprano); Nash Ensemble; Lionel Friend,
      conductor

W150. FUNNY THING (1970s)
      FOR SOPRANO AND PIANO
      Lyrics by Richard Rodney Bennett
      (Novello © 1979 - Just Friends in Print)

      Easy rock

      Written for performance by Marian Montgomery

W151. A GARLAND FOR MARJORY FLEMING
      FIVE SONGS FOR SOPRANO AND PIANO
      Text by Marjory Fleming (1803-1811) who was born in
      Kirkcaldy and died at the age of eight, leaving
      three volumes of Journals and a handful of poems,
      several of which concern her cousin and closest
      friend, Isabella Keith.
      (Novello © 1986; 9 mins.)

      Dedicated to Sasha Abrams and Peter Alexander

      1. In Isas Bed   Allegro giocoso
      2. A Melancholy Lay   Allegretto con dolore
      3. On Jessy Watsons Elopement Maestoso
      4. Sweet Isabell   Allegretto
      5. Sonnet on a Monkey   Allegro giocoso

      The score is dated: Barnsbury, 20 August, 1969

W151a 1970 (2 December); Edinburgh; BBC Studio One;
      Sasha Abrams (soprano); Peter Alexander (piano).
      This recording was subsequently played in the
      BBC Scottish Home Service on 27 December 1970

W152. I NEVER WENT AWAY
      FOR SOPRANO AND PIANO (1980s)
      (Unpublished, but handled by Novello)

Written for performance by Marian Montgomery and
featured at the Bromsgrove Festival in May 1986
with the composer at the piano

W153. JAZZ PASTORAL
FOR JAZZ SINGER AND ELEVEN PLAYERS
Text by Robert Herrick from Hesperides (1648)
(Unpublished, but handled by Universal Edition; 26
mins.)
Commissioned by the London Sinfonietta with help
for the Calouste Gulbenkian Foundation.

Alto saxophone in E-flat, tenor saxophone in
B-flat, baritone saxophone in E-flat, 2 trumpets
in B-flat, horn in F, trombone, tuba, piano,
bass and drums

Dedicated to Cleo Laine

1. Introduction ('The Argument of his Book') Up
   tempo, lightly
2. To Promroses ('To Primroses fill'd with
                   Morning-Dew') Medium
3. To the Willow-tree ('To the Willow-Tree')
                                         Slow
4. The Kisse ('The Kisse - A Dialogue') Fast
                jazz waltz
5. To Musique ('To Musique, to becalm his
                Fever')   Very slow
6. To Daffodills ('To Daffodills') Up tempo,
                   lightly

The score is dated: Barnsbury Aug-Sept 1969

Premiere

W153a 1970 (15 June): London; Queen Elizabeth Hall; Cleo
     Laine; London Sinfonietta; David Atherton,
     conductor. See:B121,193

W154. LAMENT
FOR TENOR AND GUITAR
Text by Chidiock Tichbourne, written the night
before his execution in 1586
(Unpublished, but handled by Mills Music; ? mins.)

Written for and dedicated to Peter Pears and
Julian Bream

Andante

The manuscript is dated: London ii. 1960

Premiere

W154a 1960 (21 June): Ipswich; Shrubland Park, Claydon;
     Peter Pears (tenor); Julian Bream (guitar)

W155. LET'S GO AND LIVE IN THE COUNTRY (1978)

FOR SOPRANO AND PIANO
Lyrics by Richard Rodney Bennett
Novello (c)1979 - <u>Just Friends in Print</u>)

Freely

Written for performance by Marian Montgomery on the
recording Cube HIFLY 28 (<u>See</u>: D50) and featured at
the Bath Festival in May 1978 and the Bromsgrove
Festival in May 1986 with the composer at the piano

W156.<u>THE LITTLE GHOST WHO DIED FOR LOVE</u>
FOR SOPRANO AND PIANO
Text by Edith Sitwell whose note appears in the
original manuscript: Deborah Churchill, hanged in
1708 for shielding her lover in a duel. His
opponent was killed, her love fled to Holland, and
she was hanged in his stead, according to the law
of the time. The chronicle said: "Though she died
at peace with God, this malefactor could never
understand the justice of her sentence, to the last
movement of her life".
(Unpublished, but handled by Novello; 13 mins.)

Dedicated to Jane Manning

Adagio

The manuscript is dated: Barnsbury September
7-13 '76

W156a 1977 (31 January): London; Queen Elizabeth Hall;
Jane Manning (soprano); Richard Rodney Bennett
(piano). <u>See</u>: B173, B177

W157.<u>LOVE SONGS</u>
FOR TENOR AND ORCHESTRA
Text by e.e. cummings from <u>Complete Poems</u>,
published by MacGibbon and Kee
(Unpublished, but handled by Novello; 22 mins.)
Commissioned by the BBC Philharmonic Orchestra.
<u>See</u>: B61, B249

2+2.1+1.1+1.1/2.2.2.1/timp./perc.(2)/guitar
(lightly amplified)/ piano (doubling celesta)/hp
/strings (minimum 12.10.8.6.4)
Guitar part edited by David Leisner

Dedicated to Robert Tear

1. somewhere i have never travelled - (from
   'W[ViVa]' - 1931)   Molto moderato
2. in the rain-darkness (from 'XLI Poems'-1925)
                              Allegretto
3. i carry your heart with me (from '95 Poems' -
   1958)   Allegro appassionato
4. up into the silence (from '50 Poems' - 1940)
                    Allegro giocoso
5. it may not always be so (from 'Tulips and

Chimneys' - 1923)   Adagio

The score is dated: New York City
                     Oct '82 - Jan '84

Premieres

W157a 1986 (4 March): Manchester; BBC Studios; Robert
      Tear (tenor); BBC Philharmonic Orchestra; Edward
      Downes, conductor. (A BBC recording session)

W157b 1986 (11 March): Manchester; Free Trade Hall;
      Robert Tear (tenor); BBC Philharmonic Orchestra;
      Edward Downes, conductor (Public premiere)

W157c 1987 (31 August): London; Royal Albert Hall;
      Robert Tear (tenor); BBC Philharmonic Orchestra;
      Edward Downes, conductor (Henry Wood Promenade
      Concert)

W158. THE MUSIC THAT HER ECHO IS
      FIVE SONGS FOR TENOR AND PIANO
      Text by Edward Dyer (c. 1545-1607), Thomas Campian
      (1567-1620) and 17th century anonymous
      (Universal Edition © 1970; 15 mins.)

      Written for and dedicated to Dan Klein

      1. The lowest trees have tops (Dyer) Andante
      2. Sleep, wayward throughts   (Anon) Poco
                                        allegro, inquieto
      3. April is in my mistress' face (Anon) Molto
                                        moderato
      4. Clear or cloudy   (Anon)   Allegro leggiero
      5. Follow your Saint (Campian) Lento espressivo

      [These songs were written in March and April
      1967]

      Premiere

W158a 1967 (6 October): London; Purcell Room; Dan Klein
      (tenor) and Richard Rodney Bennett (piano). See:
      B148,B149

W159. NIGHTPIECE
      FOR SOPRANO AND ELECTRONIC TAPE
      Text by Charles Baudelaire: "Les Bienfaits de la
      Lune" from Poemes en Prose.
      The tape was made by the composer using a E.M.S.
      VCS3 synthesizer and pre-recorded tapes of parts of
      the text, spoken and whispered. The tape part
      given in the score is intended only as a rough
      guide for the performer; exact synchronization with
      the events shown is not absolutely essential except
      where an arrow points from the tape part to the
      voice part. The composer would prefer that the
      work be performed in a quasi-theatrical manner,
      without a score, and using imaginative lighting.

(Universal Edition ©1976; 12 mins.)

Written for and dedicated to Jane Manning

The score is dated: Barnsbury 1972

Premieres

W159a 1972 (21 April): London; BBC Studios, Jane Manning
    (soprano) and electronic tape. This recording
    was subsequently played in the BBC's Radio 3 on
    23 May 1972.

W159b 1972 (15 May): London; Round House; Jane Manning
    (soprano) and electronic tape.
    (The first public performance, at a concert
    organised by the 1972 Camden Festival). See:
    B175

W160. ONE EVENING
    SONG FOR TENOR AND GUITAR
    Text by W.H. Auden
    (Unpublished, but handled by Universal Edition; ?
    mins.)
    Commissioned by Jupiter Records for the Jupiter
    Book of Contemporary Ballads (JUR OA 10) See:D28

    Dedicated to Wilfred Brown and John Williams

    The score is dated: Islington Nov-Dec '64

    Also included were specially composed settings
    of

    Robert Graves   (John Addison)
    Louis MacNeice   (Alan Rawsthorne)
    Patrica Beer   (Phyllis Tate)

    Recorded by Wilfred Brown (tenor) and D. Dupre
    (guitar)

W161. OPHELIA
    CANTATA FOR COUNTER-TENOR, ONDES MARTENOT, HARP AND
    NINE SOLO STRINGS (OR STRING ORCHESTRA)
    Text by Arthur Rimbaud; his poem Ophelie was
    written in May 1870, when the poet was 16 years
    old.
    (Unpublished, but handled by Novello; 15 mins.)
    Commissioned by Michael Chance.

    Ondes Martenot, harp and
    (a) 4 violins, 2 violas, 2 celli and 1 double
        bass or
    (b) 12 violins, 4 violas, 4 celli and 2 double
        basses, each violin part being taken by
        three players and the lower string parts
        being doubled. Where a line is marked SOLO
        it should always be played by one player
        only.

Dedicated to Michael Chance and Cynthia Millar

Adagio

The score is dated: New York City January 23 '87

Premieres

W161a 1987 (17 July): Cheltenham; Town Hall; Michael Chance (counter-tenor); Cynthia Millar (ondes martenot); Skaila Kanga (harp); Guildhall String Ensemble; Robert Salter, conductor. See: B388

W161b 1988 (22 April): London; St. John's Smith Square; Michael Chance (counter-tenor); Cynthia Millar (ondes martenot); London Musici; Mark Stephenson, conductor

W162. OUR OWN KIND OF DANCING
FOR SOPRANO AND PIANO (1970s)
Lyrics by Richard Rodney Bennett
(Novello © 1979 – Just Friends in Print)

Medium rock

Written for performance by Marian Montgomery and featured at the Edinburgh Festival in September 1979 ('Portraits of Ladies') with the composer at the piano

W163. QUIETLY WITH BRIGHT EYES
FOR VOICE, PIANO AND ELECTRONIC TAPE
Text by e.e. cummings
(Unpublished, but handled by Universal Edition; 10 mins.)
The word-setting was designed to give the singer considerable freedom in performance. The tape was made by the composer, using a VCS3 synthesizer.

Dedicated to Karin Krog

1. six
2. these children singing
3. here's a little mouse

[These settings were composed in 1972]

Premieres

W163a 1972 (16 November): Manchester; Royal Northern College of Music; Synthesis: Karin Krog (singer) and Richard Rodney Bennett (piano). See: B190

W163b 1972 (23 November): London; Purcell Room; Synthesis: Karin Krog (singer) and Richard Rodney Bennett (piano) See: B66,B196,B197

W164. SHE REMINDS ME OF YOU
FOR SOPRANO AND PIANO (1970s)

(Unpublished, but handled by Novello)

> Written for performance by Marian Montgomery and featured at the Bath Festival in May 1978 and the Bromsgrove Festival in May 1986 with the composer at the piano

W165. SOLILOQUY
FOR VOICE, ALTO SAXOPHONE, TENOR SAXOPHONE, TRUMPET, TROMBONE, PIANO, BASS AND DRUMS
Text by Julian Mitchell
(Unpublished, but handled by Universal Edition; 13 mins.)

> Dedicated to Cleo Laine

> Fast

> The score is dated: 26.i.67, having been started in December 1966

Premiere

W165a 1967 (4 March): London; Queen Elizabeth Hall; Cleo Laine (singer), John Dankworth Ensemble. (A concert to celebrate the opening of the Queen Elizabeth Hall). See: B15

W166. SONNET SEQUENCE
FOR TENOR AND STRING ORCHESTRA
Text by William Shakespeare
(Unpublished, but handled by Universal Edition)
Originally commissioned by the Globe Theatre Trust

> Sonnet XIX: Devouring Time, blunt thou
> Interlude
> Sonnet XII: When I do count the clock

Premiere

W166a 1972 (23 April): Southwark; Cathedral Church of St. Saviour and St. Mary Overie; Philip Langridge (tenor); London Sinfonietta; John Pritchard, conductor. See: B76, B180, B194, B295

The revised and expanded version (1974) was commissioned by the East Midlands Arts Association, to be known as the "Graham Beynon Memorial Commission"
(Unpublished, but handled by Novello; 13 mins.)

> Strings: min. 6,6,4,4,2 (players); max. 12,10,8,6,4

> Sonnet XIX: 'Devouring Time, blunt thou the lion's paw'   Maestoso
> Interlude 1

<u>Sonnet CIV</u>:   'To me, fair friend, you never can
be old'   Lirico
Interlude II
<u>Sonnet XII</u>:   'When I do count the clock that
tells the time'   Elegiaco

Certain details of the scoring were changed and the
new sonnet-setting involved an important part for
solo violin

The score is dated: 1st version: March '72
                    Revised version: Sept-Oct '74
                                     Barnsbury

<u>Premieres</u>

W166b 1974 (20 December): Milton Keynes; Stantonbury
      Theatre; Philip Langridge (tenor); New London
      Ensemble; Richard Bradshaw, conductor

W166c 1975 (8 January): London; Queen Elizabeth Hall;
      Philip Langridge; (tenor); New London Ensemble;
      Richard Bradshaw, conductor. <u>See</u>: B123, B341,
      B346

W167.TENEBRAE - CYCLE
     FOR BARITONE AND PIANO
     (Universal Edition ©1975; 17 mins.)

     Dedicated to Barry McDaniel and Aribert Reimann

     1.   Adieu, farewell earth's blisse
              Thomas Nashe, 1593   Dolente
     2.   Like to the falling of a star
              Harry King, 1664   Tranquillo
     3.   Hey Nonny No!
              Anon.   Con Slancio
     4.   Written on the eve of execution
              Chidiock Tichbourne, 1586 Desolato
     5.   Death, be not proud
              John Donne, c 1615   Declamato

     The score is dated: Barnsbury
                          11-22 October 1971

     <u>Premiere</u>

W167a 1974 (20 August): London; Queen Elizabeth Hall;
      Barry McDaniel (baritone); Aribert Reimann
      (piano). <u>See</u>: B139, B195, B240

W168.<u>this is the garden</u> - SONG
     FOR HIGH VOICE AND PIANO
     Text by e.e. cummings (1925)
     (Novello ©1985; 4 mins.)
     Commissioned for the 1985 English Song Award as the
     test piece, with funds from South East Arts

     Dedicated to Teresa Cahill

Adagio sognando

The score is dated: New York City
Sept. 15-17 1984

Premiere

W168a 1985 (14 May): Brighton; Diana Hart (soprano);
Julia Kettle (piano)
First performance of the song in the preliminary
rounds.
The actual winner of the special prize was Robin
Green (tenor), accompanied by Kathron Sturrock
in the Bennett song, who was also the overall
second-prize winner.

W169. THIS WORLD'S JOIE
FOR SOPRANO AND PIANO
Text: 14th century anonymous poem
(Mills Music © 1962; 5½ mins.)

Dedicated to Josephine Nendick

Molto adagio

[This setting was composed in 1960]

Premiere

W169a 1960 (13 November): London; Mermaid Theatre;
Dorothy Dorow (soprano); Richard Rodney Bennett
(piano)

W170. THREE SONGS
FOR SOLO TENOR
Text by Jose Garcia Villa
(Unpublished)

1. Sir, there's a tower of fire in me
2. And if the heart cannot love
3. My most, my most, O my lost

[These settings were composed in 1955 and were
originally four in total.]

Premiere

W170a 1959 (7 February): London; BBC Studios; Peter
Pears (tenor)
This recording was subsequently played in the
BBC's Third Programme on 21 September 1959

W171. TIME'S WHITER SERIES
FOR COUNTER-TENOR AND LUTE
(Unpublished, but handled by Novello; 15 mins.)
Lute part edited by Michael Blake Watkins. Version
for counter-tenor and guitar transcribed (1984) by
David Leisner.

Written for and dedicated to James Bowman

I.   Prelude (John Dryden 'Astraea Redux')
             Adagio
II.   Of Snow (F. Martens 'Voyage to
         Spitzbergen') Con moto delicato
III. Interlude I (Lute only)
             Appassionato
IV.   Bells of Grey Crystal (Edith Sitwell
      'Facade')   Molto moderato
V.   Interlude II (Lute only)
             Appassionato
VI.   A Palinode (Edmund Bolton 16th century)
             Elegiaco
VII   Postlude (Dryden)

The score is dated: Barnsbury, 23.1.74

Premieres

W171a 1975 (6 June): Aldeburgh; Jubilee Hall; James
      Bowman (counter-tenor); Anthony Bailes (lute).
      See: B154, B239

W171b 1976 (3 November): London; Cockpit Theatre, NW8;
      David James (counter-tenor); Lavinia Snelling
      (lute)

W171c 1983 (27 November): New York; Abraham Goodman
      House; Rodney Hardesty (counter-tenor); JoAnn
      Falletta (lute)

W172. TOM O'BEDLAM'S SONG
      FOR TENOR VOICE AND CELLO
      Text: Anonymous
      (Mills Music © 1964; 4 mins.)

      Written for and dedicated to Peter Pears

      Appassionato

      [This song was composed in 1961]

Premiere

W172a 1961 (22 November): Edinburgh; National Gallery;
      Peter Pears (tenor); Joan Dickson (cello)
      (The 500th lunch time concert). See: B170

W173. VOCALISE - FOUR SONGS
      FOR SOPRANO AND PIANO
      Text by Joseph Hansen
      (Unpublished, but handled by Novello; 8 mins.)

      Dedicated to Jane Manning and John McCabe

      1. Attendant   Molto adagio
      2. Vocalise   Allegro
      3. The inhabitants of the moon

                              Lento flessible
    4.   From the new cave Presto ritmico

    The score is dated: 1.   New York City 19.3.81
                           2.   New York City 20.3.81
                           3.   New York City 25.3.81
                           4.   New York City 22.3.81

       Premiere

W173a 1983 (1 March): London; Wigmore Hall; Jane Manning
    (soprano); John McCabe (piano)

VII. MUSIC FOR SPEAKER

W174. CHILDE ROLANDE TO THE DARK TOWER CAME
FOR SPEAKER AND PIANO
Text by Robert Browning
(Unpublished)

Unable to trace any details

Premiere

Unable to trace first performance

First London Performance

W174a 1962 (9 January): London; Bishopsgate Institute;
Sebastian Shaw (speaker); Richard Rodney Bennett
(piano). See: B7

VIII. MUSIC FOR CHILDREN

W175. ALL THE KING'S MEN (Universal Edition ©1968; 40 mins.)
AN OPERA FOR YOUNG PEOPLE
Libretto by Beverley Cross
Commissioned by the Coventry Schools' Music Association. See: B48, B94, B211

CAST

Royalists
King Charles I
Queen Henrietta Maria (speaking part)
Dr. Chillingworth, a scientific inventor,
                        adviser to the King
King's Herald (speaking part)
Drummer Boy
King's Generals (minimum 4)
King's Soldiers (minimum of 6, including 2 soli)
Queen's Ladies (minimum of 6, including 1 solo)

Roundheads
Colonel Massey, young Commander in charge of
  defence of Gloucester
The Messenger (speaking part)
Colonel Massey's Soldiers (minumum of 6)
Women and children of Gloucester (minimum of 6)

The action takes place within and without the City Walls of Gloucester in 1643

The ideal instrumentation for this work is as follows. The abbreviation (G) indicates a good standard of proficiency. (E) indicates an elementary standard. Instruments marked with a * are optional.

2 Flutes (G)	2 Horns (E)
* 1 Oboe (E)	2 Trumpets (E)
2 Clarinets (G)	* 1 Trombone (E)
* 1 Bassoon (E)	

Glockenspiel)
Chime Bars) 2 players (E)
* Xylophone   )

Percussion 3 players (E)

Piano duet (4 hands 1 piano) (G)
2 Violins (G)   * Violins 1 & 2 (E)
* Violins 3 and/or Violas (E)
1 Viola (or 3rd Violin) (G)
1 Cello (G)   Celli (E)
* 1 Double Bass   * Bassi (E)
Guitar (required in only 1 scene)

Dedicated to the Coventry Schools' Music Association

I.   Moderato e ritmico
II.   -
III. Molto moderato
IV.   Alla Marcia, molto ritmico
V.   Alla Marcia
VI.   Allegro
VII. Poco allegro
VIII. Senza misura
IX.   Poco allegro, agitato
X.   Allegro
XI.   Vivace
XII. Allegretto

The score is dated: Islington June 3-July 4 '68

Premiere

W175a 1969 (28   March):   Coventry;   Technical   College
Theatre;

Royalists
King Charles I   Nicolas Lawrence
Queen Henrietta Maria Alison Doig
Dr. Chillingworth   Richard Beck
King's Herald   Raymond Portelli
Drummer Boy   Christopher Coles
King's Generals   Thomas Atkins
                         Rustrum Ebrahim
                         Peter Masson
                         Christopher Morris
King's Soldiers   Christopher Birch
                         Eric Butterworth
                         Frank Hoskins
Boys with cart   Mark Harley
                         Richard Johnson
                         Martin Tellis
King's Men   Graham Allbutt
                         Ian Bird
                         Clifford Mazey
                         Philip Payne
                         Peter Scott
                         Manjit Singh

Queen's Ladies   Kathleen Banbury : Solo
                         Denise Moore
                         Julie Senior
                         Jeanne Taylor
                         Linda Williams
                         June Woodhouse

Roundheads
Colonel Massey   Matthew Campbell
The Messenger   David Mitchell
Colonel Massey's
  Soldiers   Martin Barton
                         Peter Gibbins
                         Peter Morley
Men, Women and children of Gloucester

Orchestra conducted by Peter Isherwood
Settings and costumes designed by Colin Dick
Producer: William J. Newton
See: B34, B69, B187, B212, B236, B394

W176. THE AVIARY
FIVE SONGS FOR UNISON VOICES AND PIANO
(Universal Edition ⓒ 1966; 8 mins.)
German translation by Ernst Hartmann

Dedicated to Alexander Faris

1. The Bird's Lament (John Clare)
                  Con molto
2. The Owl   (Alfred Tennyson)
                  Con brio
3. The Early Nightingale (John Clare)
                  Con tenerezza
4. The Widow Bird (P.B. Shelley)
                  Con tristezza
5. The Lark   (S.T. Coleridge)
                  Vivace

[These songs were written in 1968]

Premieres

W176a 1966 (17 January): London; BBC Studios; Dorothy
      Dorow (soprano); Richard Rodney Bennett (piano).
      (First broadcast performance)

W176b 1966 (14 February): London; Arts Council; Daniel
      Klein (tenor); Anthony Saunders (piano) (A Park
      Lane Group Concert). See: B35, B262

W177. THE BERMUDAS
FOR MIXED VOICES (HIGH VOICES (girls' or unbroken
boys' voices) TENOR AND BASSES) AND ORCHESTRA
Text by Andrew Marvell
(Universal Edition ⓒ 1974; 10 mins.)
Commissioned by Leighton Park School to celebrate
the opening of the new Hall. See: B316

2.1.2.1/2.2.1.0/timp./perc.(3)/piano   duet   (4
hands, one piano)/strings (minimum 6.6.4.4.2)

Dedicated to the Choir and Orchestra of Leighton
Park School

Con moto

The score is dated: London, Rome. Dec '71

Premiere

W177a 1972 (20 May): Reading; New Hall, Music School
      (Leighton Park School); Choir and Orchestra of
      Leighton Park School; Girls from St. Joseph's

Convent School (Director of Music: David
Andrews); David Hughes, conductor

W178.CONVERSATIONS FOR TWO FLUTES (1964)
(Universal Edition © 1965; 3 mins.)
Versions also published (1985) for 2 oboes or 2
saxophones, all in the Music for young players
series.

Dedicated to Claire and Sandra

I.   Allegretto
II.   Poco lento
III.   Vivace
IV.   Andante
V.   Con brio

Premiere

Unable to trace

W179.CROSSTALK (1966)
FOUR PIECES FOR TWO CLARINETS OR TWO BASSETT HORNS
(Universal Edition © 1967; 6 mins.)

Dedicated to Thea King and Stephen Trier

I.   Con grazia
II.   Con umore
III.   Con tristezza
IV.   Con slancio

Premiere

W179a 1966 (August): Dartington; Summer School of Music;
Thea King and Stephen Trier (clarinets)

W180.DIVERSIONS FOR PIANO (1964)
SEVEN PIECES FOR CHILDREN
(Universal Edition © 1965; 6 mins.) See: B189

Dedicated to the composer's mother

1.   Giocoso
2.   Grazioso
3.   Ritmico
4.   Legato
5.   Con brio
6.   Mesto
7.   Vivace

Premiere

Unable to trace

W181.FARNHAM FESTIVAL OVERTURE
FOR ORCHESTRA
(Mills Music © 1964; 5 mins.)

Commissioned for the Farnham Music Festival 1965 by Lloyds and Keyworth Ltd. Farnham

2.2.2.2/2.2.2.0/timp./perc.(5)/piano/strings

Allegro ritmico

The score is dated: Black River Falls, Wisconsin Aug-Sept. '64

Premiere

W181a 1965 (18 May): Farnham; Parish Church of St. Andrew; Combined orchestras of Farnham Grammar School and Tiffin School, Kingston upon Thames; Alan Fluck, conductor. See: B21, B209

W182. THE INSECT WORLD
FOUR SONGS FOR UNISON VOICES (OR SOLO VOICE) AND PIANO
(Universal Edition ⓒ 1966; 7 mins.)
German translation by Ernst Hartmann

Dedicated to Malcolm and Dolly Williamson

1. The Insect World (John Clare) Allegretto
                                          molto moderato
2. The Fly (William Oldys) Allegro ritmico
3. Glow worms (Andrew Marvell) Andante expressivo
4. Clock-a-Clay [:Ladybird] (John Clare) Alla
                                valse, leggiero e ritmico

[These songs were written in 1965]

Premieres

W182a 1966 (17 January): London; BBC Studios; Dorothy Dorrow (soprano); Richard Rodney Bennett (piano)

W182b 1966 (14 February): London; Arts Council; Daniel Klein (tenor); Anthony Saunders (piano) (A Park Lane Group concert). See: B35,B262

W183. THE MIDNIGHT THIEF (1963)
A Mexican folk story which was retold by Ian Serraillier, with music by Bennett. It was specially commissioned for the BBC's Making Music series for children 8-10, and was produced by John Hosier and presented on television during the Summer Term of 1963.
(Mills Music ⓒ 1963; 20 mins.)

One of the aims of this work is for the children themselves to provide their own accompaniment, and for this reason no piano accompaniment is given. The five songs are all quite simple and are accompanied by an equally simply melodic line, playable on any pitched percussion instrument such as chime bars, glockenspiel, or xylophone in the key of C with an additional F sharp

Characters
The Farmer
Pedro, his eldest son (large,fat,lazy)
Augusto, his next son (proud, disdainful)
Fernando, his youngest son (modest, shy)
The Toad
The Bird of Paradise
Other children could also take the parts of the Hornbill, the Toucan, the Grey-Green Cactus

The Farmer's Song (Fast and bright)
Pedro's Song (Slow and sleepy)
Augusto's Song (in march time)
Fernando's Song (Cheerfully)
The Wedding song (With a swing)

Premiere

W183a 1963 (30 March): London; BBC TV Centre; John Longstaff (singer); James Blades (percussion); Children of West Lodge Primary School, Pinner, trained by Peggy Exon and Frank Barnes (The first of 8 weekly programmes, subsequently televised on 30th April 1963)

John Longstaff introduced a complete performance of The Midnight Thief on 25 June 1963. This was pre-recorded on 4 June and in addition to the above, an instrumental ensemble was featured: Sarah Francis (oboe); Graham Evans (clarinet); Karry Camden (bassoon); Donald Blakeson (trumpet); Maria Korchinska (harp); Ron Peters (bass)

W184.OXFORD NURSERY SONG BOOK: ARRANGEMENTS (1963)
Collected by Percy Buck
(Oxford University Press [ⓒ1964])

Bennett's arrangements are not indicated in the published score. However, a recording (Jupiter jep OC 31 - See:D27) of 15 items included:

A frog he would	(page 49)
Baa-baa Black Sheep	(page 3)
I saw 3 ships	(page 62)
Jack and Jill	(page 39)
Lavender's Blue	(page 23)
Little Boy Blue	(page 15)
Little Bo-Peep	(page 33)
London Bridge	(page 57)
O Dear! What can	(page 28)
Old King Cole	(page 48)
Oranges and Lemons	(page 34)
Sing a song of Sixpence	(page 51)
The Keel Row	(page 8)
When Johnny comes	(page 75)

Where are you going   (page 25)

Premiere

Unable to trace

W185. PARTY PIECE
FOR PIANO AND SMALL ORCHESTRA
(Universal Edition © 1971; 8 mins.)
Commissioned by Youth and Music for the Farnham
Festival 1971

2+1.2.2.2/2.2.1.0/perc.(4)/solo piano/strings

Dedicated to Alexandra and Richard Franko
Goldman, in gratitude

Allegro giocoso

The score is dated: Baltimore/New York
                    Dec 18 1970

Premieres

W185a 1971 (15 May); Farnham; Grammar School; Michael
      Overbury (piano); Surrey County Youth Orchestra;
      Ernest Mongor, conductor, See: B387

W185b 1971 (20 November): London; Royal Festival Hall;
      Marios Papadopoulos (piano); Royal Philharmonic
      Orchestra; Trevor Harvey, conductor

W186. SEVEN DAYS A WEEK:
7 SHORT PIANO PIECES FOR CHILDREN (1962)
(Mills Music © 1963; 4 mins.) See: B189

Dedicated to Anne

Monday   (Tranquillo)
Tuesday   (Giocoso)
Wednesday   (Alla marcia)
Thursday   (Dolce)
Friday   (Mesto)
Saturday   (Leggiero)
Sunday   (Piacevole)

Premiere

Unable to trace

W187. SUMMER MUSIC (1982)
FOR FLUTE AND PIANO
(Novello © 1983; 10 mins.)
Used by the Associated Board for Grade VII

Dedicated to Angela and Chris

1. Allegro tranquillo
2. Siesta (Lento e dolce)

3. Games (Vivo)

Premiere

W187a 1982 (23   November);   London;   Burgh   House,
    Hampstead;   Ann   Radzinowicz   (flute);   Roger
    Steptoe (piano)

W188.UP BOW, DOWN BOW (BOOK ONE)
    FOR VIOLIN AND PIANO
    7 first-position pieces used for Grades I and II
    (Novello ©1979; 7 mins.)

        Dedicated to Michael Easton

        1. Serenade   (Lightly)
        2. Air   (Slow and gentle)
        3. Ghost story   (Stealthy)
        4. A quiet conversation (Andante)
        5. Hide and seek   (Lively and rhythmic)
        6. A little elegy   (Tenderly)
        7. Merry-go-round   (Lively and rhythmic)

        The score is dated: London, July 21-23, 1979

    Premiere

        Unable to trace

W189.UP BOW, DOWN BOW (BOOK TWO)
    FOR VIOLA AND PIANO
    6 first - position pieces, used by the Associated
    Board for Grade III
    (Novello ©1980; 6 mins.)

        1. A country walk   (Grazioso)
        2. Work song   (Alla marcia)
        3. Romance   (Lento)
        4. Fives   (Scherzando)
        5. Cradle song   (Andante)
        6. Windmills   (Giocoso)

        The score is dated: London, July 29-Aug 6, 1979

    Premiere

        Unable to trace

W190.A WEEK OF BIRTHDAYS
    SEVEN SHORT PIECES FOR PIANO
    (Mills Music ©1961; 8 mins.) See: B1, B2, B189

        Dedicated to Lindsay, Charlotte, Adam, Tamsin
        and Tully

        Monday's Child   (Moderato)
        Tuesday's Child   (Waltz tempo)
        Wednesday's Child   (Slow)
        Thursday's Child   (Flowing)

Friday's Child   (Peacefully)
Saturday's Child   (Vigorous, but not too
                         fast)
The child that is born
on the Sabbath Day   (Gaily)

<u>Premiere</u>

Unable to trace

IX. FILM MUSIC

W191.AFRICAN AWAKENING: DOCUMENTARY FILM (1962)
Directed by Peter Hopkinson
Production company: World Wide for Unilever

Duration of film : 38 mins.

Release date: September 1962

W192.THE ANGRY HILLS : FEATURE FILM (1958)
Directed by Robert Aldrich
Production   company: Raymond   Strass-Cineworld
Productions. Script by A.I. Bezzerides from the
book by Leon Uris

Duration of film : 105 mins.

Release date: 9 March 1959

W193.BILLION DOLLAR BRAIN: FEATURE FILM (1967)
Directed by Ken Russell
Production Company: Lowndes Productions
Script by John McGrath from the book by Len
Deighton

Duration of film: 111 mins.

Musical director: Richard Rodney Bennett who
played one of the three pianos featured in the
score.

Release date: 14 January 1967

W194.BILLY LIAR: FEATURE FILM (1963)
Directed by John Schlesinger
Production company : Joseph Janni
Script by Keith Waterhouse and Willis Hall from the
book by Keith Waterhouse and the play by Waterhouse
and Hall

Duration of film: 98 mins.

Release date: 16 September 1963

W195.BLIND DATE: FEATURE FILM (1959)
US Title: Chance Meeting
Direction by Joseph Losey
Production Company: Independent Artists
Script by Ben Barzman and Millard Lampell from the
book by Leigh Howard

Duration of film: 95 mins.

Musical director: Malcolm Arnold

Release date: 21 September 1959

W196.THE BRINKS JOB: FEATURE FILM (1978)

Directed by William Friedkin
Production company: Dino De Laurentiis Corporation
for Universal
Script by Walon Green from the book <u>Big Stick up at</u>
<u>Brink's</u> by Noel Behn

Duration of film: 103 mins.

Musical director: Angela Morley

Release date: September 1979

W197.<u>THE BUTTERCUP CHAIN</u>: FEATURE FILM (1970)
Directed by Robert Ellis Miller
Production company: John Witney-Philip Waddilove
Productions
Script by Peter Draper from the book by Janice
Elliott

Duration of film: 95 mins.

Release date: October 1970

W198.<u>CIRCUS DRAWINGS</u>: DOCUMENTARY FILM (1962)
Directed by Richard Williams
The score was written but the film was left
unfinished and never completed

W199.<u>THE DEVIL NEVER SLEEPS</u> : FEATURE FILM (1961)
US Title: Satan never sleeps
Directed by Leo McCarey
Production company: Leo McCarey
Script by Claude Binyon and Leo McCarey from the
book <u>China Story</u> by Pearl S. Buck

Duration of film: 127 mins.

Musical director: Muir Mathieson

Release date: April 1962

W200.<u>THE DEVIL'S DISCIPLE</u>: FEATURE FILM (1958)
Directed by Guy Hamilton
Production company: Hecht-Hill-Lancaster/Brynaprod
Script by John Dighton and Roland Kibbee from the
play by George Bernard Shaw

Duration of film: 82 mins.

Musical director: John Hollingsworth

Release date: 5 October 1959

W201.<u>THE ENGINEERS</u>: DOCUMENTARY FILM (1965)
Directed by John Gates Armstrong
Production Company: Athos production Co. for Hawker
Siddeley

Duration of film: 26 mins.

Release date: October 1967. <u>See</u>:B4

W202.<u>EQUUS</u>: FEATURE FILM (1977)
Directed by Sidney Lumet
Production company: The Winkast Co. in association
with Persky-Bright
Script by Peter Shaffer from his own play

Duration of film: 137 mins.

Musical director: Angela Morley

Release date: November 1977

W203.<u>EUROPEAN TAPESTRY</u>: DOCUMENTARY FILM (1965)
Directed by Terry Gould
Production company: Athos Film Productions for
British Overseas Airways Corporation
Script by Henry Sandoz

Duration of film: 23 mins.

Release date: unable to trace

W204.<u>A FACE IN THE NIGHT</u>: FEATURE FILM (1956)
US Title: Menace in the Night
Directed by Lance Comfort
Production company: Gibraltar Films
Script by Norman Hudis and John Sherman from the
book <u>Suspense</u> by Bruce Graeme

Duration of film: 75 mins.

Musical director: Philip Martell

Release date: unable to trace

W205.<u>FAR FROM THE MADDING CROWD</u>: FEATURE FILM (1967)
Directed by John Schlesinger
Production company: Appia films/Vic
Script by Frederic Raphael from the book by Thomas
Hardy. <u>See</u>: B47

Duration of film: 168 mins.

Musical director: Marcus Dods

2+1.1+1.0.1/4.2.2+1.1/timp./perc.(3)/hp/2 pianos
/strings

Release date: 27 October 1968. <u>See</u>: B120

W206.<u>FIGURES IN A LANDSCAPE</u>: FEATURE FILM (1970)
Directed by Joseph Losey
Production company: Cinecrest Films/Cinema Center
Script by Robert Shaw from the book by Barry
England

Duration of film: 110 mins.

Musical director: Marcus Dods

Release date: December 1970

W207. <u>HEAVENS ABOVE</u>!: FEATURE FILM (1963)
Directed by John Boulting
Production   Company: Boulting   Bros   (Charter
Productions)
Script by Frank Harvey and John Boulting from an
idea by Malcolm Muggeridge

Duration of film: 118 mins.

Musical director: John Hollingsworth

Release date: 8 September 1963

W208. <u>L'IMPRECATEUR</u>: FEATURE FILM (1977)
Directed by Jean-Louis Bertuccelli
Production Company: Action Films
Script by Rene-Victor Pilhes, S. Becker and
Jean-Louis Bertuccelli from the book by Rene-Victor
Pilhes

Duration of film: 102 mins.

Release date: reviewed at Salle Ponthieu, Paris
25 August 1977

W209. <u>INDISCREET</u>: FEATURE FILM (1958)
Directed by Stanley Donen
Production company: Grandon Production
Script by Norman Krasna from his play <u>Kind Sir</u>

Duration of film: 98 mins.

Release date: 20 October 1958

W210. <u>INTERPOL</u>: FEATURE FILM (1956)
<u>US Title</u>: Pickup Alley
Directed by John Gilling
Production company: Warwick Productions
Script by John Paxton from the book by A.J. Forrest

Duration of film: 92 mins.

Release date: April 1957. <u>See</u>: B25

W211. <u>LADY CAROLINE LAMB</u>: FEATURE FILM (1972)
Directed by Robert Bolt
Production   company: GEC/Pulsar   Productions   of
London
Script by Robert Bolt

Duration of film: 123 mins.

Music played by the New Philharmonia Orchestra
Peter Mark (viola)
Musical director: Marcus Dods

2+1.2+1.2+1.2/2.2.0.0/timp./perc.(2)/harpsichord
/hp/strings(10.8.6.6.4) including solo viola

Elegy for viola and orchestra   Molto vivo
        Duration: 16 mins.   Dated: August 1972
    9.M.1 Byron's carriage   Alla marcia
        Duration: 1 min. 20 secs. (Recorded 24.7.72)
    9.M.3 Caroline in the rain (Solo viola) Inquieto
        Duration : 16 secs.   (Recorded 24.7.72)
    10.M.1. William returns home Lento
        Duration : 1 min. 20 secs. (Recorded 24.7.72)
    11.M.2. The Ride   Molto vivo
        Duration: 38 secs. (Recorded 24.7.72)
    14.M.1. William and Caroline Andante con moto
        Duration: 5 mins. 30 secs.
    14.M.2. End Titles   Maestoso
        Duration: 1 min. 30 secs.

    Release date: December 1972

W212.THE MAN INSIDE: FEATURE FILM (1958)
     Directed by John Gilling
     Production company: Warwick Film Productions
     Script by Richard Maibaun and John Gilling from the
     book by M.E. Chaber

     Duration of film: 97 mins.

     Release date: 8 September 1958

W213.THE MAN WHO COULD CHEAT DEATH: FEATURE FILM (1959)
     Directed by Terence Fisher
     Production company: Hammer Films
     Script by Jimmy Sangster from the play The Man in
     Half Moon Street by Barre Lyndon

     Duration of film: 83 mins.

     Musical director: John Hollingsworth

     Release date: 30 November 1959

W214.THE MARK: FEATURE FILM (1961)
     Directed by Guy Green
     Production company: Raymond Stross/Sidney Buchman
     Script by Sidney Buchman and Stanley Mann from the
     book by Charles Israel

     Duration of film: 127 mins.

     Musical director: John Hollingsworth

     Release date: 26 January 1961

W215.MURDER ON THE ORIENT EXPRESS: FEATURE FILM (1974)
     Directed by Sidney Lumet
     Production company: G.W. Films for EMI
     Script by Paul Dehn from the book by Agatha
     Christie. See: B47

Duration of film: 131 mins.

Musical director: Marcus Dods
Richard Rodney Bennett (piano)

2+1.1.2+1.0/4.0.0.0/timp./perc.(3)/piano
(doubling celesta)/2 harps/strings
Rhythm guitar, bass and drums also in some
numbers

1.M.1. Main title   Grandioso
    Duration: 2 mins. 6 secs.
1.M.2. Kidnapping   Adagio
    Duration: 3 mins. 22secs.
1.M.3. Ferry Crossing   Adagio
    Duration: 58 secs.
3.M.1. The Orient Express (i)   Tempo di valse
    Duration: 3 mins. 43 secs.
3.M.2. Orient Express(ii)   Tempo di valse
    Duration: 3 mins. 7 secs.
4.M.1. Orient Express (iii)   Tempo di valse
    Duration: 39 secs.
4.M.2. Melodrama   Tempo di valse
    Duration: 2 mins. 41 secs.
4.M.3. The Body   Adagio
    Duration: 38 secs.
6.M.1. Remembering Daisy   Moderato
    Duration: 2 mins. 20 secs.
7.M.1. Snowdrift
    Duration: 35 secs.
8.M.1. Kennst du das Land?
    Duration: 1 min.
8.M.2. Princess Dragomiroff   Adagio
    Duration: 2 mins. 15 secs.
9.M.1. The Kimono   Vivo
    Duration: 28 secs.
10.M.1. The Knife   Lento
    Duration: 1 min. 21 secs.
11.M.1. Paulette   Lento
    Duration: 56 secs.
13.M.1. Prelude to Murder   Adagio
    Duration: 3 mins. 50 secs.
13.M.2. The Murder   Adagio
    Duration: 3 mins. 38 secs.
14.M.1. Finale   Allegro-Lento-Allegro
    Duration: 4 mins. 32 secs.

The score is dated: 18. viii. 1974

Release date: November 1974

Theme and Waltz theme: arranged for piano solo
(EMI Film and Theatre Music Limited. ©1974)

W216.MURDER WITH MIRRORS: FEATURE FILM (1985)
    Directed by Richard Lowry
    Production company: Warner Bros/Hajeno Productions
    Inc.

Script by George Eckstein from the book by Agatha Christie

Duration of film: 120 mins.

Release date: 20 February 1985 (1st showing on CBS TV)

W217. THE NANNY: FEATURE FILM (1965)
Directed by Seth Holt
Production company: Hammer Films
Script by Jimmy Sangster for the book by Evelyn Piper

Duration of film : 93 mins.

Musical director: Philip Martell

Release date: 7 November 1965

W218. NICHOLAS AND ALEXANDRA: FEATURE FILM (1971)
Directed by Franklin Schaffner
Production company: Horizon
Script by James Goldman and Edward Bond from the book by Robert K. Massie. See: B47

Duration of film: 189 mins.

Music played by the New Philharmonia Orchestra
Musical director: Marcus Dods

Release date: November 1971

W219. OF JEWELS AND GOLD: DOCUMENTARY FILM (1973)
Directed by G.L. Weinbren and Peter Bucknall
Production company: Athos Film Production/Gazelle Film Productions for Intergold
Script by Patrick O'Donovan

Duration of film: 28 mins.

Release date: unable to trace

W220. ONE WAY PENDULUM: FEATURE FILM (1964)
Directed by Peter Yates
Production company: Woodfall
Script by N.F. Simpson from his own play

Duration of film: 85 mins.

Music played by The Tommy Scott Quintet
Musical director: Marcus Dods

Release date: 4 February 1965

W221. ONLY TWO CAN PLAY: FEATURE FILM (1961)
Directed by Sidney Gilliat
Production company: Launder-Gilliat

Script by Bryan Forbes from the book <u>That Uncertain Feeling</u> by Kingsley Amis

Duration of film: 106 mins.

Musical director: Muir Mathieson

Release date: unable to trace

W222. <u>OUT OF HARMONY</u>: DOCUMENTARY (AMATEUR) FILM (1960)
Directed by Oscar Riesel

Duration of film: 14 mins.

One of the "Amateur Cine World 10 Best 1960" films

W223. <u>A PENNY FOR YOUR THOUGHTS</u>: FEATURETTE (1966)
Directed by Donovan Winter
Production company: Donwin
Script by Donovan Winter

Duration of film: 40 mins.

Release date: unable to trace

W224. <u>PERMISSION TO KILL</u>: FEATURE FILM (1975)
Directed by Cyril Frankel
Production company: Warner Bros/Sascha-Film
Script by Robin Estridge from his own book

Duration of film: 97 mins.

Music played by the Vienna Volksoper Orchestra, featuring Art Farmer (flugel horn)
Musical director: Robert Opratko

Release date: December 1975

W225. <u>THE PURPLE STREAM</u>: DOCUMENTARY FILM (1961)
Directed by Clive Donner
Production company: Aurelia Productions for Beecham Foods
Script by Henry Bentinck

Duration of film: 28 mins.

Musical director: John Hollingsworth

Release date: unable to trace

W226. <u>THE QUEST FOR PERFECTION</u>: DOCUMENTARY FILM (1962)

Unable to trace any details

W227. <u>A QUESTION OF SPRINGING</u>: DOCUMENTARY FILM (1960)
Part 3 of "How a Motor Car Works"
Directed by John Armstrong

Production company: World Wide Pictures for Shell
Petroleum

Duration of film: 18 mins.

Musical director: Richard Rodney Bennett

Release date: unable to trace

W228. THE R-AND-B MAN: DOCUMENTARY FILM (1965)

Unable to trace any details

W229. THE RETURN OF THE SOLDIER: FEATURE FILM (1982)
Directed by Alan Bridge
Production company: Brent Walker Pictures/Barry R
Cooper Productions/Skreba Films
Script by Hugh Whitemore from the book by Rebecca
West

Duration of film: 102 mins.

Musical director: Marcus Dods

Release date: June 1982

W230. THE SAFECRACKER: FEATURE FILM (1957)
Directed by Ray Milland
Production company: Coronado Productions
Script by Paul Monash from the book by Lt.-Col.
Rhys Davies and Bruce Thomas

Duration of film: 96 mins.

Release date: 28 April 1958

W231. SECRET CEREMONY: FEATURE FILM (1968)
Directed by Joseph Losey
Production company: Universal/World Films
Script by George Tabori from the short story by
Marco Denevi. See: B47, B97

Duration of film: 109 mins.

Musical director: Marcus Dods
Thea Musgrave (harpsichord)

2 percussion/piano/celesta/Hammond organ/harpsi-
chord/harp

Release date: 7 June 1969

W232. SHERLOCK HOLMES IN NEW YORK: FEATURE FILM (1976)
Directed by Boris Sagal
Production company: 20th Century Fox/NBC TV
Script by Alvin Sapinsley, based on the character
created by Arthur Conan Doyle

Duration of film: 120 mins.

Musical director: Leonard Rosenman

Release date: 18 October 1976 (1st showing on US TV)

W233. SONG OF THE CLOUDS: DOCUMENTARY FILM (1956)
Directed by John Armstrong

Unable to trace any details

W234. THEY TOOK US TO THE SEA: DOCUMENTARY FILM (1961)
Directed by John Krish
Production company: Graphic Films

Duration of film: 26 mins.

Release date: unable to trace

W235. VOICES: FEATURE FILM (1973)
Directed by Kevin Billington
Production company: Warden Productions
Script by George Kirgo and Robert Enders from the play by Richard Lortz

Duration of film: 91 mins.

Musical director: Marcus Dods

Release date: July 1973

W236. THE WITCHES: FEATURE FILM (1966)
US Title: The Devil's Own
Directed by Cyril Frankel
Production company: Hammer Films
Script by Nigel Kneale from the book The Devil's Own by Peter Curtis

Duration of film: 91 mins.

Musical director: Philip Martell

Release date: 9 December 1966

W237. THE WORLD ASSURED: DOCUMENTARY FILM (1956)
Directed by Reginald Jeffryes
Production company: World Wide Pictures for the British Insurance Association

Duration of film: 20 mins.

Musical director: John Hollingsworth

Release date: December 1956

W238. THE WRONG ARM OF THE LAW: FEATURE FILM (1962)
Directed by Cliff Owen
Production company: Romulus Films
Script by John Warren and Len Heath from an original story by Ivor Jay and William W. Smith

Duration of film: 94 mins.

Release date: 22 April 1963

W239. YANKS: FEATURE FILM (1979)
Directed by John Schlesinger
Production company: Joseph Janni-Lester Persky
Prods.
Script by Colin Welland and Walter Bernstein from a
story by Colin Welland

Duration of film: 140 mins.

Musical director: Marcus Dods

Release date: October 1979

X.   INCIDENTAL MUSIC

W240.ABIDE WITH ME: TV DRAMA (1976)

by Julian Mitchell
From "A Child in the Forest" by Winifred Foley
Directed by Moira Armstrong

Commissioned by BBC Television

Premiere

W240a 1976 (24 November): Transmitted on BBC Television
(BBC2). See: B326
Duration of music: 18 mins.

W241.ARENA: LA DAME AUX GLADIOLAS (1979)

- The Agony and the Ecstasy of Edna Everage.
A television documentary following a day in the
life of Dame Edna Everage.
Directed by Julian Jebb

Commissioned by BBC Television

Premiere

W241a 1979 (19 March) : Transmitted on BBC Television
(BBC2). Bennett took part in the programme,
playing the piano in a song (Moonee Blues),
specially composed for the occasion. Barry
Humphries sang the vocal line.
Duration of music: 25 secs.

W242.THE ATTIC : THE HIDING OF ANNE FRANK: TV DRAMA
(1988) by William Hanley

Directed by John Erman

Commissioned by Television Music Limited (a
subsidiary company of Yorkshire Television) in
association with Telecom Entertainment Inc., New
York

Saxophone/oboe/cor anglais/ 2 horns/hp./
piano/ondes martinot/ percussion(2)/strings
(12.10.8.6.4)

Premiere

W242a 1988 (4 September); Transmitted on the ITV network
(a Yorkshire Television production)

Music recorded at CTS Studios, Wembley on 20
February 1988.
Musical director: Neil Richardson

W243.THE CHARMER: TV DRAMA (1987)

by Allan Prior, in 6 episodes
Directed by Alan Gibson

Commissioned by London Weekend Television

Soprano saxophone/alto saxophone/tenor saxophone /baritone saxophone/ondes martinot/
percussion/harp/synthesiser/drums/   double
bass

Main titles/signature tune: an arrangement of
You're the Top   50 secs.

Episode 1:
1.M.2 The morning after   16 secs.
1.M.3 Mr. Stimpson   34 secs.
1.M.4 Suspicion   1 min. 2 secs.
1.M.5 The Letter   1 min. 2 secs.
1.M.6 Stealing the car   1 min. 4 secs.
1.M.7 Seducing Stimpson 1 min. 11 secs.
1.M.9 Clarince   2 mins.37 secs.
1.M.10 "It's gone"   28 secs.
1.M.11 Phone call   41 secs.
1.M.12 Joan's room   1 min. 11 secs.
End/Closing titles   )   55 secs.
written with two extra) 1 min. 10 secs.
endings   ) 1 min. 18 secs.

Episode 2:
2.M.2 Bedroom   1 min. 55 secs.
2.M.3 Worry   43 secs.
2.M.4 Going to the bank   55 secs.
2.M.5 Stimpson   1 min. 2 secs.
2.M.6 Watching Ralph   18 secs.
2.M.7 Bedroom waltz   1 min. 22 secs.
2.M.8 Money   20 secs.
2.M.9 The housemaid   11 secs.
2.M.10 Ralph at the bank 2 mins.20 secs.
2.M.11 Driving to the Ritz(i) 1 min. 16 secs.
2.M.11 Driving to the Ritz(ii)1 min. 17 secs.
2.M.13 At the station   12 secs.

Episode 3:
3.M.1 Bunty   25 secs.
3.M.2 Joan and Donald   33 secs.
3.M.4 Bunty and Mr Bennett 1 min. 49 secs.
3.M.5 Moving along   1 min. 57 secs.
3.M.6 Blackmail   25 secs.
3.M.7 Pamela   25 secs.
3.M.8 "Nothing more to say"   44 secs.

Episode 4:
4.M.1 After the wedding   47 secs.
4.M.2 Ralph and Pamela   1 min. 12 secs.
4.M.3 Donald and Pamela   54 secs.
4.M.4 The Burning House 3 mins.32 secs.
4.M.5 Funeral Cortege   51 secs.
4.M.6 After the wake   19 secs.
4.M.7 Ralph wonders   13 secs.

4.M.8	Suspicion		40 secs.
4.M.9	Ralph at the garage		41 secs.

Episode 5

5.M.1	Leaving the army		38 secs.
5.M.2	The Pier		48 secs.
5.M.3	Alison leaves		25 secs.
5.M.4	The name tag		42 secs.
5.M.5	In the pub	1 min.	29 secs.
5.M.6	The sea-front		45 secs.
5.M.7	The detectives		17 secs.
5.M.8	"Everything!"		14 secs.

Episode 6:

6.M.1	The Morgue		27 secs.
6.M.2	Joan sees Ralph	1 min.	14 secs.
6.M.3	Joan and Alison		46 secs.
6.M.4	"You're a fake"		20 secs.
6.M.5	Murder	1 min.	46 secs.
6.M.6	Ralph escapes	1 min.	46 secs.
6.M.7	Relief		11 secs.
6.M.8	On the train	1 min.	55 secs.
6.M.9	Prison cell		24 secs.
6.M.10	Joan	1 min.	13 secs.
6.M.11	Death sentence		39 secs.

Premiere

W243a 1987 (18 October): Episode 1 transmitted on the
     ITV network (A LWT production)

          The music was recorded:
          Signature tune: 20 November 1986 at CBS 2
          Incidental music: 8 March 1987 at Angel,
          Islington
          Musical director: Neil Richardson

W244. THE CHRISTIANS: TV DOCUMENTARY (1977)
     Written and presented by Bamber Gascoigne, in 13
     parts.

          Directed by Carlos Pasini

          Commissioned by GRANADA Television

Premiere

W244a 1977 (2 August): Part 1 transmitted on Thames
     Television (A GRANADA TV Production)
     Musical director: Marcus Dods

W245. CURTMANTEL: THEATRE PLAY (1962)
     by Christopher Fry

          Directed by Stuart Burge

          Commissioned by the Royal Shakespeare Company

Premiere

W245a 1962 (4 September): Edinburgh; Lyceum Theatre;
    Royal Shakespeare Company (World premiere at the
    Edinburgh Festival)

> Music recorded by The Royal Shakespeare
> Theatre Wind Band (leader: Alec Whittaker);
> Musical director: Brian Priestman, See: B188

First London performance

W245b 1962 (9 October): London, Aldwych; Royal
    Shakespeare Company

W246.THE DIARY OF NIJINSKY: RADIO FEATURE (1965)
    Translated and edited by Romola Nijinsky

> Produced by H.B. Fortuin

> Commissioned by the BBC

> 2+1.2.2.2/4.2.2+1.0/timp./perc.(1)/hp/strings

> Music written to link the three parts of the
> diary: Life, Death and Feelings

Premiere

W246a 1965 (11 April); Transmitted on the BBC Third
    Programme

> Music (previously recorded on 22 March 1965)
> played by the BBC Welsh Orchestra;
> Musical director: Marcus Dods
> Duration of music: 28 mins.

W247.DISMISSAL LEADING TO LUSTFULNESS: TV DRAMA (1967)
    By Thomas Whyte

> Directed by Rex Tucker

> Commissioned by BBC Television

Premiere

W247a 1967 (12 April): Transmitted on BBC Television
    (BBC1)

> Music played by an ad hoc orchestra;
> Musical director: Buxton Orr
> Duration of music: 11 mins.

W248.THE EBONY TOWER: TV DRAMA (1984)
    by John Fowles, dramatised by John Mortimer

> Director by Robert Knights

> Commissioned by GRANADA Television

Premiere

W248a 1984 (9 December): Transmitted on the ITV network
(A GRANADA TV Production)

Music played by ad hoc musicians (including
Susan Bradshaw and John McCabe (pianos) and
Cynthia Millar (ondes martenot));
Musical director: Marcus Dods

W249. THE ENTERTAINERS - "JUMPING AT THE WEEKEND"
Cartoon used by London Weekend Television to
advertise forthcoming programmes.

Devised by Pat Gavin

Commissioned by London Weekend Television

2 alto saxophones/2 tenor saxophones/baritone
saxophone/4 trumpets/2 trombones/bass
trombone/ piano/guitar/bass/drums

Promo I	15 secs
Promo II	29 secs
Promo III	45 secs
Promo IV	59 secs
Slower-Drama	30 secs

Premiere

W249a 1986 (29 August): Transmitted by London Weekend
Television

Music (previously recorded on 23 June 1986)
played by ad hoc musicians;
Musical director: Neil Richardson

W250. EUSTICE AND HILDA: TV DRAMA (1977)

A Trilogy by L.P. Hartley

Screenplay by Alan Seymour
Directed by Desmond Davis

Commissioned by BBC Television

1. The Shrimp and the Anemone
2. The Sixth Heaven
3. Eustice and Hilda

Premiere

W250a 1977 (30 November))
     1977 (7 December)) Transmitted on BBC
     1977 (14 December)) Television (BBC2)

Music played ad hoc musicians;
Musical director: Marcus Dods
Duration of music: 12 mins; 8 mins; 11 mins.

Theme from Eustace and Hilda: arranged for
piano solo by Bennett (Novello © 1978)

W251.HAMLET AT ELSINORE: TV DRAMA (1963)
    by William Shakespeare

        Directed by Philip Saville

        Commissioned by BBC Television

    Premiere

W251a 1964 (19 April): Transmitted on BBC Television

            Music played by ad hoc musicians;
            Musical director: John Hollingsworth
            Duration of music: 16 mins.

W252.HEREWARD THE WAKE: TV DRAMA (1965)
    by Charles Kingsley

        Dramatised by Anthony Steven
        Directed by Peter Hammond

        Commissioned by BBC Television

        0.1+1.0.1/1.1.0.0/perc.(1)/harp

    Premiere

W252a 1965 (12 September): Episode 1 transmitted on BBC
        Television (BBC1)

            Music (previously recorded on 3 August 1965)
            played by ad hoc musicians;
            Musical director: Marcus Dods
            Duration of music:
            Opening titles 20 secs.
            Link Music   1 min. 17 secs.
            Closing music   45 secs.

W253.JUDITH: THEATRE PLAY (1962)
    by Jean Giraudoux
    Adapted by Christopher Fry

        Directed by Harold Clurman

        Commissioned by Roger L. Stevens, William
        Zeckendorf and H.M. Tennent

    Premiere

W253a 1962 (28 May): Oxford, New Theatre

        Music composed in collaboration with Daphne Oram

    First London Performance

W253b 1962 (20 June): London; Her Majesty's Theatre,
        Haymarket. See B43

W254.KNOCKBACK : TV DRAMA (1984)

A film in two parts by Brian Phelan, based on the book by Peter Adams and Shirley Cooklin

Directed by Piers Haggard

Commissioned by BBC Television

<u>Premiere</u>

W254a 1985 (27 January): Transmitted on BBC Television (BBC 2)

> Music played by 8 ad hoc musicians;
> Musical director: David Snell
> Duration of music (15 sections): 16 mins.

W255.<u>THE LONG-DISTANCE PIANO-PLAYER</u> : RADIO DRAMA (1962)
A parable for radio by Alan Sharp
Produced by Christopher Holme

Commissioned by the BBC

<u>Premiere</u>

W255a 1962 (17 August): Transmitted on the BBC Third Programme

> Music (previously recorded on 2 August 1962) played by Richard Rodney Bennett (piano) and Denis McCarthy (percussion)
> Duration of music: 26 mins. 21 secs.
> <u>See</u>: B207, B359

W256.<u>MALATESTA</u> : TV DRAMA (1964)
by Henry de Montherlant
Translated by Jonathan Griffi
Directed by Christopher Morahan

Commissioned by BBC Television

<u>Premiere</u>

W256a 1964 (2 December): Transmitted on BBC Television (BBC1)

> Music played by ad hoc musicians;
> Musical director: Marcus Dods
> Duration of music: 6 mins.

W257.<u>THE ORDER</u> : TV DRAMA (1966)
by Fritz Hochwälder
Translated by Patrick Alexander
Directed by Basil Coleman

Commissioned by BBC Television

<u>Premiere</u>

W257a 1967 (18 January): Transmitted on BBC Television (BBC1)

Music played by 10 ad hoc musicians;
Musical director: Marcus Dods
Duration of music: 8 mins. 43 secs.

W258.POOR LITTLE RICH GIRL: TV DRAMA (1982)
5-part mini series produced by ITC for NBC
Television.

Unable to trace any details

W259.STEPHEN D: TV DRAMA (1963)
from "A Portrait of the Artist as a Young Man" and
"Stephen Hero" by James Joyce. TV adaptation by
Hugh Leonard.
Directed by Anthony Page

Commissioned by BBC Television

Premiere

W259a 1963 (30 October): Transmitted on BBC Television

Music played by ad hoc musicians;
Musical director: John Hollingsworth
Duration of music: 13 mins. 30 secs.

W260.STRANGE INTERLUDE: TV DRAMA (1987)
by Eugene O'Neill
Directed by Herbert Wise

Commissioned by Harlech Television

Premiere

W260a 1988 (13 July): Episode 1 transmitted on Channel 4

Music played by ad hoc musicians;
Musical director: Neil Richardson

W261.SURVIVAL: TV DOCUMENTARY (1976)
Wild-life film series, produced by Anglia TV.

Bennett wrote incidental music for:

(i) "Come into my Parlour" and
(ii) "Orangutan: Orphans of the Forest" (US
     title: "Orangutan: Orphans of the Wild")

Commissioned by Anglia Television

Premieres

W261a Come into My Parlour:
Instrumentation included harpsichord, cimbalom,
harp and percussion.

Recorded at CTS Wembley on 19 and 20 July
1976
Transmitted in UK : 4 January 1976
Transmitted in USA: 12 August 1976

W261b Orangutan: Orphans of the Forest
        Recorded at CTS Wembley on 16 March 1976
        Transmitted in UK: 9 September 1976
        Transmitted in USA: 21 April 1976

        In both cases, music played by ad hoc musicians;
        Musical director: Angela Morley

W262.TALKING PICTURES (1987)
        Music for a 10-part documentary series; written and
        presented by Barry Norman
        Produced by Judy Lindsay

        Commissioned by BBC Television

        Both Main Title and End Title are scored for 4
        horns, 3 trumpets, 3 trombones, tuba, ondes
        martenot, timpani, percussion (2), piano, harp
        and 8 violins

        Main Title: Allegro Maestoso   16 secs.
        End Title: Allegro Maestoso - three versions of
                     varying length: 40 secs, 50 secs,
                     and 1 min.

Premiere

W262a 1988 (25 January): First part transmitted on BBC
        Television (BBC1)

                Music (previously recorded on 18 May 1987 at
                the BBC TV Music Studio, Lime Grove) played
                by ad hoc musicians;
                Musical director: Chris Gunning

W263.TEA JINGLES (1960s)
        to accompany TV commercials for Horniman's Dividend
        Tea

        Unable to trace any details

W264.TENDER IS THE NIGHT: TV DRAMA (1985)
        by F. Scott Fitzgerald
        Screen play in six parts by Dennis Potter
        Directed by Robert Knights

        Commissioned by BBC Television

Premiere

W264a 1985 (23 September): First part transmitted on BBC
        Television (BBC2)

                Music played by 12 ad hoc musicians,
                including ondes martenot (Cynthia Millar) and
                saxophone (John Harle);
                Musical director: David Snell
                Duration of music: 12 mins.

1. Nicole's Theme and 2. Rosemary's Waltz
- arranged for piano solo by Richard
Rodney Bennett (Novello © 1985;2
mins. 35 secs.)

Premiere

W264b 1985 (30   June): London;   BBC   Studios;   Richard
Rodney Bennett (piano) - Radio 2 (previously
recorded on 21 June 1985)

2. Nicole's Theme and Rosemary's Waltz
arranged for ondes martenot and string
quartet by the composer. (Unpublished but
handled by Novello)

Premiere

W264c 1986 (18 October): Little Missenden; Parish Church
of St. John Baptist; Cynthia Millar (ondes
martenot); Brindisi String Quartet

3. Nicole's Theme and Rosemary's Waltz
arranged for soprano saxophone by John
Harle (Unpublished but handled by Novello)
See: D37

W265.TIMON OF ATHENS: THEATRE PLAY (1965)
by William Shakespeare
Directed by John Schlesinger

Commissioned by the Royal Shakespeare Company

1+1.0.1.1/1+crumhorn.2.1.0/perc./guitar   (and
lute)

Premiere

W265a 1965 (1 July); Stratford-upon-Avon; Royal Shakespeare Theatre; music (18 cues) played by the
Royal Shakespeare Wind Band. See: B335

W266.THE TOURELLE SKULL:TV DRAMA (1963)
by Jonnie Archambault
Produced by Rex Tucker

Commissioned by BBC Television

Premiere

W266a 1963 (25 March): Transmitted on BBC Television

Music played by Richard Rodney Bennett
(harpsichord and celesta). Composed in
collaboration with the BBC Radiophonic
Workshop.
Duration of music: 9 mins. 22 secs.

W267.TWENTY FOUR HOURS: TV SIGNATURE TUNE (1969)

Commissioned by BBC Television. <u>See</u>: B336

4 horns, timpani (4), vibraphone, glockenspiel
and piano duet (4 hands)

```
A - Main titles   :    40 secs
B - Headlines     :     2 secs  (a)
  - Headlines     :     2 secs  (b)
  - Headlines     :     2 secs  (c)
  - Final Headlines :   3 secs  (d)
C - Closing Sequence:  2½secs   (I)
  - Credit Titles   :  24 secs  (II)
D - Special Title   :   5 secs
```

<u>Premiere</u>

W267a 1969 (8 April): Transmitted on BBC Television
       (BBC1)

        Music played by ad hoc musicians;
        Musical director: Richard Rodney Bennett

XI. MUSIC FOR CONCERT BAND

W268. MORNING MUSIC
(Novello © 1987; 16 mins.)
Commissioned by the British Association of Symphonic Bands and Wind Ensembles with funds provided by the Arts Council of Great Britain

Piccolo, 2 flutes, 2 oboes, cor anglais, clarinet in E-flat, 2 clarinets, bass clarinet in B-flat, 2 bassoons, double bassoon, 2 alto saxophones in E-flat, tenor saxophone in B-flat, baritone saxophone in E-flat, 4 horns in F, 3 trumpets in B-flat, 2 trombones, bass trombone, tuba, timpani, percussion (3), piano, harp and double basses

Dedicated to Carol Sloane

The score is prefaced with the following:

'This city now doth like a garment wear
The beauty of the morning, silent, bare.
Ships, towers, domes, theatres, and temples lie
Open unto the fields and to the sky,
All bright and glitt'ring in the smokeless air...'
                                William Wordsworth

I.	Prelude	(Molto moderato)
II.	Ships	(Allegro giocoso)
III.	Towers	(Molto mosso)
IV.	Domes	(Andante tranquillo)
V.	Theatres	(Vivo)
VI.	Temples	(Molto moderato)
VII.	Finale	(Presto con brio)

(played without a break)

The score is dated: New York City
                     July 19 - Aug 17 '86

Premieres

W268a 1987 (25 July): Boston (Massachusetts); Sherman Union, Boston University Campus; Northshore Concert Band; Timothy Reynish, conductor
(The 3rd International Conference of the World Association of Symphonic Bands and Ensembles)

W268b 1987 (31 October): Manchester; Royal Northern College of Music concert hall; RNCM Wind Orchestra; Timothy Reynish, conductor

W268c 1987 (16 November): London; Royal College of Music concert hall; RCM Symphonic Wind Band, Timothy Reynish, conductor

XII. ADDITIONAL LIST

W269. THE AZTECS: TV DRAMA (1964)
     by J. Lucarotti

   Directed by John Crocket

   Commissioned by BBC Television

   Premiere

W269a 1964 (23 May): Transmitted on BBC Television – the
     first of a four-part 'Dr. Who' story

W270 CONCERTO FOR 10 BRASS PLAYERS (1988-9)
     (Unpublished, but handled by Novello)

   Unable to trace any details

Premiere

W270a 1989 (27 June): London; Queen Elizabeth Hall;
     London Brass.

W271. THE FLOWERS OF THE FOREST: REFLECTIONS ON A
     SCOTTISH FOLK SONG FOR BRASS BAND (1989)
     (Unpublished, but handled by Novello)

   Commissioned by the BBC

Premiere

W271a 1989 (6 August): London; Royal Albert Hall;
     National Youth Brass Band of Great Britain;
     Charles Groves, conductor

W272. IPHIGENIA IN TAURUS (1966)
     by Goethe, translated by Roy Pascal

   Produced by H.B. Fortuin

   Commissioned by the BBC

Premiere

W272a 1967 (3 February): Transmitted in the BBC Third
     Programme

W273. PARALLELS FOR TRUMPET AND PIANO (1955)
     (Unpublished)

   Unable to trace any details

W274. SONATA FOR VIOLA (1955)
     (Unpublished)

   Unable to trace any details

XIII.PUBLISHING DIRECTORY

MILLS MUSIC LTD - no longer extant.

NOVELLO & Co LTD., 1-3 Upper James Street, London W1R 4BP.
United States representative: Theodore Presser Co.,
Presser Place, Bryn Mawr, Pennsylvania, 19010.

OXFORD UNIVERSITY PRESS LTD., Music Department, Walton
Street, Oxford. OX2 6DP.

UNIVERSAL EDITION, 2/3 Fareham Street, London W1V 4DU.

Discography

This selected discography includes long playing records currently available or deleted, mono or stereo.

The "see" references, e.g. See: B133, identify citations in the "Bibliography" section.

D1. ALBA FOR ORGAN (W44)

> Vista VPS 1034. 1977.
> Jonathan Bielby (organ)
> See: B385

D2. ALL THE KING'S MEN (W175)

> Abbey XMS 703. 1971.
> Michael Flaxman, Paul Male, Jonathan Gaunt, Bill Tucker, Ashley Stafford, Colin Greenstreet and Stephen Cornwall with the Trinity Boy's Choir and a section of the Trinity School Orchestra conducted by David Squibb
> See: B111

D3. AUBADE (W9)

> Argo ZRG 907. 1980.
> Philharmonic Orchestra conducted by David Atherton
> See: B181,B393

D4. THE AVIARY (W176)

> HMV 7EG 8943. 1966.
> Finchley Children's Music Group conducted by John Andrewes with Richard Rodney Bennett (piano)

D5. BILLION DOLLAR BRAIN (W193)

> UA ULP 1183. 1967.
> J. Loriod (ondes martenot) and orchestra conducted by Marcus Dods

D6. CALENDAR FOR CHAMBER ENSEMBLE (W46)

>   HMV ASD 640. 1965.
>   Melos Ensemble conducted by John Carewe
>   See: B67,B172,B291
>
>   Reissued in
>   Argo ZRG 758. 1975.
>   See: B292

D7. CAPRICCIO FOR PIANO DUET (W48)

>   Argo ZRG 704. 1972.
>   Richard Rodney Bennett and Thea Musgrave (piano duet)
>   See: B130,B293

D8. COMMEDIA IV (W52)

>   Argo ZRG 813. 1975.
>   Philip Jones Brass Ensemble
>   See: B250

D9. CONCERTO FOR GUITAR AND CHAMBER ORCHESTRA (W12)

>   RCA SB 6876. 1973.
>   Julian Bream (guitar) and Melos Ensemble conducted by David Atherton
>   See: B191
>
>   Reissued in
>   RCA ARL3 0997. 1976.
>   See: B354

D10. CONCERTO FOR PIANO AND ORCHESTRA (W18)

>   Philips 6500 301. 1972.
>   Stephen Bishop (piano) and London Symphony Orchestra conducted by Alexander Gibson
>   See: B192

D11. CROSSTALK FOR TWO BASSET HORNS (W179)

>   Discourses All About Music ABM24. 1979.
>   Georgina Dobree and Thea King (basset horns)
>   See: B251, B301

D12. FANFARE FOR BRASS QUINTET (W58)

>   Argo ZRG 851. 1977.
>   Philip Jones Brass Ensemble
>   See: B252

D13. FARNHAM FESTIVAL OVERTURE (W181)

>   Waverley LLP 1039. 1966.
>   Schools orchestras from the Farnham and Aldershot areas conducted by Alan Fluck
>   See: B144

D14. <u>FIVE CAROLS</u> (W123)

> Abbey LPB 655. 1970.
> Choir of St. Matthew's Church, Northampton directed
> by Michael Nicholas

D15. <u>FIVE IMPROMPTUS FOR GUITAR</u> (W65)

> RCA RL 25419. 1982.
> Julian Bream (guitar)
> <u>See</u>: B137

D16. <u>FIVE STUDIES FOR PIANO</u> (W60)

> Philips Fourfront 4FM 10002. 1968.
> Shura Cherkassky (piano)
> <u>See</u>: B115

> Reissued <u>in</u>
> ASV ALH 9<del>6</del>5. 1986.
> <u>See</u>: B141

> Argo ZRG 704. 1972.
> Richard Rodney Bennett (piano)
> <u>See</u>: B130,B293

D17. <u>FOUR PIECE SUITE</u> (W62)

> EMI EL749116 – 1. 1988.
> David Nettle and Richard Markham (piano – 4 hands)
> <u>See</u>: B353

D18. <u>HEARE US, O HEARE US, LORD</u> (W145)

> Abbey LPB 783. 1977.
> Gloucester Cathedral Choir directed by John Sanders
> <u>See</u>: B386

D19. <u>THE HOUSE OF SLEEPE</u> (W125)

> EMI EMD 5521. 1975.
> The King's Singers
> <u>See</u>: B261

D20. <u>IMPROMPTU FOR SOLO FLUTE</u> (W63)

> Universal Edition UE 15043. 1969.
> Members of the Pierrot Players

D21. <u>THE INSECT WORLD</u> (W182)

> HMV 7EG 8943. 1966.
> Finchley Children's Music Group conducted by John
> Andrewes with Richard Rodney Bennett (piano)

> Unicorn RHS 316. 1974.
> Simon Woolf (treble) and Steuart Bedford (piano)
> <u>See</u>: B384

D22. JAZZ CALENDAR (W66)

> Philips 6500 301. 1972.
> London Jazz Ensemble conducted by John Lanchberry
> See: B192

D23. LADY CAROLINE LAMB (W211)

> HMV CSD 3728. 1973.
> New Philharmonia Orchestra conducted by Marcus Dods
> See: B304

> HMV ASD 3797. 1979.
> City of Birmingham Symphony Orchestra conducted by
> Marcus Dods
> See: B269
> Reissued in
> HMV Greensleeves ED290109-1. 1984.
> See: B140

> Elegy, arranged for organ by Christopher Palmer
> Vista VPS 1052. 1978.
> Roger Fisher (organ)

D24. THE MIDNIGHT THIEF (W183)

> HMV DLP 1216. 1964.
> Choir of West Lodge Junior Mixed School, Pinner;
> Percussion and instrumental ensemble conducted by
> John Longstaff
> See: B145

D25. MURDER ON THE ORIENT EXPRESS (W215)

> EMI EMC 3054. 1975.
> Royal Opera House Orchestra, Covent Garden
> conducted by Marcus Dods
> See: B305

D26. NICHOLAS AND ALEXANDRA (W218)

> Bell 202. 1972.
> National Philharmonic Orchestra conducted by Marcus
> Dods
> See: B306

> Columbia TWO 398. 1972.
> London Symphony Orchestra conducted by John Keating

D27. NURSERY SONG ARRANGEMENTS (W184)

> Jupiter jep OC31. 196?.
> Dorothy Dorow (soprano), John Carol Case
> (baritone), Maria Korchinska (harp), Thea King
> (clarinet and bass clarinet) and William Bennett
> (flute)

D28. ONE EVENING (W160)

Jupiter JUR OA10. 1965.
Wilfred Brown (tenor) and Desmond Dupre (guitar)

D29. OUT OF YOUR SLEEP (W123)

Cabaletta CDN 5001. 1981.
Croydon Singers directed by Matthew Best
See: B331

D30. RETURN OF THE SOLDIER (W229)

That's Entertainment Records TER 1036. 1983.
Music conducted by Richard Rodney Bennett

D31. SERENADE (W31)

Alpha ACA 508. 1982.
King Edward VI School Orchestra, Chelmsford
conducted by Peter Cross.

D32. SONATA FOR SAXOPHONE (W96)

Hyperion KA 66246 (cassette)
        CDA 66246 (compact disc). 1988.
John Harle (soprano saxophone) and John Lenehan
(piano)
See: B253

D33. THE SORROWS OF MARY (W138)

Argo ZRG 5499. 1966.
Elizabethan Singers directed by Louis Halsey
See: B118

D34. SPELLS (W139)

Argo ZRG 907. 1980.
Jane Manning (soprano), Bach
Choir, Philharmonia Orchestra conducted by David
Willcocks
See: B181,B393

D35. SYMPHONY NO. 1 (W37)

RCA Victor SB 6730. 1968.
Royal Philharmonic Orchestra conducted by Igor
Buketoff
See: B199,B317

D36. TELEGRAM (W110)

Pearl SHE 537. 1977.
Richard Deering (piano)
See: B198

D37. TENDER IS THE NIGHT - Theme (W264)

Hannibal/Harmonia Mundi HNBL 1331 (cassette)
                HNCD 1331 (compact disc). 1988.

John Harle (saxophone) and John Lenehan (piano)
See: B254

D38. TOM O'BEDLAM'S SONG (W172)

Argo ZRG 5418. 1964.
Peter Pears (tenor) and Joan Dickson (cello)
See: B146

Reissued in
Argo ZK 28. 1978.
See: B200

D39. TRIO FOR FLUTE, CLARINET AND OBOE (W115)

Argo ZRG 5475. 1966.
William Bennett (flute), Gervase de Peyer
(clarinet) and Peter Graeme (oboe)
See: B255

D40. TWO LULLABIES (W144)

Abbey XMS 727. 1972.
The choir of Leeds Parish Church directed by Donald
Hunt

Abbey LPS 764. 1976.
The choristers of Worcester Cathedral directed by
Donald Hunt

D41. A WEEK OF BIRTHDAYS (W190)

Jupiter JEP OC26. 1962.
Richard Rodney Bennett (piano)
See: B319

D42. WINTER MUSIC (W118)

Delta SDEL 18005. 1963.
William Bennett (flute) and Susan Bradshaw (piano)
See: B167,B296

D43. YANKS (W239)

HMV ASD 3797. 1979.
City of Birmingham Symphony Orchestra conducted by
Marcus Dods
See: B269

Reissued in
HMV Greensleves ED290109-1. 1984.
See: B140

ARRANGEMENTS

D44. CONCERT COLLECTION - KING'S SINGERS

One Day - Michel Legrand
EMI CSD 3766. 1976.

D45. KING'S SINGERS

Ask Yourself Why - Michel Legrand
Columbia SCX 6531. 1972.

D46. OUT OF THE BLUES - KING'S SINGERS

Dayton Ohio - 1903 - Randy Newman
The Half-of-it-dearie blues - George Gershwin
It's a great little world - George Gershwin
EMI EMC 3023. 1974.

D47. A SURE THING - MUSIC OF JEROME KERN

All the things you are
Don't ever leave me
Go, little boat
I'm old fashioned
Long ago and far away
Smoke gets in your eyes
Sure thing
Till the clouds roll by/Look for the silver lining
Up with the lark
The way you look tonight
Why do I love you?
Yesterdays

Barry Tuckwell (horn), instrumental group
(including Richard Rodney Bennett on keyboards)
conducted by Neil Richardson
EMI ASD 3844. 1980.

D48. SURPRISE, SURPRISE

includes:

Blues in the Night -	H. Arlen
Chelsea Morning -	J. Mitchell
Dayton Ohio - 1903 -	R. Newman
Give me the simple life -	R. Bloom
I hear music -	B. Lane
Just a little lovin' -	H. Von Tilzer
Midnite Blue -	M. Manchester
Miss Otis Regrets -	C. Porter
Softly as in a morning sunrise -	S. Romberg
Tea for two -	V. Youmans
You make me feel so young -	J. Myrow

Marian Montgomery and Richard Rodney Bennett
Cube Records HIFLY 24. 1977.

D49. TENTH ANNIVERSARY CONCERT - KING'S SINGERS

Dayton Ohio - 1903 - Randy Newman
EMI KC 1002. 1978.

D50. <u>TOWN AND COUNTRY</u>

includes:

Any place I hang my hat is home –	H. Arlen
Ballad of the sad young man –	T. Wolf
Do you know the way to San Jose? –	B. Bacharach
The Eagle & Me –	H. Arlen
The Folks who live on the Hill –	J. Kern
I'm always drunk in San Francisco –	T. Wolf
Let's go and live in the country –	R.R. Bennett
<u>See</u>: W155	
New York State of Mind –	B. Joel
Night Owl –	J. Taylor
Peaceful –	K. Rankin
Save the sunlight –	J.R. Cobb
Skylark –	H. Carmichael
Summerhouse –	M. Montgomery, etc.

Marian Montgomery and Richard Rodney Bennett
Cube Records HIFLY 28.   1978.

Bibliography

"See" references refer to individual works and particular performances of those works as described in the "Works and Performances" section (e.g. <u>See</u>: W133) and in the "Discography" (e.g. <u>See</u>: D33).

B1. Addison, Richard. "Listen, Look, Learn." <u>Music Teacher and Piano Student</u>, 49 (January 1970), p.13.

>   An analysis of <u>Tuesday's Child</u> from <u>A Week of Birthdays</u>, written for the pianist, in a series of articles intended to make "you <u>think</u> about what you play, to think about how the composer might have worked and about how, and even why, he put his music together." <u>See</u>: W190

B2. Addison, Richard. "Listen, Look, Learn." <u>Music Teacher and Piano Student</u>, 49 (March 1970), p.12.

>   A similar article to the above analysing <u>Saturday's Child</u>. <u>See</u>: W190

B3. Anderson, ? "Juilliard School of Music." <u>Music Journal</u> (New York), 26 (March 1968), p.104.

>   A review of the first performance in America of <u>The Mines of Sulphur</u> at the Juilliard School of Music in New York. <u>See</u>: W2e

B4. Anon. "Arousing an interest". <u>The Times</u> (London), 30 October 1967, p.23.

>   A mention of <u>The Engineers</u>, "one of the most outstanding examples of...film seen during the past 12 months...from the Hawker Siddeley group". <u>See</u>: W201

B5. Anon. "Bennett's one-act opera 'The Ledge' at Krefeld – Monchengladbach." <u>Melos</u>, 31 (March 1964), p.95-6.

A review, in German, of <u>The Ledge</u> which praises the extremely effective stage set by Hans Aeberli, the good performances and the music. <u>See</u>: W1b

B6. Anon. "Cautious Dive in Symphonic Ocean." <u>The Times</u> (London), 11 February 1966, p.17.

An account of the first performance of Bennett's First Symphony. "The orchestral colours are pleasing, cool and functional, whether in cocktail-shaken percussive chunks or in heady high string melodies or shrill calls from the brass choir. As his music has usually suggested...Bennett is concerned first and last with communication to an existing audience, and therefore with saying new things in familiar language. As so in this symphony he gives us an exhilarating first movement, a sultry, amorous Andante with a smashing climax, and a busy but rather more elliptical finale which is seen in the end to have absorbed the flavour of the earlier movements and added a firmer streak of its own." <u>See</u>: W37a

B7. Anon. "Childe Roland as Melodrama." <u>The Times</u> (London), 10 January 1962, p.13.

"Richard Rodney Bennett...is more traditional in his setting of Browning's <u>Childe Roland</u>, of which he and Mr Sebastian Shaw gave the first performance at the City Music Society's lunchtime concert yesterday. Here the music is quite frankly designed as an accompaniment to the poem, subordinate except in its brief moments of independence." <u>See</u>: W174a

B8. Anon. "Composer in Ordinary." <u>The Sunday Telegraph</u> (London), 21 October 1962, p.11.

An early interview with Bennett who "...has been commissioned to write three operas...." Mention is made of his fluency and his plans for the future including an opera on a Muriel Spark subject which "...I'd love to do, but that's not fixed...."

B9. Anon. "(A) Composer of the New Generation." <u>The Times</u> (London), 15 August 1962, p.13.

A discussion about Bennett and his work in which it is observed that "it is unusual for an English composer to establish a reputation while he is still in his twenties, and perhaps even more surprising for a young creative artist in our age of stylistic confusion to have found his own way and defined it with simple clarity. Although his style is contemporary and serialist, he does not regard himself as a member of the avant garde.... Mr Bennett is a serialist whose aim is to 'compose serial music that sounds well'. He feels that serial techniques have often been handled by composers with a degree of self-consciousness that made them forget about harmonic consistency and the 'aural elements' of their music."

B10. Anon.   "Concerto premiered." The Windsor, Slough and Eton Express, 7 October 1983, p. 62.

An account of the first performance of Memento, written in memory of the British jazz pianist Pat Smyth, who died three weeks before its completion. See: W70a

B11. Anon. "Editorial Notes." Strad, 75 (October 1964), p. 195.

"An English evening on the following day...introduced the sonic-sounding Aubade (for John Hollingsworth) by the highly ingenious Richard Rodney Bennett. This 12-minute epic revealed an assured hand with instrumental colour which was prodigally displayed with a muted intensity as its name suggests." See: W9a

B12. Anon. "First Opera of Bennett." The Times (London), 13 September 1961, p. 14.

A review of the premiere of The Ledge, Bennett's first opera. Bennett is called the most able British composer of his generation and his music "...striking, atmospherically suggestive, especially in the beautiful interlude for orchestra alone, and vocally gratifying at almost all times." See W1a

B13. Anon.   "First Performance of Tribute to John Hollingsworth." The Times (London), 12 September 1964, p. 12.

"The music [of Aubade]...is in a sense a lament for the transience of all living beauty rather than an expression of individual grief; the point is made through sonority of an ethereal, translucent kind of fragility, rather than through more obvious tugs at the heart-strings. The vistas opened up are new, strange and often hauntingly beautiful for Bennett has a remarkable aural imagination of an uncommonly rarefied kind." See: W9a

B14. Anon.   "'Golden' oboe sounds long-awaited notes." Seaton News (Devon), 28 October 1983, p. ?

An account of the premiere of After Syrinx in which "...Richard Rodney Bennett used Debussy's marvellous solo flute piece Syrinx as his starting point, developing the theme on serial lines, rather than as variations, dissonance and atonalism being more apparent in the piano part than that for the oboe." See: W42a

B15. Anon. "In jazz idiom."   The Times (London), 6 March
         1967, p.8.

         "Jazz was represented at the inaugural concerts in
         the Elizabeth Hall by a programme given by Miss
         Cleo Laine with the John Dankworth Ensemble on
         Saturday night.   It included two new relatively
         extended works in jazz idiom composed for the
         occasion. Soliloquy, by Mr Richard Rodney Bennett
         is a dramatic scene to a text by Mr Julian
         Mitchell, in which four song-movements are
         introduced by a spoken prologue and linked by a
         recitative - like refrain.   The words express
         feminine feelings at the severance of an emotional
         relationship, given distinctive musical form and
         subtly coloured by the scoring for seven-piece
         ensemble. The ideas and harmonic progressions are
         inventive and imaginatively varied." See: W165a

B16. Anon. "Isadora." About the House 6(3) 1981, p. 16-19.

         A photographic record of the premiere of Bennett's
         ballet Isadora. See: W5a

B17. Anon.   "(A) Lyrical View of London."   The Times
         (London), 14 July 1962, p. 4.

         A report about a concert in the City of London
         Festival and mention of a new piece
         "...commissioned by the Lord Mayor from Richard
         Rodney Bennett....The title, London Pastoral, at
         once makes clear by its apparent contradiction that
         this is no attempt to hold a musical mirror up to
         the Great Wren and reflect its vastness, its
         grandeur, and its horror directly.
         The essence of the work, in fact, is lyrical rather
         than dramatic, and its three main sections
         represent not so much aspects of London herself as
         moods engendered by her. " See: W127a

B18. Anon.   "Macnaghten new music group."   The Times
         (London), 24 February 1953, p.5.

         "A work of the utmost promise came forward in a
         theme with variations for unaccompanied oboe by
         Richard Bennett, who is still at school. Bennett
         masters a difficult and, save for Britten's
         Metamorphoses, unexplored medium with suave
         assurance, and treats his modest yet cogent theme
         with an imagination that Miss Joy Boughton
         gratefully transmitted to her audience." See:
         W117a

B19. Anon. "(A) Master of Precision and Feeling." The Times
         (London), 10 July 1963, p. 13.

         "If one were looking for a single quality that
         distinguishes Mr Richard Rodney Bennett, while
         still in his twenties, as the most naturally gifted

of the youngest generation of English composers, it would surely be precision. Not only does he show an instinctive understanding of the capacity of whatever medium he writes for; he also has the much rarer gift of feeling for pace and proportion. There is no generalisation in his music; each image is focused and particular.
All this is true of his new suite of three Nocturnes, commissioned by the Cheltenham Festival Committee and given their first performance in this country...(by special permission there had been an earlier one in Vancouver last March). Scored for wind quintet, harp and string orchestra they evoke in ravishingly beautiful sonorities three aspects of night suggested by three fragments of prose and poetry prefixed to the score...." See: W30b

B20. Anon. "Monotonous Rhythms." The Times (London), 9 January 1962, p.5.

"...the other novelty (was) an oboe sonata by Richard Rodney Bennett. This is an elegant piece of work - lyrical as befits its medium, but taut and cool in expression. Miss Susan Bradshaw...negotiated her part in the Bennett with consummate skill." See: W94a

B21. Anon. "Music with a smiling face." The Times (London), 19 May 1965, p.8.

"A brand new Farnham Festival Overture by Richard Rodney Bennett, again commissioned by a local business firm, brought a second concert of the Farnham school children's festival of contemporary music to a lively end in the parish church....
This was music with a smile on its face, music with tunes to whistle, rhythms to set every foot tapping, besides orchestral colours and bold dynamic contrasts to arrest the ear." See: W181a

B22. Anon. "NATO Anniversay Concert." The Times (London), 5 June 1959, p.4.

An account of the NATO Anniversary Concert in the Royal Festival Hall when Music for an Occasion was performed and which is described as "...distinguished in conception, cunning in design and brilliantly orchestrated." See: W28a

B23. Anon. "New Bennett Quartet." The Times (London), 7 May 1965, p.18.

"The quartet, which is Bennett's fourth, quite strongly recalls the opera Mines of Sulphur...because the same composer wrote both, and fairly close together.
...the quartet is strongly dramatic, full of fierce contrasts...and its music is close to song in character, melodious, human and impetuous in its

themes, elaborated as though by <u>dramatis personae</u>."
<u>See</u>: W78a

B24. Anon. "No 'Fashions' for Richard Rodney Bennett." <u>The</u>
<u>Times</u> (London), 7 February 1966, p.5.

An interview with Bennett with mention of
influences, "...perhaps I am most in sympathy with
Thea Musgrave, Malcolm Williamson and Nicholas Maw.
My admiration for Thea Musgrave is unbounded in
that she has written an opera without a commission.
I couldn't do that."

B25. Anon. "Odeon: Interpol." <u>The Times</u> (London), 8 April
1957, p.3.

A preview of <u>Interpol</u> which is described as "...a
routine crime <u>film</u>...." <u>See</u>: W210

B26. Anon. "Pianist in World Premiere." <u>The Armidale</u>
<u>Express</u> (New South Wales), 29 May 1985, <u>p.14</u>.

An announcement that the world premiere of <u>Noctuary</u>
would be featured in a piano recital <u>by</u> John
McCabe, distinguished British pianist and composer.
"It is a scintillating piece which consists of a
set of variations on a theme by Scott Joplin."
<u>See</u>: W6a

B27. Anon. "Real Emotional Impact." <u>The Times</u> (London), 8
June 1962, p.6.

"For all the economy of its texture (there is not a
single octave doubling in the entire piece) Richard
Rodney Bennett's <u>Fantasy</u> for piano shows all the
marks of being composed by a skilled pianist. It
lies well under the hands, and is written with a
real feeling for piano sonority. ...in spite of
its cool harmonic palette this is a work with real
emotional impact." <u>See</u>: W59a

B28. Anon. "Richard Rodney Bennett's Vocation for Opera."
<u>The Times</u> (London), 26 February 1965, p.16.

An article describing and discussing Bennett's
second opera <u>The Mines of Sulphur</u>, "...a dark,
violent, rather melodramatic, concentrated story."

B29. Anon. "Rodney Bennett's Epithalamion." <u>The Times</u>
(London), 17 April 1967, p.6.

A review of the premiere of <u>Epithalamion</u> in which
"Mr Bennett employs free serial technique
throughout but cunningly contrived so that it
polarizes around strong tonal centres. Thus he
strikes a balance, uneasy at times, between the old
and the new.
<u>Epithalamion</u> demonstrates again his sensitivity to
words, his skill in inventing significant motives,

his unerring feeling for new and exciting orchestral sonorities, his fertile inventiveness and astonishing facility." See: W121a

B30. Anon. "Seminar '65." Opus, 1 (Spring 1966) p. 19-20.

An edited transcription from tape of part of the discussion that was held at an informal open seminar, chaired by Dr Arnold Whittall of the University of Nottingham's music department, on Sunday 14 November 1965. The piece of music under discussion was Richard Rodney Bennett's Fantasy for piano. See: W59

B31. Anon. "Serial Technique of Young Composers." The Times (London), 9 January 1961, p.3.

"Richard Bennett's Winter Music... possessed many of his special qualities. Most satisfying in the long, lyrical melodies of the first and last movements, it displayed a most imaginative understanding of the special characteristics of the instrument." See: W118a

B32. Anon. "Singers on firm ground." Worcester Evening News, 24 August 1984, p.8.

"Richard Rodney Bennett's Sea Change, a set of four chamber choir songs especially written for the singers, received its first performance and was well presented but nonetheless difficult to accept." See: W137a

B33. Anon. "Taut, Fierce Plot in New Opera." The Times (London), 25 February 1965, p.16.

A review of Bennett's first full-length opera. "The Mines of Sulphur" has a taut, fierce plot, distinctive among modern librettos in its atmosphere and tension of character and situation. The music is ambitious and attractive: it deserves an article to itself. Mr Colin Davis made much of its sensuousness and of its dynamism too...." See: W2a

B34. Anon. "That World Premiere Smile." Coventry Evening Telegraph, 28 March 1969, pp. 30-1.

A preview of All the King's Men, commissioned by Coventry Schools Music Association, and photograph of the composer with members of the children's choir. See: W175a

B35. Anon. "Vivid Songs for Children." The Times, 15 February 1966, p.13.

"The creative versatility of Richard Rodney Bennett can embrace the post-Webern world of his

symphony...and the cheerful diatonic fancies of two
song cycles, written for children....
Both are vividly imagined, so that children who
sing or listen to them will get a strong impression
of each creature and its song. The Insect World
contains the more distinguished music...and in The
Aviary the tones and rhythms now and again fall
into the humdrum, though Bennett's setting of
Shelley's 'The Widow Bird' very nicely captures the
forlorn, gelid atmosphere of the poem." See:
W176b, W182b

B36. Aprahamian,F.["Concerto for Violin and Orchestra"]. The
Sunday Times, 4 April 1976, p.36.

An account of the "... magnificent new Violin
Concerto by Richard Rodney Bennett, a worthy
successor to the Piano Concerto which also reached
London by way of Birmingham. The poetic fantasy
resides in the music which itself stems from
poetry, for each of the work's two extended
movements reflect quotations from
Herrick....Bennett's twelve-tone allegiance or
formal cerebration, like Berg's is secondary to the
total clarity with which an expressive message or
poetic mood is communicated. His Violin Concerto
progresses from a bright awakening to a most
beautiful, nocturnal ending." See: W22b

B37. Aprahamian,F. ["Zodiac"]. The Sunday Times, 5 September
1976, p.29.

A review of Zodiac in which "...Bennett, with his
usual facility, has created a sophisticated guide
to the orchestra, exploiting a different tessitura
and group of timbres in each section. The result
is a succinctly brilliant score, kaleidoscopic in
mood as well as colour." See: W40b

B38. Atticus. "Young Classic." The Sunday Times, 6 February
1966, p.9.

An informal interview with the composer.

B39. B.,A. "A Penny for a Song." Opera, 18 (December 1970),
pp. 1020-22.

An appreciation of Bennett's opera, "...one of the
chief pleasures of (the) score (being) the way he
slips in and out of each mood. He has used
individual instruments and motives subtly to
delineate his characters - the lugubrious bassoon
for Lamprett, the delicate winding of an oboe for
Dorcas, a clarinet for Hallam Mathews, the
world-weary rake." See: W3a

B40. B.,D.J. "Richard Rodney Bennett." Film Dope, 3 (August
1973), pp. 27-8.

A few biographical details about the composer, together with a list of his film scores composed between 1956 and 1973. "You don't need the fingers of one hand to count the number of accomplished composers working in British movies today, so Bennett's regular contributions are to be loudly acknowledged."

B41. B.,H.M. "New Bennett Concerto." Music and Musicians, 24 (March 1976), pp. 12+14.

A report about "an important premiere for the City of Birmingham Symphony Orchestra in March will be that of Richard Rodney Bennett's Violin Concerto, with Ralph Holmes, the dedicatee, as soloist." A description of each movement follows. See: W22a

B42. Barker, F.G. "London." Opera News (New York), 31 (January 1968), p. 32.

A report about the world premiere of Penny for a Song, in which "Bennett undoubtedly has achieved...instrumental writing of delicacy and imagination; the web of sound is brilliantly atmospheric. His vocal line, too, is clear and direct, though it affords the singers no real chances to shine individually." See: W3a

B43. Barnes, Clive. "Virgin Undergrowth." Plays and Players, 9 (August 1962), pp. 50-51.

A review of Judith, but with no direct reference to the incidental music by Bennett. See: W253b

B44. Barrett, M. "Composer taking pulse of Denver." Rocky Mountain News, 27 April 1972, p. 58+61.

An interview with Bennett who "is in Denver to become acquainted with the area, the Denver Symphony Orchestra and members of the English Speaking Union who has commissioned him to compose a work for the orchestra to be premiered in February 1974. " See: W17

B45. Barry, M. "Marian Montgomery." Music and Musicians 26 (February 1978), p. 65.

An account of a Bennett/Montgomery concert - "...a superbly professional performance with not a hair out of place...."

B46. Barry, M. "Modern." Music and Musicians, 23 (October 1974), pp. 56-8.

An review of the U.K. premiere of Bennett's Concerto for Orchestra in which "Bennett intended...to demonstrate the modern orchestra as a virtuosi body of players....He...makes clear his formal schemes - a modified arch in the first movement, ternary in the second and a theme and variations in the third. He uses the row melodically, deriving from it themes for the second and third movements. His sections are clear, his melodies are provided with accompaniments and harmonic bases are thus set up. The row is also presented initially in stark single notes and then provided with a contrast by means of a tonal triad. The whole is certainly accessible and well constructed." See: W17b

B47. Bazelon, Irwin. "Knowing the score: notes on film music." New York, Van Nostrand, 1975, pp. 55-60,85,98,103,139,143,155,207-13.

A discussion about film music, with reference to Bennett's scores for Far from the madding crowd, Murder on the Orient Express, Nicholas and Alexandra and Secret Ceremony including an example of the manuscript score. Also included is an interview between Bennett and Pat Gray. See: W205,W215,W218,W231

B48. Bennett, Richard Rodney. "All the King's Men." Music in Education, 33 (March/April 1969), pp. 75-6.

An account by the composer of the background to the commission for, and writing of, All the King's Men. See: W175

B49. Bennett, Richard Rodney "(A) Changing Musical World or the Circus Moves on." Peabody Notes, XXIV (November 1970), p.1.

Portions of a 'provocative talk' given by Bennett (whilst composer-in-residence at the Peabody Institute) in the Wednesday Noon Hour series.

B50. Bennett, Richard Rodney. "(A) Composer on his Opera." Music and Musicians, 10 (September 1961), pp. 18+38.

A detailed explanation and introduction by Bennett of his first opera, The Ledge in which he "...was given an entirely free hand about questions of length, scale, subject matter and style." See: W1

B51. Bennett, Richard Rodney. "In defence of Tavener, 1." Music and Musicians, 18 (February 1969), p. 69.

A letter protesting that "...Ates Orga's attack on John Tavener (M & M, December 1968) should have never been printed in your columns."

B52. Bennett, Richard Rodney. "Jazz in the Third." Radio Times, 28 May 1964, p. 60.

An introduction to Jazz Calendar, a piece "I wanted to write...which would satisfy me as a serious composer, particularly in terms of form and integrated style, and which, perhaps, would please the jazz-minded listener." See: W66

B53. Bennett, Richard Rodney.   "Letter from...." Opus, 2 (Spring 1967), p. 24.

A reply to some of the points raised in the discussion (See: B30) about Bennett's Fantasy for piano. See: W59

B54. Bennett, Richard   Rodney.   "Maturity's   benefits." Crescendo International, 21(3), 1982, pp. 16-17.

An interview with the composer, with mention of his thoughts about contemporaries in the field - "Of that older generation, William Walton is the one I've always been closest to. We share the same birthday and I think we were born on the same day of the week - in different years, of course - and at the same time of day. Which is very nice, and kind of curious."

B55. Bennett, Richard Rodney.   "(The) Mines of Sulphur." Radio Times, 25 February 1965, p.62.

A general introduction to the first broadcast performance (on 5 March 1965) of The Mines of Sulphur by the BBC. See: W2

B56. Bennett, Richard Rodney. "My double lifetime in music." Crescendo International, 20(9), 1982, pp. 6-8.

An   absorbing   interview   with   the   composer, emphasising his interest in jazz and "...high-class popular music."

B57. Bennett, Richard Rodney.   "(The) need to have a free hand."   Crescendo International, 20(12), 1982, pp. 12-13.

Bennett's views on certain musical subjects, with mention of working with Barry Tuckwell on 'A Sure Thing', and other recordings.

B58. Bennett, Richard Rodney. "Neglect of Jazz." The Times (London), 28 July 1973, p.13.

A letter for Bennett and others (including James Blades, David Atherton and Kenneth Tynan) about the "...serious neglect of jazz music by the media in this country in particular by radio and televison."

B59. Bennett, Richard Rodney. "New Music." Radio Times, 28 February 1963, p. 13.

A description of The Approaches of Sleep, "...the first of six vocal works written between 1959 and 1963 which are settings chiefly of seventeenth and eighteenth-century texts." See: W120

B60. Bennett, Richard Rodney. "(A) Penny for a Song." The
     Times (London), 19 September 1967, p.14.

          Bennett's view that Penny for a Song and "...music
          is more relaxed in style. It has been a pleasure
          to write, and working on it has been like a
          holiday." See: W3

B61. Bennett, Richard Rodney. "(The) romantic side of
     Richard." Radio Times, 8-14 March, 1986, p.15.

          Some quotes which reveal that Richard Rodney
          Bennett "...says that his recent composition Love
          Songs...marks an important change of direction for
          him. He has set five love poems by e.e. cummings
          and says they find him in more romantic mood than
          earlier works. They have turned me in a completely
          different direction and inspired a much more
          lyrical vein." See: W157

B62. Bennett, Richard Rodney. "Some Responses to 'A Personal
     Credo' - Ruth Gipps." Composer, no. 54 (Spring
     1975), p.32.

          A letter in which Bennett writes, "Dr. Ruth Gipps
          would have done better to keep her Credo entirely
          to herself than to have published the incredible
          farrago printed in your Spring '75 issue. We may
          safely ignore her splendidly confused statements
          that amplified pop music leads straight to drug
          addiction and crimes of violence, that 'Schoenberg,
          poor man, tried hard to become a composer' or that
          Stravinsky's late works constitute the sin against
          the Holy Ghost."

B63. Bennett, Richard Rodney. "Symphony." Musical Events,
     21(February 1966), p.9.

          An analysis, movement by movement, of the
          composer's first symphony. See: W37

B64. Bennett, Richard Rodney. "Technique of the jazz
     singer." Music and Musicians, 20 (Feburary 1972),
     pp. 30-5.

          An article about the characteristic 20th-century
          form of vocal expression, "...the extensions and
          varied uses of the voice in jazz." Billie Holiday,
          Ella Fitzgerald, Anita O'Day, Carmen Macrae, Chris
          Connor and Karin Krog are amongst the singers
          discussed. Reprinted in Educator, 5(3),1973,
          pp.2-4+

B65. Bernstein, Elmer. "A conversation with Richard Rodney
     Bennett." Film-music Notebook, 2(1), 1976, pp.
     16-25.

A detailed and revealing conversation with the composer about his early life, technique, influences and work in films.

B66. Bird, C. "Krog/Bennett." <u>Melody Maker</u>, 2 December 1972, p. 73.

A review of a concert in which 'Synthesis' (Bennett and the Norwegian singer Karin Krog) gave the performance of Bennett's "...own tape and piano settings of three poems by e.e. cummings (which) were very attractive, particularly the middle section where the sound of children's voices, like distant church bells, were oddly moving." <u>See</u>: W163b

B67. Blake, D. "Calendar." <u>The Musical Times</u>, 106 (September 1965), pp. 688 + 690.

A review of the HMV recording ASD 640 in which the critic says that "...it provides effective contrast...(and) the performance seems to be excellent." <u>See</u>: D6

B68. Blezzard, J. "Liverpool." <u>The Musical Times</u>, 126 (February 1985) p. 109.

"Two new pieces by Richard Rodney Bennett received first performances at the Chester Music Festival. The National Youth Choir of Great Britain...were clearly enthusiastic about <u>Nonsense</u>....The texts by Mervyn Peake are long and colourful, and their macabre humour is undermined by vivid, almost extravagant music that makes no claims to profundity but leaves an abiding impression of sheer fun and energy. The piece is ideal for a young choir and its first performance was an admirable display of accomplished singing.... Teresa Cahill gave the first performance of Bennett's <u>Five Sonnets of Louise Labé</u>....These short pieces are diverse in emotional range, reflecting musically the intensely passionate love poetry of their 16th-century authoress." <u>See</u>: W131a, W149a

B69. Blyth, Alan. "Bennett's musical tale of Humpty Dumpty." <u>The Times</u> (London), 29 March 1969, p. 21.

An account of the first performance of <u>All the King's Men</u> in which "...Bennett has predictably provided singable tunes, racy orchestration and the occasionally more complex structure. His ever fertile pen provides a kaleidoscope of styles from the jaunty Roundhead melody, through the almost musical comedy touches to the Cavaliers' entrance, to the seventeenth-century pastiche of the charming guitar nocturne for the Queen and her maids. Rather more recognisable Bennett comes in the prayer of the Gloucester ladies and the tremendous climax of Humpty Dumpty's collapse." See: W175a

B70. Blyth, Alan. "Penny for an opera." Music and Musicians, 16 (November 1967), pp. 22-3.

A talk with the composer about his opera A Penny for a Song which "...deals with the futility of war and the heartlessness of a brief, summer love-affair. To this extent it is satire, although as Bennett pointed out there is no element of parody in the music." See. W3

B71. Bosman, Lance. "Reflections on Richard Rodney Bennett's Sonata for Guitar." Guitar International, November 1985, pp. 16-20.

A survey of Bennett's career and useful background to the Guitar Sonata which is briefly analysed movement by movement. See: W92

B72. Bosman, Lance. "Serialism." Guitar, 9 (July 1981), pp. 9+11.

A brief analysis of Bennett's Impromptus for Guitar with notes on the serial schemes for each piece in the set. See: W65

B73. Bowen, Meirion, "Guildhall Ensemble." The Guardian, 22 May 1985, p.11.

"Richard Rodney Bennett's Reflections on a Theme of William Walton was tailormade for the group.... Taking as his starting point a 12-note theme from the last movement of Walton's second symphony, Bennett had constructed here a shapely set of variations grouped around a central interlude, whose free use of pizzicato and glissando effects and flexible tempo enabled the work to achieve briefly a sense of repose. Bennett's work was blessed with a premiere of which the composer would have been proud." See: W82a

B74. Bowen Meirion. "Northern Sinfonia." The Guardian, 16 March 1974, p. 8.

A review of the London premiere of Bennett's Viola Concerto which is described as a "...tough, gritty piece which leads the listener through a sequence of three continuous movements with impeccable logic and dramatic timing." See: W21b

B75. Bowen Meirion. "Pegasus." The Guardian, 29 October 1984, p. 12.

"Pegasus is an enterprising amateur choir conducted by Richard Crossland.
Bennett's Seachange...drew upon texts contemporary with the 16th-century epic voyages of discovery.

The first and last movements set lines from
Shakespeare's The Tempest in an idiom extending
Vaughan Williams by means of an octotonic scale;
the third movement relied overmuch on onomatopoeia
in its treatment of Spenser's version of Jaws; the
neatest and most adept movement (and the firmest in
performance) was the second, Marvell's The
Bermudas...." See: W137b

B76. Bowen, Meirion. "Shakespeare." The Guardian, 24 April
1972, p. 8.

"Two sonnets by the bard himself inspired one of
Richard Rodney Bennett's most successful
compositions, one that owed less to Britten than at
first appeared the case, and sustained its
invention well right up to the final dramatic
couplet of 'When I do count the clock.' The work
was superbly sung by Philip Langridge." See: W166a

B77. Brace, Reginald. "Bars of Virtuosity." The Yorkshire
Post, 17 August 1979, p. 10.

A discussion with Bennett about his unusually
diverse life as a musician and composer.

B78. Bradbury, Ernest. "Festive Leeds." Music and
Musicians, 15 (June 1967), p. 28.

A consideration of the 1967 Leeds Festival's
commissioned piece, Richard Rodney Bennett's
Epithalamion which "...rather marked a new and
interesting stage in his own development. ...the
main impression is one of sweet, if brief, melodic
interest and general loveliness of texture. This
is translucent and swift, with crotales,
glockenspiel, vibraphone, xylophone, piano, celesta
and harp adding their own distinctive colours in
the general fabric of sound." See: W121a

B79. Bradbury, Ernest. "Mines of drama." The Yorkshire
Post, 26 March 1980, p. 12.

An interview with the composer at the time of the
revival of The Mines of Sulphur by ENON. See: W2g

B80. Bradbury, Ernest. "New work in true spirit of day."
The Yorkshire Post, 17 April 1967, p. 9.

A description of Epithalamion after its first
performance in Leeds Town Hall, a commission which
"...has been splendidly fulfilled: not necessarily
because Bennett has created a masterpiece...but
because he has added something of contemporary
significance to the Festival scene, something
enjoyable moreover, for both performers and
listeners." See: W121a

B81. Bradbury, Ernest.   "Opera."   The Yorkshire Post,   28
     March 1980, p.7.

         A review of The Mines of Sulphur when revived by
         ENON at the Grand Theatre in Leeds. The opera is
         described as "...a gripping entertainment...."
         See: W2g

B82. Bradbury, Ernest.   "Virtuoso parts for all."   The
     Yorkshire Post, 4 July 1973, p.3.

         An account of the first performance of the Viola
         Concerto in which Bennett is said to have
         "...written virtuoso parts for the entire chamber
         orchestra, so that it is in some ways a concerto
         for all the players." See: W21a

B83. Bradbury, Ernest.   "Yorkshire."   The Musical Times, 14
     (September 1973), p. 927.

         "...Bennett's Viola Concerto (was) splendidly
         played   by   Roger   Best   and   the   Northern
         Sinfonia....Cast in a single movement of some 20
         minutes, with a nobly elegiac central section, the
         concerto   contains   economical   but   immediately
         apprehensible ideas, elegantly and clearly
         expressed and resourcefully elaborated." See: W21a

B84. Bradshaw, Susan. "Bennett's Versatility." The Musical
     Times, 125 (July 1984), pp. 381-4.

         A survey of Bennett's most recent works, continuing
         the article written in 1982 (B88)

B85. Bradshaw, Susan.   "Mines of Sulphur."   Music and
     Musicians, 13 (February 1965), pp. 16-17.

         An examination of and detailed introduction to
         Bennett's opera. See: W2.

B86. Bradshaw, Susan.   "(The) Music of Richard Rodney
     Bennett." The Listener, 69 (28 February 1963), p.
     396.

         A brief survey of Bennett's life and music
         including mention of Boulez, and Bennett's interest
         in jazz.

B87. Bradshaw, Susan.   "Richard Rodney Bennett."   The
     Listener, 81 (13 February 1969), p. 217.

         An account of Bennett's musical background, and an
         analysis of the Second Symphony. See: W38

B88. Bradshaw, Susan.   "Richard Rodney Bennett: the last
     decade." The Musical Times, 123 (September 1982),
     pp. 609-11.

A detailed and extensive survey of the "...last ten years of Richard Rodney Bennett's career (which) have seen a surge of creative activity unusual even for a composer as naturally prolific as he. Perhaps sparked off by a change of publisher in the early 1970s, his music has also broadened both in scope and in range of harmonic emphasis during these years as well as acquiring what several critics have referred to as something of a sharper profile."

B89. Bradshaw, Susan.   "Victory."   The Musical Times, 111 (April 1970), pp. 370-2.

An interview with the composer about his opera Victory. See: W4

B90. Bradshaw, Susan and Bennett, R.R.   "Anthony Payne and his Paean." Tempo, no. 100 (Spring 1972), pp. 40-44.

A detailed analysis, with musical examples, of Payne's Paean for piano, written in 1971.

B91. Bradshaw, Susan and Bennett, R.R.   "Elizabeth Lutyens's Stage Works." Tempo, no. 120 (March 1977), pp. 47-8.

A survey of Lutyens's stage works, many unperformed, prompted by recent performances of Isis and Osiris.

B92. Bradshaw, Susan and Bennett, R.R.   "In search of Boulez." Music and Musicians, 11 (January 1963), pp. 10-13.

The first part of an article describing Boulez's life, career and compositions.

B93. Bradshaw, Susan and Bennett, R.R.   "In search of Boulez." Music and Musicians, 11 (August 1963), pp. 14-18 +50.

The second part of the article about Boulez and his music. With musical examples.

B94. Brewer, M.   "All the King's Men." Music Teacher, 57 (May 1978), pp. 18-19.

An interesting and useful analysis, section by section, of All the King's Men. See: W175

B95. Bucht, B.K.   "Sweden." Opera, 18 (December 1967), p. 1007.

Mention of the performance at the Stockholm Festival, of The Mines of Sulphur. See: W2d

B96. Buckle, Richard.   "Pop goes the nursery." The Sunday Times, 14 January 1968, p.49.

An account of the first performance of the ballet
Jazz Calendar in which the music is described as
attractive, the designs as clever, the choreography
as professional and the performance as spirited.
See: W66b

B97. Butler, Ivan. "The Making of Feature Films: a guide."
Harmondsworth, Penguin Books, 1971, pp. 161-3.

Bennett's views about composing music for films,
with mention of Secret Ceremony. See: W231

B98. Caps, John.   "In conversation with Richard Rodney
Bennett." Soundtrack Collector's Newsletter, 2 (July
1976), pp. 3-9.

An interview with Bennett about film music in
general, and his in particular.

B99. Caps, John.   "In conversation with Richard Rodney
Bennett (2)." Soundtrack Collector's Newsletter, 2
(October 1976), pp. 17-21.

A continuation of the interview with Bennett with
many references to his film music.

B100.Caps, John.   "(An) Interview with Richard Rodney
Bennett." Hi-Fi/Musical America, 27 (June 1977), pp.
58-62.

A discussion with Bennett about his work in the
concert hall and the cinema.

B101.Cardew, Cornelius. "The Ledge." The Musical Times, 102
(November 1961), p.707.

An explanation of the story and the music of The
Ledge which "...for a first opera...cuts a
remarkable distance into the ice, without actually
breaking it." See: W1a

B102.Chanan, M. "Bennett's second." Music and Musicians, 17
(April 1969), p. 62.

"Bennett's Second   Symphony is a concise
uninterrupted span which falls into three sections.
An Allegro, equivalent to a first movement, is
followed by a Moderato. A Vivace is introduced,
which alternates with the Moderato until the end.
This scheme produces the only really poignant
movement in the score, which is otherwise a
confident,   well   orchestrated   compendium   of
everything one expects it to be." See: W38b

B103.Chanan, M.   "Songs for a mad King."   Music and
Musicians, 17 (July 1969), pp. 78-9.

"The Pierrot Players once again brought off an
outstanding recital...when almost the entire

programme consisted of new music by no less than 12
different composers.
Eleven of them had written short pieces which
together contribute A Garland for Dr. K - a tribute
to the music publisher Alfred Kalmus on his 80th
birthday....The pieces included an unpretentious
flute solo (Bennett, excellently played by Judith
Pearce)...." See: W63a

B104.Chapman, E. "The Ledge." Musical Events, 16 (November
       1961), p. 24.

A review of Bennett's first opera in which he "...
certainly has the ability to conjure up atmosphere,
to create expressive orchestral sonorities, and to
write singable vocal lines. The work leaves no
doubt as to his resourceful craftsmanship in an
advanced Schoenbergian idiom." See: W1a

B105.Chapman, E. "Macnaghten Concert." Musical Events, 20
       (February 1965), p 28.

"Of the new carols Richard Rodney Bennett's The
Sorrows of Mary stood out for its refinement and
certainty of effect...." See: W138a

B106.Chapman, E. "Mines of Sulphur." Musical Events, 28
       (November 1973), pp. 26-28.

A review of the 1973 revival. "Bennett has now
tightened the effect of the whole by omitting the
interval between the second and third acts, running
them straight on. A wise move, for the action was
formerly held up at a crucial moment. The music
has punch and assurance, though lyricism -
particularly in the music for the actress Jenny -
is also there in welcome measure." See: W2f

B107.Chapman, E. "Musica Viva." Musical Events, 17 (April
       1962), p. 13.

A brief mention of Bennett's Clarinet Quintet which
is described as "...unassuming but skilful." See:
W79a

B108.Chapman, E. "New Bennett and Wagner operas." Musical
       Events, 20 (April 1965), pp. 12-13.

"Richard Rodney Bennett has travelled far since his
first opera....In his new full length work The
Mines of Sulphur...he is much more ambitious, moves
with greater confidence, and probes much deeper,
dramatically and musically.
...the work is a splendid piece of musical theatre,
and Bennett's music, serially based , evokes most
skilfully the sinister, phantasmagorical atmosphere
of the tale. His vocal writing is grateful and the
orchestration abounds in colourful touches." See:
W2a

B109.Chapman, E. "The new Bennett opera." Musical Events,
     22 (December 1967), pp. 6-9.

          A review of Penny for a Song which is described as
          "...Bennett's tricky, shimmering score." See: W3a

B110.Chapman, E. "Prom Commissions." Musical Events, 19
     (October 1964), p. 28.

          "The most successful of this year's commissions was
          Richard Rodney Bennett's Aubade, written in memory
          of John Hollingsworth. Sensuously romantic in the
          Bergian manner but cooler in tone, the work seemed
          perfectly realised in every detail...." See: W9a

B111.Chislett, W.A. "All the King's Men." The Gramophone,
     49 (November 1971), p. 912.

          A review of the Abbey recording XMS 703. "As might
          be expected Richard Rodney Bennett has brought the
          right feeling of youth to his attractive music."
          See: D2

B112.Chissell, Joan.   "Bradshaw/Bennett."   The   Times
     (London), 3 December 1977, p. 12.

          Details of the first performance of Bennett's
          Kandinsky Variations which "...was   directly
          inspired   by   pictures,   or   rather   musical
          connotations of their names." See: W67a

B113.Chissell, Joan. "Cheltenham Festival." The Times
     (London), 10 July 1978, p. 11.

          "Lasting about 20 minutes, Music for Strings' four
          movements...live up to their titles with that
          elegance of craftsmanship and ear for sensitively
          fanciful sonority, not least in the supernatural
          flights of the second movement, so characteristic
          of this composer." See: W29a

B114.Chissell, Joan. "English Bach Festival: Oxford." The
     Times (London), 17 April 1972, p. 9.

          "The programme also included the premiere of
          Richard Rodney Bennett's Commedia I, commissioned
          by the festival.
          ...the idea was delightful and the scoring
          masterly." See: W49a

B115.Chissell, Joan. "Five Etudes for solo piano." The
     Gramophone, 46 (November 1968), p. 692.

          A review of the Philips Fourfront recording 4FM
          10002.
          "All are highly complex in rhythm and strikingly
          imaginative in sonority." See: D16

B116. Chissell, Joan. "Last night's concerto and recitals."
The Times (London), 26 February 1969, p. 13.

"Easily the most enjoyable performance was a
dashing one of Mr Bennett's own Capriccio, a
brilliant, effervescent piece of writing." See:
W48a

B117. Chissell, Joan. "Nash Ensemble: Queen Elizabeth Hall."
The Times (London), 27 February 1973, p. 11.

"Bennett was represented...by a brand new Commedia
III for chamber ensemble....The four main sections
are...joined by three important cadenzas in which
woodwind,   strings   and   brass   assert   their
individuality in turn....
...the sequence of events emerged more organic and
close-knit here...." See: W51a

B118. Chissell, Joan.   "The   Sorrows   of   Mary."   The
Gramophone, 44 (December 1966), p. 327.

A review of the Argo recording ZRG 5499, a
collection of contemporary carols. "Richard Rodney
Bennett provides a much more extended composition
of great beauty...." See: D33

B119. Clarke, Mary. "Isadora." Dancing Times, 71 (June
1981), pp. 608-10.

A detailed survey of Isadora and its first
performance. "Richard Rodney Bennett's score is
vivdly theatrical and he cleverly uses pastiche
music in the style of Isadora's favourite composers
- Brahms, Liszt, Chopin and Mendelssohn - for her
dances. He provides a score that is both danceable
and dramatic...." See: W5a

B120. Cook, P. "The Sound Track." Films in Review, 19
(January 1968), pp. 38-40.

An account of Bennett's score for Far from the
Madding Crowd. See: W205

B121. Crighton, Ronald. "Banks, Bennett." The Musical Times,
111 (August 1970), p. 816.

"Richard Rodney Bennett's Pastoral...shows his
usual fluency and skill....Cleo Laine, although she
hit some gorgeously rich notes, only made her words
clear when she dropped her amplified voice nearly
to a whisper." See: W153a

B122. Crighton, Ronald. "The Mines of Sulphur." Financial
Times, 31 March 1980, p. 13.

A review of the revival of Bennett's opera, the
music of which "...while hardly achieving the
toughness he claims for it, helps greatly. His

orchestra, eerie horn-calls and all, is strongly
atmospheric.   The   vocal   lines,   while   ranging
widely, are not ungratefully jagged.   Above all,
Bennett is adroit in his sparing employment of the
typically English medium-paced arioso writing....
See: W2g

B123.Crighton, Ronald. "New Music." The Musical Times, 116
(March 1975), p. 264.

"Richard Rodney Bennett's Sonnet Sequence consisted
originally of two Shakespeare sonnets set for tenor
and piano: a third has now been added and the whole
scored for string orchestra....
The writing contains Bennett's vocal clarity,
assurance and polished craftsmanship...with genuine
depth of feeling." See: W166c

B124.Crisp, Clement. "About the ballet Isadora." About the
House, Spring 1981, pp. 14-17.

An interview with Kenneth MacMillan about Isadora,
with a question about the music. "Richard produced
a   working   score   for   me   composed   for   two
pianos...except for the fact that we can't afford
two pianists at every rehearsal. So he also
provided me with a two-piano tape recording." See:
W5

B125.Cross, Anthony. "Birmingham." The Musical Times, 117
(June 1976), p. 509.

A review of the Violin Concerto.   "The first
movement evokes morning with predominantly bright,
transparent sonorities and a brilliant scherzo
section....The   slow   second   movement...has   a
nocturnal atmosphere which emerges even more
strongly in the impressionistic coda.... A very
experienced composer's hand is evident in both the
structure and the perfectly judged balance between
soloist and orchestra." See: W22a

B126.Cross, Anthony. "Birmingham." The Musical Times, 127
(August 1986), p. 453.

"Richard Rodney Bennett was featured and his Fifth
Quartet (Lamento d'Arianna), a concentrated and
resourceful working out of the opening of
Monteverdi's famous madrigal, received a confident
first performance by the Medici Quartet". See:
W68a

B127.Cross, Beverley "Novel into Libretto." Opera, April
1970, pp.286-290.

Valuable background about the preparation and
writing of the libretto for Bennett's opera
Victory. See: W4

B128. Davies, Richard. "Composing for Isadora." _Classical Music_, 16 May 1981, p.27.

> A talk with the composer about his score for Kenneth MacMillan's ballet _Isadora_. See:W5

B129. Davis, Peter. "New York sees opera by Bennett". _The Times_ (London), 2 February 1968, p.7.

> A review of the American premiere of _The Mines of Sulphur_, the production of which "... reached an astonishing level of smooth professionalism." See: W2e

B130. Dawes, Frank. "Record Reviews" _The Musical Times_, 114 (March 1973), p.267.

> A review of the Argo recording ZRG 704, containing Bennett's _Five studies for piano_ and _Capriccio for piano duet_. See: D7,D16

B131. Dean, Winton. "The Mines of Sulphur". _The Musical Times_, 106 (April 1965), pp. 281-2.

> "The composer has identified himself completely with the libretto, and the result is a memorable theatrical experience with a gripping climax. Bennett has an undoubted feeling for character; his vocal lines, influenced now and then by the Britten of _Billy Budd_, are often expressive and his sense of orchestral texture is outstanding." See: W2a

B132. Dean, Winton. "A Penny for a Song". _The Musical Times_, 108 (December 1967), p.1127.

> "Bennett's fine ear for instrumental sonorities, especially among the woodwind, is everywhere in evidence. His vocal writing is not ungrateful, and the exquisite portrait of Dorcas reveals a sensitive feeling for character that will surely develop". See: W3a

B133. Dean, Winton. "Victory" _The Musical Times_, 111 (June 1970), pp.622-3.

> A discussion about the first performance of Bennett's opera, _Victory_, at the Royal Opera House, Covent Garden. See: W4a

B134. Downes, Edward. "A man of principle." _Music and Musicians_, 18 (May 1970), pp. 30+73.

> An explanation of _Victory's_ plot in detail with a discussion of the music. "Like most of Bennett's music, _Victory_ is a serial composition - that is, the music is entirely based on pre-arranged series of notes." See: W4

B135.Downes, Edward. "Victory." About the House, 3 (1970),
        pp.34-9.

>   An examination of the story, based on Conrad's
>   novel, and detailed examination of each Act.
>   Drawings of the sets and costume designs for the
>   opera are also included. See: W4

B136.Dromgoole, N. "Ashton's Jazz Ballet." The Sunday
        Telegraph, 14 January 1968, p.12.

>   "... there can be no doubt that his [Frederick
>   Ashton] latest work, Jazz Calendar, with music by
>   Richard Rodney Bennett, and designs by Derek
>   Jarman, is a rampaging success.
>   ... Ashton in Jazz Calendar has made marvels with
>   Bennett's score...." See: W66b. Also printed in
>   About the House 1968(2), p.45.

B137.Duarte, J. "Five Impromptus for guitar." Gramophone, 59
        (April 1982), p. 1397.

>   A review of the RCA Red Seal digital recording (RL
>   25419) of Bennett's 5 Impromptus for Guitar which
>   are described as "... five contrasted growths from
>   one note-row (which) have become standard guitar
>   repertory...." See: D15

B138.East, Leslie. "Modern British." Music and Musicians,
        20 (July 1972), p.67.

>   "With a technique like Holliger's at his disposal
>   one can perhaps excuse Richard Rodney Bennett for
>   writing what is unashamedly a vehicle for the
>   soloist. His concerto... is in two movements
>   linked by an extended cadenza. Hardly any ideas of
>   impact come from the ... string orchestra, all the
>   material development rests with the soloist, and
>   although the solo writing makes a striking and
>   sympathetic blend of both traditional and new-found
>   qualities of the oboe, one wonders whether anybody
>   other than Holliger could put over the work as
>   convincingly." See: W16d

B139.East, Leslie. "South Bank Summer Music". Music and
        Musicians, 23 (November 1974), p.46.

>   A review of the world premiere of Tenebrae, the
>   opening number of which is described as "... being
>   outstanding." See: W167a

B140.Edwards,A. "British Music for Film and Television."
        Gramophone, 62 (October 1984), pp. 535-6.

>   A review of the HMV Greensleeve recording
>   ED290109-1 which includes the themes from Lady
>   Caroline Lamb and Yanks. See: D23,D43

B141.Fanning, D.J. "Five Etudes for solo piano." <u>Gramophone</u>, 63 (February 1986), p. 1052.

> A review of the ASV recording ALH 965. "The Richard Rodney Bennett studies sound quite effective in Cherkassky's impressionistic renderings...." <u>See</u>:D16

B142.Fawkes, R. "Richard Rodney Bennett at Edinburgh" <u>Music and Musicians</u>, 28 (September 1979), pp.28-30.

> A consideration of the Bennett - Barry Tuckwell association with mention of their Kern recording and <u>Actaeon</u>.
> Also included is an interview with Bennett and Marian Montgomery about their "man-woman relationship as defined in popular song."

B143.Finn, Robert. "Composer at home writing for concerts or films." <u>Cleveland Plain Dealer</u>, 9 February 1983, Section F, p.10.

> A report of an address by Bennett to students at the University of Akron.

B144.Fiske, Roger. "Farnham Festival 1965" <u>The Gramophone</u>, 43 (February 1966), p.404.

> A review of the Waverley recording LLP 1039 which includes Bennett's <u>Farnham Festival Overture</u>, "... an irresistible piece of music...." <u>See</u>:D13

B145.Fiske, Roger. "(The) Midnight Thief." <u>The Gramophone</u>, 42 (December 1964), p.292.

> A review of the HMV recording DLP 1216, "... (a) record... full of good ideas, and every Primary School in the country should get a copy...." <u>See</u>: D24

B146.Fiske, Roger. "Twentieth-Century English Songs." <u>The Gramophone</u>, 42 (November 1964), p.339.

> A recording (ZRG 5418) which includes Bennett's <u>Tom O'Bedlam's Song</u>, "...a splendid 'scena' (which) Peter Pears sings... with marvellous intensity and understanding, and Joan Dickson's 'cello playing in <u>Tom O'Bedlam</u> is very good indeed." <u>See</u>:D38

B147.Fluck, Alan. "Festival of Youth". <u>Composer</u>, no.25 (Autumn 1967), pp.14-17.

> The Farnham Festival organiser looks back after the third biennial Festival at Farnham, Surrey. First aim at Farnham has been to encourage serious composers to write for young performers. To date, 27 new works, including the <u>Farnham Festival Overture</u> from Bennett, had been commissioned locally.

B148.French, Peter. "The London Concert Scene". <u>Musical Opinion</u>, 91 (November 1967), pp. 71-2.

"Klein gave an outstanding and most impressive performance [of <u>The Music that her Echo is</u>], showing a voice of great colour and character. ... he caught the exact atmosphere of the assorted Elizabethan verses; and Bennett's piano accompaniment was suitable and off-setting...." <u>See</u>: W158a

B149.French, Peter. "New Elizabethan cycle." <u>Music and Musicians</u>, 16 (December 1967), p.51.

"... (Klein's) voice had a timbre that emphasised the feeling of unrequited love that pervades the five Elizabethan verses set, and he was able to provide both delicacy and lugubrious power as required. His performance was admirable...." <u>See</u>: W158a

B150.Giffin, G. "Composer Bennett Adept at Classical Music, Film Scores." <u>The Denver Post</u> (Round UP Magazine), 30 April 1972, pp.3+8.

An interview with Bennett, "... a young British composer who moves easily between film-score assignments and classical, serious composition."

B151.Giffin, G. "Symphony Euphoric on World Premiere." <u>The Denver Post</u>, 26 February 1974, p.24.

An account of the world premiere of Bennett's <u>Concerto for Orchestra</u>, a work in which "...Bennett challenges both his players and listeners to stretch their abilities." <u>See</u>: W17a

B152.Gilardino, Angelo. "La musica contemporanea per chitarra in Gran Bretasna" (Contemporary guitar music in Great Britain). <u>Fronimo</u> 1 (October 1973), pp. 8-14

An article in Italian, discussing works for guitar by several twentieth-century British composers (including Bennett) against the background of performances by English virtuosos Julian Bream and John Williams.

B153.Goodwin, Noel. "Aldeburgh Festival." <u>Music and Musicians</u>, 20 (October 1971), pp. 68-9.

"A new Oboe Concerto by Richard Rodney Bennett was ...(given) its first performance...on 6 June. It is a thoughtful, carefully worked piece in two movements, of tougher imaginative fibre than is usually found in Bennett's music and exploiting some resources of Holliger's individual technique without making this a focal feature. A compelling performance...." <u>See</u>: W16a

B154.Goodwin, Noel. "Aldeburgh Festival." Music and
     Musicians, 23 (August 1975), pp. 47-8.

> "...Time's Whiter Series...provides the cycle with
> prelude and postlude. Three wintry texts are
> enclosed within it, together with two interludes
> for lute solo, and the effect is gentle, elegant -
> fastidiously written for the resources of
> counter-tenor, and sparingly for the lute in its
> support...." See: W171a

B155.Goodwin, Noel. "Bennett's Victory." Music and
     Musicians, 19 (June 1970), pp. 23-4.

> An account of the premiere of Victory at the Royal
> Opera House, Covent Garden. "Bennett, I believe,
> has successfully enlarged the dimensions of his
> musical imagination in this opera...." See: W4a

B156.Goodwin, Noel. "(The) Cheltenham Festival." The
     Musical Times, 101 (September 1960), pp. 572-3.

> "Five Pieces for Orchestra by Richard Rodney
> Bennett...are contrasting mood-pieces, written four
> years ago when the composer was aged twenty. They
> seemed little more than symphonic chapter-headings,
> too short-winded and heavily scored for the thin
> musical argument, and showing no evidence that the
> composer can sustain musical ideas as fluently as
> he created them." See: W23b

B157.Goodwin, Noel. "Cheltenham Festival." The Musical
     Times, 104 (September 1963), p. 641.

> "Signs that Richard Rodney Bennett is developing
> beyond fluency of invention and technique were
> revealed by his Nocturnes for Chamber
> Orchestra....The work has a depth and intensity of
> feeling hitherto unusual in the composer's writing.
> The work deserves, and should achieve a welcome
> place in the repertory of small orchestras." See:
> W30b

B158.Goodwin, Noel. "Cheltenham's problems." Music and
     Musicians, 12 (September 1963), p. 38.

> "Bennett's Nocturnes for chamber orchestra, evoking
> feelings associated with three aspects of night,
> had a new intensity of imagination and expression,
> and immediate appeal." See: W30b

B159.Goodwin, Noel. "Jazz sounds." Dance and Dancers, 19
     (February 1968), pp. 16-17+22.

> Useful background to Bennett's Jazz Calendar and a
> detailed account of the ballet version's first
> performance at the Royal Opera House, Covent
> Garden, movement by movement. See: W66b

B160.Goodwin, Noel. "London Pastoral." <u>Music and Musicians</u>, 11 (September 1962), p. 36.

"A setting for tenor and small orchestra of three poems having to do with London, it reflects a sensitive feeling for words on the composer's part, an ear for attractive instrumental colour and a sense of musical shapeliness." <u>See</u>: W127a

B161.Goodwin, Noel. "(The) Mines of Sulphur." <u>Opera</u>, 16 (February 1965), pp. 85-88.

An interview with the composer about the work, its music and the composer's attitude towards opera. <u>See</u>: W2

B162.Goodwin, Noel. "More English Eccentrics." <u>Music and Musicians</u>, 16 (January 1968), pp. 26-7.

A review of a <u>A Penny for a Song</u>. "At first impression I found it instantly attractive in the light, graceful manner that formerly occupied a now-deserted middle-ground between music-drama and musical comedy. In character it is the antithesis of his previous opera..., not simply in reverting from a serial basis to a more conventional harmonic technique, but in its conception as a conversation-piece for singers, in allowing music to support words from underneath, and in its often bold use of simplicity of means to achieve quite an intricate pattern of effect. ...I think Bennett deserves more credit than he has so far been given for the subtlety and skill of the opera's instrumental writing." <u>See</u>: W3a

B163.Goodwin, Noel. "Symphonic Bennett." <u>Music and Musicians</u>, 14 (May 1966), p. 50.

"The three compact movements, lasting just over 20 minutes, at times recall Walton's <u>First Symphony</u> in their frank eloquence of expression, their skill in orchestral colour and often dazzling impact. But the bright, sharp-featured sounds and rhythms are very much of the 1960s, and Bennett shows a distinctive flair for evolving appealing melodic lines from themes and textures rooted in serial technique." <u>See</u>: W37a

B164.Goodwin, Noel. "Taking a chance." <u>Music and Musicians</u>, 11 (December 1962), p. 16.

"Surprisingly little notice has so far been taken of the most significant item in Norman Tucker's recent announcement of future plans for Sadler's Wells. When we are told that one composer, still in his twenties, has been invited to write 'one, two or three full-length operas' for the company, the implications go beyond the apparent casualness with which the statement was made. The composer,

Richard Rodney Bennett, is the subject of a major
development in operatic policy.
In Richard Rodney Bennett I think that Sadler's
Wells has made an extremely clever choice. His
first opera, The Ledge, a tense one-act drama of a
would-be suicide, made a distinctive impression
when it was presented by 'Rostrum' at Sadler's
Wells just over a year ago. It was evident that
the composer had a sound grasp of character and
situation and the means to illuminate it in music -
not altogether surprising after his considerable
experience in writing music for films."

B165. Graham, Colin. "Introducing 'A Penny for a Song'."
Opera, 18 (November 1967), pp. 870-73.

An introduction to Bennett's third opera by Colin
Graham who wrote the libretto, based on John
Whiting's play who "...himself would have been
delighted that Richard Rodney Bennett has hit the
nail so well on the head: his conception of the
piece seems entirely at one with the charm and
sparkle of the play." See: W3

B166. Greenfield, Edward. "(The) Mines of Sulphur." The
Guardian, 25 February 1965, p.9.

"The first performance last night more than
confirmed the high confidence of the Sadler's Wells
authorities who gave (Bennett), when still in his
mid-twenties, a multiple commission for operas,
something that the British composer (certainly not
one so young) has ever had before.
As to the musical idiom, Bennett has solved with
enormous confidence the perennial problem facing
modern composers - how far should atonal principles
be sacrificed in order to make the vocal line
singable or - going further still - tuneful." See:
W2a

B167. Greenfield, Edward. "Winter Music." The Musical Times,
104 (July 1963), p. 500.

A review of the Delta recording SDEL 18005,
including Bennett's Winter Music which is described
as "...deliberately lighter and more immediately
attractive." See: D42

B168. Grier, Christopher. "At the Proms." Radio Times, 3
September 1964, p. 52.

A preview of Aubade, a commission from the BBC and
written in memory of John Hollingsworth. See: W9

B169. Grier, Christopher. "CBSO/Fremaux." The Guardian, 1
April 1976, p. 8.

"...the   [violin]   concerto   has   two
movements...though   within   those   general

specifications there are considerable fluctuations
of pace and mood not to mention a generous ration
of cadenzas in the Allegro.
First impressions suggest that in this case the
composer's inspiration was essentially lyrical."
See: W22b

B170.Griffiths, David. "More Scottish Strings." Music and
Musicians, 10 (January 1962), p. 37.

Mention of the first performance of Tom O' Bedlam's
Song, composed for the 500th concert at the
National Gallery in Edinburgh. See: W172a

B171.Griffiths, Paul. "Bennett's Comedies." The Musical
Times, 115 (August 1974), pp. 649-50.

A survey and useful analysis of Bennett's Commedia
pieces. See: W49, W50, W51, W52

B172.Griffiths, Paul. "Calendar." The Musical Times, 116
(September 1975), p. 797.

A review of the Argo recording ZRG 758, the ninth
disc in the Gulbenkian series and a reissue of a
recording once available from EMI. "Bennett's
Calendar for chamber group is perhaps the sort of
music Gershwin might have written if he had come
into contact with Webern." See: D6

B173.Griffiths, Paul. "Jane Manning." The Times (London), 1
February 1977, p.9.

"Her [Jane Manning] accompanist was Richard Rodney
Bennett, who was also at the piano for the first
performance of his own The Little Ghost who Died
for Love.
...Bennett responds with music of elegant
accomplishment." See: W156a

B174.Griffiths, Paul. "(The) Mines of Sulphur." The Musical
Times, 114 (December 1973), pp. 1252-3.

An account of the brief revival of Bennett's opera
at the Coliseum in September 1973. See: W2f

B175.Griffiths, Paul. "New Music." The Musical Times, 113
(July 1972), p. 686.

Bennett's Nightpiece...(his) first electronic work,
is a beautiful piece which successfully transmits
the oneiric imagery of the text. Jane Manning gave
a brilliant performance: her response to every
phrase, whether sung or whispered in speech-song,
was absolutely right." See: W159b

B176.Griffiths, Paul. "New Music." The Musical Times, 117
(June 1976), p. 508.

Reviews of the first London performances of
Bennett's Oboe Quartet and the Violin Concerto.
See: W22b, W74b

B177. Griffiths, Paul. "New Music." The Musical Times, 118
(April 1977), pp. 319-20.

"Setting a poem by Edith Sitwell [The Liitle Ghost
who Died for Love]...is a subtle, strange and
elegant transcription of the thoughts of a poor,
puzzled spirit...." See: W156a

B178. Griffiths, Paul. "Proms." The Musical Times, 117
October 1976), pp. 841-2.

A review of the first British performance of
Zodiac, "...a piece (which) showed once more
Bennett's technical accomplishment, and also his
facility." See: W40b

B179. Griffiths, Paul. "Proms." The Musical Times, 118
(October 1977), p. 841.

"Actaeon...is a work that fits into the sequence of
Bennett's concerto already numerous, in that it is
brilliantly conceived for the solo instrument and
abounds in fluent orchestral writing." See: W7a

B180. Griffiths, Paul. "Shakespeare's Birthday." The Musical
Times, 113 (June 1972), p. 577.

"Very different was the gentle setting by Richard
Rodney Bennett of two sonnets on the inexorable
progress of time. This Sonnet Sequence was finely
sung by Philip Langridge, and the accompaniment of
strings sounded superb in this acoustic." See:
W166a

B181. Griffiths, Paul. "Spells/Aubade." The Musical Times,
121 (April 1980), p. 248.

A review of the Argo recording ZRG 907 of Spells in
which "...Bennett runs true to form in providing a
thoroughly effective but rarely surprising musical
weave, atmospheric, sensitive to the qualities and
quantities of the text, effortlessly well written
for the resources.
Otherwise the main treasure (on the disc) is the
Aubade of 1964, a beautiful orchestral aquatint
which is prettily played under David Atherton."
See: D3, D34

B182. Griffiths, Paul. "Susan Milan." The Times (London), 18
August 1981, p. 7.

A review of the first performance of Bennett's Six
Tunes for the Instruction of Singing Birds in which
"five different avian songsters are imitated in
idealised fashion, the starlings coming both first

and last to frame what is a very attractive little
suite, beautifully played here by Susan Milan."
See: W89a

B183.Grimley, Terry. "A tribute to Gershwin." The
Birmingham Post, 6 February 1988, p. 31.

An article describing Bennett's affinity with the
music of George Gershwin - "witness the cabaret
show, Fascinatin' Rhythmn...."

B184.Grundy, Michael. "World premiere is a scoop for
festival!" Worcester Evening News, 21 August 1987,
p. 21.

Details of the "...new symphony which will receive
its world premiere at the Three Choirs Festival in
Worcester Cathedral....It is the Elgar Commission
(for which)...Bennett originally told the Three
Choir organisers he was writing a short orchestral
piece called 'Tapestry'...but has since extended
the work to become his Third Symphony." See: W39

B185.Guidi, G. "Milan." Opera News (USA), 7 May 1966, pp.
25-6.

An account of the Italian premiere of The Mines of
Sulphur at the Teatro alla Scala. See: W26

B186.H.,C.C. "Heart-warming cello tone in Bennett
composition." Evening News (Edinburgh), 4 September
1979, p.9.

A review of Bennett's Sonnets to Orpheus,
commissioned by the Edinburgh Festival and played
by the Halle Orchestra "...at the top of its form
and having as soloist Heinrich Schiff, a player
with a heart-warming broad cello tone." See: W33a

B187.H.,R.L. "Opera theme taken from Civil War." The Daily
Telegraph, 29 March 1969, p.17.

"With his usual intuitive grasp of exactly what is
needed in any given situation, Bennett's music (in
All the King's Men) is fresh, lively and
economical. Not only does it sound enjoyable both
to sing and to play, but it makes use of a largish
body of performers of extremely variable ability
with considerable skill, moving at a pace which
never allows them to become bored." See: W175a

B188.Hamilton, Peter. "Edinburgh Festival." Plays and
Players 10 (November 1962), p. 60.

A review of the British premiere of Christopher
Fry's play Curtmantle, but with no mention of
Bennett's incidental music. See: W245a

B189.Harris, R.L.   "Contemporary   piano   music."   <u>Music Teacher</u>, 66 (September 1987), pp. 25+27.

> Part two in a series aimed at encouraging teachers to explore less familiar piano pieces from the contemporary repertoire, with mention of some of Bennett's pieces. <u>See</u>: W180, W186, W190

B190.Harrison, David. "MICA Concert." <u>Manchester Evening News</u>, 17 November 1972, p. 10.

> An account of the concert when Bennett and Karin Krog gave the first performance of the composer's <u>Quietly with Bright Eyes</u>, scored for voice, piano and electronic tape. <u>See</u>: W163a

B191.Harrison M. "Contemporary British Guitar Works." <u>The Gramophone</u>, 51 (October 1973), pp. 690+695.

> A review of the RCA recording SB 6876 which includes Bennett's guitar concerto.
> "...Bennett sensibly uses a chamber ensemble whose scope for intimacy matches that of the guitar itself. The music deserves the fine performance it receives and the performance deserves the excellent recording." <u>See</u>: D9

B192.Harrison, M. "Jazz Calendar/Piano Concerto." <u>The Gramophone</u>, 49 (March 1972), p. 1522.

> A review of the Philips recording, 6500 301, of the <u>Piano Concerto</u> and <u>Jazz Calendar</u>. <u>See</u>: D10, D22

B193.Harrison, M. "Jazz devices." <u>The Times</u> (London), 17 June 1970, p.8.

> "More disappointing still was...Bennett's <u>Jazz Pastoral</u>....This marked no advance at all on his earlier 'Soliloquy'...its crippling weakness being the lack of any distinction in its musical ideas." <u>See</u>: W153a

B194.Harrison, M. "Shakespeare gala." <u>The Times</u> (London), 24 April 1972, p.8.

> "Richard Rodney Bennett's <u>Sonnet Sequence</u>...was a bit more astringent, even if it amounted to no more than a demonstration of this composer's well-known fluency. " <u>See</u>: W166a.

B195.Harrison, M. "Summer Music." <u>The Times</u> (London), 21 August 1974. p. 8.

> "...Bennett's <u>Tenebrae</u>...(is) a dark, pessimistic work, consist(ing) of five settings of sixteenth and seventeenth century verses which all take human transience as their subject. The piano commentary - behind the voice and in interludes between verses

- is particularly striking in the opening piece...." See: W167a

B196. Harrison, M. "Synthesis: Rodney Bennett/Krog." The Times (London), 24 November 1972, p. 9.

"Synthesis is Karin Krog, the Norwegian jazz singer and Richard Rodney Bennett, the English composer....
...one is happy to hear a 'straight' composer such as Mr. Bennett looking into Joplin, a jazz singer like Miss Krog tackling - and more successfully, be it noted - Cage or Berberian." See: W163b

B197. Harrison, M. "Synthesis." Jazz and Blues 2 (February 1973), p.32.

"A new composition of his Quietly with bright eyes seemed at first hearing to be little more than a modish exercise, Krog speaking three e.e. cummings texts over the usual electronic noises pre-recorded on tape and with keyboard injections." See: W163b

B198. Harrison, M. "Telegram (1976)." Gramophone, 54 (May 1977), p. 1714.

A review of the Pearl recording SHE 537, part of a recital given by Richard Deering at the Purcell Room in July 1976, in celebration of Elizabeth Lutyens's 70th birthday. "Among the works by other hands, Bennett's Telegram is simply an amusing variant on 'Happy Birthday to you'...." See: D36

B199. Harvey, T. "Symphony No. 1." The Gramophone, 45 (January 1968), p. 373.

A review of the RCA Victor recording SB 6730 which includes the first symphony. The reviewer ends by saying "...don't miss this record, especially for Bennett's symphony". See: D35

B200. Harvey, T. "Tom O'Bedlam's Song." Gramophone, 55 (January 1978), p.1283.

A review of the ARGO recording ZK28, a reissue of ZRG 5418, two discs devoted to English songs and including Bennett's Tom O'Bedlam's Song...a superb poem imaginatively set and strikingly original." See: D38

B201. Henderson, R.L. "The heirs of Webern." Weekly Post, 10 December 1960, p. 38.

A discussion about the music of Bennett and Henze. "Richard Bennett is still in his early twenties and...these latest compositions...show a new depth of experience, a maturity of expression."

B202. Henderson, Robert. "In memory of jazz..." The Daily

Telegraph, 11 November 1983, p. 17.

"The _Momento_ for flute and strings that Richard
Rodney Bennett composed earlier this year...is a
work of a characteristically urbane sprucely
tailored fluidity." _See_: W70b

B203.Henderson, Robert. "Some younger British composers."
Music in Britain, no. 1967 (Winter 1964/5), pp.
18-21.

A survey of the younger generation of British
composers, including Bennett who is described as a
brilliant practical musician, equally at home in
the world of modern jazz (and) "...arguably the
most prodigiously talented composer of his
generation."

B204.Heyworth, Peter. "Complacency in a cool climate?" _The
Observer_ (Review), 5 November 1967, p. 24.

"In sheer craftsmanship Richard Rodney Bennett
stands head and shoulders above the many young
British composers who have recently turned their
hand to opera. Not since Britten have we been
blessed with a creative musician who is so
consummate a master of his calling and as a result
his latest opera _A Penny for a Song_...is
refreshingly free from the miscalculations,
ineptitude and downright clumsiness that are so
liable to dog British composers when they turn to
the strange and tricky world of the theatre. Mr
Bennett's ear is miraculously exact. His use of
the orchestra is restrained, subtle and yet
dramatically effective. His vocal writing...is
unfailingly grateful to sing, yet admirably pointed
in its handling of words." _See_: W3a

B205.Heyworth, Peter. "(The) judgement of the ear." _The
Observer_ (Review), 23 February 1969, p. 26.

"There is a great deal to admire in Richard Rodney
Bennett's _Second Symphony_....In the first place, it
sounds wonderfully clear, brilliant and lustrous
and every instrumental inflection is calculated
with the precision of a master." _See_: W38b

B206.Hofacre, M.J. "The use of tenor trombone in twentieth-
century brass quintet music: a brief historical
overview with comprehensive listing of original,
published twentieth-century quintets and a discussion
of tenor trombone excerpts from selected compositions." Doctor of Musical Arts Dissertation,
University of Oklahoma, 1986, 253 pp.

Included are details of Bennett's _Commedia IV_,
"...(one) of the most significant works in the
twentieth-century brass quintet repertoire." _See_:
W52

B207.Holme, C.   "Long-Distance Piano-Player."   Radio Times, 9
      August 1962, p. 43

            "The music...is bound to be of equal importance
            with the speech in such a conception, and here it
            is the hands of Richard Rodney Bennett, one of the
            most talked-of composers...(who) plays the piano in
            this production...."   See: W255a

B208.Hughes, Eric and Day, Timothy.   "Discographies of
      British Composers: 14 - Richard Rodney Bennett."
      Recorded Sound no. 81 (January 1982), pp. 59-77.

            The discography lists all known commercial discs,
            together with BBC transcription discs held at the
            National Sound Archive. In addition to music, the
            tapes listed include talks given by the composer.

B209.Hurd, Michael.   "Farnham 1965."   Music in Education 29
      (1965), pp. 173-5.

            A survey of the 1965 Farnham Festival which
            included the first performance of Bennett's Farnham
            Festival Overture. See: W181a

B210.Hutchinson, Peter.   "Munich."   Opera, 19 (May 1968), pp.
      367-9.

            A review of the first German performance of A Penny
            for a Song which is described as "...a delightful
            work in many ways...."   See: W3b

B211.Sherwood, Peter.   "All the King's Men at Coventry."
      Music (Schools Music Association), 3 (1969), p. 34-5.

            Background information about the commissioning and
            production of the opera. "Things were on the way
            and it was very exciting to receive the manuscripts
            as Richard Bennett proceeded with the work...."
            See: W175

B212.Jacobs, A.   "Bennett's New Piece for Children."
      Opera, 20 (May 1969), pp. 456-7.

            A review of the first performance of All the King's
            Men, the music of which is "...delightful..." and
            the piece"...most agreeable...."   See: W175a

B213.Jacobs, A.   "The Ledge."   Opera, 12 (October 1961), pp.
      670-2.

            A criticism of Bennett's first opera in which (the
            composer) "...was well served by his singers and
            poorly by the production."   See: W1a

B214.Jacobs, Arthur.   "London Music: Henze and Bennett."   The
      Musical Times, 102 (January 1961), p. 38.

"The occasion also provided the first performance of Richard Rodney Bennett's...<u>Calendar</u>. In a ten-minute span...it displays true invention, individual and consciously modern without being freakish, and confirms the rising status of this young composer." <u>See</u>: W46a

B215. Jacobs, Arthur. "(The) Mines of Sulphur." <u>Opera</u>, 31 (May 1980), pp. 499-500.

An account of the revival of Bennett's opera at the Grand Theatre, Leeds in March 1980. See: W2g

B216. Jacobs, Arthur. "(The) Mines of Sulphur." <u>Opera</u>, 16 (April 1965) pp. 301-5.

A detailed criticism of the first performance of <u>The Mines of Sulphur</u> at Sadler's Wells. <u>See</u>: W2a

B217. Jacobson, Bernard. "Friday's Child." <u>Music and Musicians</u>, 13 (November 1964), p. 17.

Background information and useful detail about Bennett's <u>Jazz Calendar</u>, and a performance of one of the movements, 'Friday's Child' by William Russo's jazz orchestra. <u>See</u>: W66

B218. Jacobson, Bernard. "Pianists' Pianist." <u>Music and Musicians</u>, 13 (December 1964), p. 40.

"Richard Rodney Bennett's <u>Five Studies</u> received their first piano performance: this is inventive and enjoyable music...." <u>See</u>: W60a

B219. Joachim, Heinz. "Richard Rodney Bennett's Ballade in Moor." <u>Neue ZFM</u>, 128 (May 1967), pp. 178-9.

An article, in German, describing the first performance of Bennett's <u>Mines of Sulphur</u> at the Cologne Opera House. <u>See</u>: W2c

B220. K., A.H. "Savouring a personal style." <u>Newbury Weekly News</u>, 21 May 1987, p. 32.

"The highlight of the evening was the European premiere of the <u>Sonata for Wind Quintet and Piano</u> by Richard Rodney Bennett. This is a one-movement work that will become an essential part of the repertoire. With the composer taking the piano part, it was a moving experience to hear a work played by the people for whom it was written." <u>See</u>: W100b

B221. Kay, Norman. "Bennett's Piano Concerto." <u>Tempo</u> no. 86 (Autumn 1968), pp. 17 and 19.

A short analysis of Bennett's <u>Piano Concerto</u>, movement by movement. <u>See</u>: W18

B222.Kay, Norman. "Richard Rodney Bennett: London Pastoral."
     The Musical Times, 103 (September 1962), p. 615.

          A review of the first performance of London
          Pastoral in the Guildhall, London in July 1962.
          See: W127a

B223.Kay, Norman. "Richard Rodney Bennett's Victory."
     Tempo, no. 92 (Spring 1970), pp. 32-4.

          A description of Victory and the broad technical
          musical means used by the composer. See: W4

B224.Keller, Hans. "Bennett's Actaeon." Tempo, no. 123
     (December 1977), pp. 50-51.

          A mention of Actaeon's first performance which
          "...raised seven points of lasting importance, none
          of them as much as touched upon by any music
          critic." These are listed accordingly. See: W7

B225.Kennedy, Michael. "Harrogate Festival/Joplin
     variations." The Daily Telegraph, 7 August 1985, p.
     11.

          "The exception was Mr McCabe's performance of
          Richard Rodney Bennett's Noctuary.... This is a
          most attractive addition to the pianist's
          repertory, an absorbing and brilliant piece which
          makes a creative virtue out of eclecticism in its
          array of styles from Ravel and Gershwin to
          Bennett's own idiom. See: W6b

B226.Kennedy, Michael. "The Mines of Sulphur." The Daily
     Telegraph, 29 March 1980, p. 13.

          "I enjoyed Richard Rodney Bennett's opera The Mines
          of Sulphur much more at the Grand Theatre,
          Leeds...when it entered the North's repertory than
          I did 15 years ago when it was new. ...it is his
          vocal writing which one admires most..., See: W2g

B227.Kennedy, Michael. "Three Choirs Festival: an East
     European flavour." The Daily Telegraph, 26 August
     1987, p. 8.

          A review of the Third Symphony's first performance
          at Worcester.
          "There has always been a lyrical and reflective
          side to Bennett's music and here he indulges it
          fully as if the name Elgar has inspired him to
          rediscover the virtues and possibilities of
          tonality in a symphonic context. The symphony is
          lightly scored and eschews outward display, yet it
          does not lack colour, though the shades are pastel
          rather than anything more garish." See: W39a

B228.Koegler, Horst. "Cologne." Opera, 18 (May 1967), p.
     378.

An account of the German premiere of <u>The Mines of Sulphur</u> in Cologne. "...what really decided the success of the production was the marvellous conducting of Christoph von Dohnanyi." <u>See</u>: W2c

B229. Koegler, Horst. "Englische Oper am Spree". <u>Music and Musicians</u>, 18 (July 1970), pp. 24-25.

An account of the Covent Garden visit to West Berlin and mention of a performance of <u>Victory</u> which "... suffered a total defeat from a rather sparsely filled house, with vehement boos carrying from everywhere.... However the public made it quite clear that they certainly appreciated the contributions of the individual singers... and of course the composer himself (was) spared no hostility." <u>See</u>: W4b

B230. Kolodin, Irving. "New York." <u>Opera</u>, 19 (April 1968), p.293.

"The first American production of ... Bennett's <u>The Mines of Sulphur</u> at the Juilliard School of Music... did not convey the impression of wholly successful venture by the composer and his librettist... but it did make one curious as to what Bennett might achieve in another opera, with a less artificial subject. <u>See</u>: W2e

B231. Kozinn, Allan. "The Guitar Literature: beyond Segovia's influence". <u>Guitar Review</u> 1984 (Summer), pp. 10-17.

Mention of Bennett's <u>Impromptus</u> and <u>Guitar Concerto</u> which "... leans further in the direction of atonal density... yet the composer is a master of dramatic manipulation which cuts through the harshness and angularity of his language and makes an appeal of its own." <u>See</u>: W12, W65

B232. Kozinn, Allan. "How a composer and choreographer create a new ballet." <u>The New York Times</u>, 28 June 1981, pp.17-18.

An article describing the writing of <u>Isadora</u> which, according to the composer, "... is a <u>hugh</u> task, the largest and most difficult job I've ever undertaken." <u>See</u>: W5

B233. Kozinn, Allan. "Percussive and Lyric Works". <u>The New York Times</u>, 22 March 1988, p.C16.

"Particularly appealing was a new <u>Concerto</u> (<u>for marimba</u>) by Richard Rodney Bennett. Cast in Mr. Bennett's familiar blend of free atonality and glowing lyricism, the work sets the marimba against gorgeous string writing, and a soloistic tapestry of winds, giving Mr. Moersch two athletic cadenzas. <u>See</u>: W15b

B234.Larner, Gerald. "Leeds Festival". The Musical Times, 108
       (June 1967), p.535.

       "Epithalamion... is a brilliantly scored piece with
       a finely judged combination of challenge and
       accessibility in the choral parts and a constantly
       fascinating orchestral texture. The audience like
       it." See: W121a

B235.Larner, Gerald. "Viola Concerto". The Guardian, 4 July
       1973, p.10.

       "Bennett has preserved something of the viola's
       traditional irascibility and melancholy; he has
       also presented the instrument as one with very
       subtle seductive charms. Brilliance he does not
       demand from it, but he sets it always in high
       relief against the orchestra by skilfully achieved
       contrasts of sound, so that the soloist has a
       consistently heroic role without having to play out
       of character." See:W21a

B236.Lawrence, Nicholas K. "What the cast thought of it..."
       Music (Schools Music Association), 3 (1969), pp.
       35-6.

       A view of All the King's Men by a member of the
       original cast who played King Charles I. "The
       music was easy to learn and hard to forget...."
       See: W175a

B237.Levi, Peta. "Just how much is a composer worth?" The
       Sunday Times, 6 March 1977, p.35.

       An investigation into the hazards and rewards of
       composers, including mention of Bennett, Hoddinott
       and Williamson.

B238.Lohmuller, Helmut. "Napoleon zieht nicht ins Munchner
       Nationaltheatre ein." Melos, 35 (February 1968),
       pp.67-8.

       A review (in German) of the production of A Penny
       for a Song at the National Theatre in Munich. See:
       W3b

B239.Loppert, Max. "Aldeburgh." The Musical Times, 116
       (August 1975), p.724.

       A review of the 1975 Aldeburgh Festival with brief
       mention of Time's Whiter Series. See: W171a

B240.Loppert, Max. "South Bank Summer." The Musical Times,
       115 (October 1974), p. 863.

       "Bennett's... Tenebrae: five 16th or 17th century
       poems, selected for the different faces they
       present to the spectre of death, and set in that
       neat, skilful Bennett manner... did little to

approach or contain the power of the poetry." <u>See</u>:
W167a

B241. Loveland, Kenneth. "Cheltenham." <u>The Musical Times</u>,
124 (September 1983), p.564.

An account of the 1983 Cheltenham Festival which
celebrated the 80th birthday of Sir Lennox
Berkeley, and which "... began with a delightful
tribute... <u>Bouquet for Lennox</u> (in which) Richard
Rodney Bennett included Lady Berkeley through
'Freda's Fandango'...." <u>See</u>: W24a

B242. Loveland, Kenneth. "Cheltenham" <u>The Musical Times</u>, 127
(September 1986), p. 507.

"Although Nicolas Cox was a strong advocate for
Richard Rodney Bennett's new <u>Duo Concertante</u> for
clarinet and piano..., I found it too shrill."
<u>See</u>: W56a

B243. Loveland, Kenneth. "Fishguard." <u>The Musical Times</u>, 121
(October 1980), p.647.

Richard Rodney Bennett's "... <u>Metamorphoses</u>... was
given a strongly committed first performance....
It is not simply a set of variations, but a
successful adventure in transforming the actual
nature of the material, from the sombre cello
start... through a gradually evolving pattern of
contrasted but smoothly interlinked textures to
something finally brilliant and rhythmically
lively. <u>"See</u>: W71a

B244. Loveland, Kenneth. "Metamorphoses." <u>The Times</u> (London),
23 July 1980, p.13.

Another account of the Fishguard Festival and the
first performance of Bennett's <u>Metamorphoses</u> which
"... poses few problems for the listener, but some
for the performers (though it is completely
practicable)." <u>See</u>: W71a

B245. Loveland, Kenneth. "Three Choirs." <u>The Musical Times</u>,
116 (November 1975), p.995.

"The new work (<u>Spells</u>) is imaginatively planned.
It really is a fine piece, lively and articulate
yet accommodated to the probable technical level of
a festival choir in a craftsmanlike way." <u>See</u>:
W139a

B246. Loveland, Kenneth. "Worcester." <u>The Musical Times</u>, 128
(November 1987), p. 646.

"In his first symphony Bennett flirted with
serialism; here (in the third symphony) he has a
positive affair with tonality.... ... the manner
here is restrained, the effort going into

thoughtful craftsmanship, clothed in a more modest orchestration.
The symphony has shape, and suggests perhaps an important corner turned; it is a predominantly serious work inviting serious attention, though never taxing the listener." See: W39a

B247. Luttwitz, H. von. "Einakter." [One Act] Musica (Kassel), 18 (1964), pp.76-7.

A review (in German) of Bennett's first opera The Lodge performed at Krefeld. See: W1b

B248. M.,F. "New York." Opera News, 32 (17 February 1968), p.30.

"... Bennett's Mines of Sulphur... received a characteristically handsome American premiere production at the Juilliard School of Music.
... it is post-Berg music, astringent but not forbidding, and it suggests a man who has a gift for both theatre and sound." See: W2e

B249. McBurney, Gerard. "Time for dreams." The Listener, 118 (27 August 1987), pp. 30-1.

An examination of Bennett's music in light of a performance of Lovesongs at the 1987 Promenade Concerts. See: W157

B250. Macdonald, M. "Commedia IV." Gramophone, 53 (December 1975), p.1066.

A review of the Argo recording ZRG 813 by members of the Philip Jones Brass Ensemble.
Included is Bennett's Commedia IV where "... there is a splendid variety of reasonably continuous colour assembled into a propulsive and endlessly intriguing texture." See: D8

B251. Macdonald, M. "Contemporary clarinet." Gramophone. 56 (January 1979), p. 1302.

A review of the Discourse All Above Music recordings ABM 24-5 which includes Bennett's Crosstalk for two basset horns.
"... here two basset horns duet on the most amicable and expressive of terms." See: D11

B252. Macdonald, M. "Music for Brass." Gramophone, 55 (July 1977), p. 201.

A review of the Argo recording ZRG 851 (PJBE). Included is Bennett's Fanfare for brass quintet which "... will be expected as always, to do its job, and so it does...." See: D12

B253. Macdonald, M. "Sonata for saxophone." Gramophone, 66 (July 1988), pp. 178+180.

A review of the Hyperion compact disc recording CDA 66246 which includes Bennett's <u>Saxophone Concerto</u>, played by John Harle and John Leneham, which is described as "... the most effectively constructed, offering a sense of purpose throughout its four movement...." <u>See</u>: D32

B254.Macdonald, M. "Tender is the Night" <u>Gramophone</u>, 66 (July 1988), pp. 178+180.

A review of the Hannibal/Harmonia Mundi compact disc recording HNCD 1331 which includes John Harle's arrangement (for saxophone and piano) of the theme from Bennett's music for <u>Tender is the Night</u>. <u>See</u>: D37

B255.Macdonald, M. "Trio for flute, clarinet and oboe." <u>The Gramophone</u>, 44 (November 1966), p. 268.

A review of the argo recording ZRG 5475 featuring modern instrumental music and including Bennett's <u>Trio for flute, clarinet and oboe</u>. <u>See</u>: D39

B256.Mann, William. "Aldeburgh Festival." <u>The Times</u> (London), 7 June 1971, p.8.

"The novelty was Richard Rodney Bennett's <u>oboe concerto</u>, commissioned by the English Chamber Orchestra and written for Heinz Holliger who was here to play it.
Whatever Hollinger plays seems like marvellous music. Bennett's concerto is itself sufficiently full of character to remain in the head, as a structure and for many striking individual ideas, some hours after it is over." <u>See</u>: W16a

B257.Mann, William. "An opera to argue about: Covent Garden - Victory." <u>The Times</u> (London), 14 April 1970, p.20.

"There is plenty of vocally ingratiating music, but after two hearings and much study of the score, I believe he has kept his lyrical invention too discreetly in the background.
As it sounds, the music (which also means the dramatic impact) of <u>Victory</u> improves as it goes on. The third act is the strongest of all.
... Bennett's music does quite helpfully differentiate the many characters in <u>Victory</u>, even if not as strongly as one might wish." <u>See</u>: W4b

B258.Mann, William. "Bennett's brilliant concerto." <u>The Times</u> (London), 20 September 1968, p.14.

"The emotional range is hearteningly broad, perhaps because there was a special stimulus of a confrontation between Bennett the pianist and Bennett the orchestral composer.

Since the concerto is greatly enjoyable, and gives
the soloist a field day to remember, I may be
perplexing myself unnecessarily". See: W18a

B259. Mann, William. "Bennett Guitar Concerto: Queen Elizabeth
     Hall." The Times (London), 20 November 1970, p.15.

"The work Bennett has... written is perfectly,
idiomatic, nicely and quite boldly scored for
guitar and chamber ensemble.... It should be
gratefully accepted by solo guitarists everywhere,
especially those on good terms with a chamber
ensemble." See: W12a

B260. Mann, William. "CBSO/Fremaux." The Times (London), 1
     April 1976, p.15.

"The latest acquisition is Richard Rodney Bennett's
Violin Concerto which the CBSO brought to London
last night....
The solo part is brilliant, including several big
cadenzas and frequent excursions into the violin's
highest positions where Ralph Holmes usually
excels....
The orchestral writing is lean but allows plentiful
activity and some sumptuous moments to which the
orchestra did not properly rise although, Mr.
Fremaux seemed much in sympathy with the content of
the music." See: W22b

B261. Mann, William. "The House of Sleepe". Gramophone, 53
     (June 1975), p.80.

A review of the EMI recording EMD 5521 by the
King's Singers.
"Richard Rodney Bennett's text comes from an old
translation of Ovid, and the music is sober,
expansive, dreamily euphonius, quite intricate."
See: D19

B262. Mann, William. "London Music." The Musical Times, 107
     (April 1966), p. 325.

"The song-cycles (The Aviary and The Insect World)
were written for boys and girls, and the language
is tonal and uncomplicated." See:W176b, W182b

B263. Mann, William. Macnaghten New Music Group." The Musical
     Times, 94 (April 1953), p. 182.

"Richard Bennett, who has written a set of
variations for solo oboe, is indeed still on
schoolboy; his theme was modest but striking and he
varied it with lively imagination, seizing each
time on a salient facet of the theme and basing a
variation on that facet. His idiom is not
sophisticated nor elaborate, but it is not
unenterprising either. The work is attractively
laid out for the instrument with much variety; most

important, it sounded complete, never giving the
impression that the composer had been too lazy to
supply a piano part." See: W117a

B264.Mann, William. "The Mines of Sulphur." The Times
(London), 31 March 1980, p.9.

"If The Mines of Sulphur is hokum, it remains
attractive hokum, enhanced by music that has not
lost its aural appeal – the duet for two sopranos
at the end of the first act falls on the ear as
gracefully as ever, and the whole score still seems
expertly paced and balanced...." See: W2g

B265.Mann, William. "Music in London." The Musical Times,
110 (June 1969), p.645.

"Dr. Alfred Kalmus, who runs the London branch of
Universal Edition, was 80 last month and to
celebrate this occasion 11 of the composers, whose
work he has published, composed together a
symposial tribute called A Garland for Dr. K.
The composers had been told to write for the
available strength of the Pierrot Players. Richard
Rodney Bennett wrote an impromptu for flute solo, a
slow and gently poetic piece." See: W63a

B266.Mann, William. "Music in London: Concerts." The Musical
Times, 106 (July 1965), p. 526.

"The Quartet (No. 4) is in two movements with
similar thematic ideas....It sounds beautiful and
exciting as well as being powerfully argued." See:
W78a

B267.Mann, William. "New wind quintet by Bennett." The
Times (London), 18 March 1968, p. 6.

"The Bennett quintet demands virtuosity of its
players but is essentially pleasing to listen to.
The first performance...was full of gusto and
attractive in timbre and sonority." See: W81a

B268.Mann, William. "Whiting comedy as new opera." The
Times (London), 1 November 1967, p. 7.

"...A Penny for a Song provides an enjoyable and
amusing evening at the opera.
...the opera is nicely varied in pace and scored
with expertise and a nice sense of humour.... The
vocal writing, if not often melodious, is very
often memorable and apparently gratifying to the
singers." See: W3a

B269.March, Ivan. "British music for film and television."
Gramophone, 57 (December 1979), p. 1024.

A review of the HMV recording ASD 3797 which
includes Bennett's themes from Lady Caroline Lamb,

which is described as an "evocative" portrait, and the similarly "nostalgic" theme from Yanks. See: D23, D43

B270.Marston, Marlene G. "The serial keyboard music of Richard Rodney Bennett. " Doctor of Philosophy (Music) Dissertation, University of Wisconsin, 1968, 284 pp.

Detailed analysis of Bennett's Fantasy for Piano, Five Studies for Piano and Sonata for Piano. See: W59, W60, W95

B271.Mason, Colin. "Bland sweetness of Epithalamion." The Daily Telegraph, 17 April 1967, p. 17.

"It showed Bennett's unexcelled professionalism, facility and good judgement in meeting a specific musical requirement and in suiting his style to the resources at his disposal.
Skilfully and considerately written for the chorus, with enough problems to be challenging but not discouraging, it uses a bland harmonic idiom with many familiar echoes of the 'English choral tradition', much of it almost Delian in its nostalgic sensuousness and sweetness." See: W121a

B272.Mason, Eric. "The phantoms at the opera." Daily Mail, 25 February 1965, p. 14.

"Bennett's music employs 12-note technique, though with strong tonal implications which make that fact unobtrusive.
Broad tunes in the ordinary sense are not to be expected. Yet the whole score proceeds melodically, with very singable vocal lines flowering repeatedly into an agreeable arioso.
The orchestral writing shows enormous assurance, allied to an acutely sensitive judgement of colours and textures in maintaining atmosphere and pointing parallels between the crime and the play-within-the-opera. Certainly, the music holds one's attention, and dramatic tension mounts steadily to the grim climax." See: W2a

B273.Maw, Nicholas. "Richard Rodney Bennett." The Musical Times, 103 (February 1962), pp. 95-7.

An early and very useful survey of Bennett's life and music. "...he possesses one of the most extraordinary talents that have arrived on the scene since the young Britten startled the world 30 years ago."

B274.Meikle, Robert. "Birmingham." The Musical Times, 109 (November 1968), p. 1041.

A description of the first performance of Bennett's Piano Concerto. "Completely individual...and the

brilliant scoring and piano writing, the easy
fluency of the melodies and the continuous control
of the musical material within these conventions."
<u>See</u>: W18a

B275.Millington, Barry. "Orchestral, choral, electronic."
<u>The Musical Times</u>, 126 (March 1985), p. 165.

"<u>Moving into Aquarius</u> uses melodic fragments
familiar from Tippett's works without attempting to
mimic his idiom. The enterprise was notable
chiefly for its seamless fusion of two different
composers' styles." <u>See</u>: W27a

B276.Milnes, Rodney. "The Mines of Sulphur." <u>Opera</u>, 24
(November 1973), pp. 1034-36.

A review of the revival of Bennett's opera at the
Coliseum in September 1973.
"As a theatrical experience this is an absolute
winner." <u>See</u>: W2f

B277.Mitchell, Donald. "London Concerts: Chamber Music."
<u>The Musical Times</u>, 96 (March 1955), p. 152.

"Mr Bennett has long shown exceptional promise and
his new quartet (no. 3) shows real achievement. On
the basis of these two movements (1 and 2), it is
now possible to prophesy with some conviction to a
fruitful creative future for the maturity of Mr
Bennett's outstanding talent.
The whole piece...displayed a very convincing and
personal use of the twelve-note method. Mr Bennett
should go far." <u>See</u>: W77a

B278.Mitchell, Donald. "London Concerts – some first
performances." <u>The Musical Times</u>, 97 (June 1956), p.
316.

"No more arduous...was Richard Rodney Bennett's
<u>Ricercar</u> for unaccompanied chorus....It was, I
thought, a better piece than his recent choral
setting.... The Ricercar was neat in form, fresh
and direct in utterance, and its counterpoint
allied to a lively rhythmic scheme, built up to a
satisfying point of climax." <u>See</u>: W136a

B279.Mitchell, Donald. "London Music – some first
performances." <u>The Musical Times</u>, 95 (November
1954), p. 615.

"If Mr Bennett's age is taken into account, it may
be safely said that his quartet (no. 2) shows not
only promise but achievement; the slow introduction
to his last movement...disclosed a real sensibility
and a fine feeling for quartet texture – this was a
truly creative patch of composition which argues
well for the future." <u>See</u>: W76a

B280.Mitchell, Donald. "London Music: some first performances." The Musical Times, 95 (December 1954), p. 667.

"...Mr Bennett (chose) one of Donne's most complex poems.
...however (it) would seem (not) to have been a very fruitful experiment." See: W130a

B281.Mitchell, Donald. "London Music: some first performances." The Musical Times, 96 (April 1955), p. 211.

"A sonatina for solo flute (1954) by Richard Rodney Bennett was the most accomplished piece to be heard in an otherwise thoroughly mediocre studio recital.... ...Mr Bennett made something fresh out of it, though there was some note-spinning and some inconsistencies of style." See: W102a

B282.Mitchell, Donald. "London Music: some first performances." The Musical Times, 97 (August 1956), p. 429.

A report of a Royal Academy New Music Club concert on 5 June 1956 when Bennett and Cornelius Cardew gave the first performance in the UK of Pierre Boulez's Structures.

B283.Mitchell, Donald. "London Music: some first performances." The Musical Times, 98 (February 1957), p. 90.

"The central problem of composition was much better solved in Mr Bennett's Four Improvisations for solo violin...whose melodic organisation was charged with spontaneity; there were some contrived passages, but for the most part the pieces unfolded many fresh and effective developments and continuations. Mr Bennett's talent sustains its promise of creative substance." See: W61a

B284.Mitchell, Donald. "London Music, Concerts and Opera: some first performances." The Musical Times, 97 (May 1965), p. 264.

"The Elizabethan Singers, under Louis Halsey, gave the first performance of The Tillaquils by Richard Rodney Bennett. ...Mr Bennett's setting of an obscure text by Laura Riding had little to commend it. Its continuous metrical variations did not result in rhythmical fluidity, and a marked lack of contrapuntal interest did not lead in this instance to an enriched melodic sphere." See: W142a

B285.Monelle, Raymond. "Effortless sophistication." The Scotsman, 6 September 1979, p. 6.

An account of the Bennett/Montgomery concert at the 1979 Edinburgh Festival.

B286.Monelle, Raymond.   "Lyrical Sonnets."   The Scotsman 4 September 1979, p. 12.

A review of the first performance of Sonnets to Orpheus, a work which is described as having "...lyricism and delicate atmosphere...."   See: W33a

B287.Montagu, George.   "Festival of The City of London." Musical Opinion, 85 (September 1962), p. 711.

"The first performance of London Pastoral by ...Richard Rodney Bennett was also heard.... Alexander Young gave a fine performance, eloquently accompanied by conductor and orchestra...."   See: W127a

B288.Moorhouse, Geoffrey.   "The anatomy of an opera."   The Guardian, 14 March 1970, p. 9.

A description of the birth of Bennett's fourth opera, Victory, based on Joseph Conrad's novel. See: W4

B289.Myers,   Rollo   H.   "British   Music."   Canon,   14 (January/February 1961), pp. 107-111.

A survey of five new symphonies by British composers, with also a mention of two young avant-garde composers - Peter Maxwell Davies and Richard Rodney Bennett.

B290.Neukirchen,   Alfons.   "Krimi   und   Erlosungsdrama." Opernwelt, May 1967, pp. 40-1.

A review (in German) of the Cologne performance of The Mines of Sulphur.   See: W2c

B291.Noble,   Jeremy.   "Calendar."   The   Gramophone,   43 (September 1965), p. 144.

A review of the HMV recording ASD 640.   Included is Calendar in which "...one cannot help being struck by his far more fluent command of his medium." See: D6

B292.Noble, Jeremy.   "Calendar."   Gramophone, 52 (May 1975), p. 2000.

A review of the Argo recording ZRG 758, a re-issue of ASD 640 (see B291).   "...Calendar...is attractive and well-made...."   See: D6

B293.Noble,   Jeremy.   "Capriccio/Five   Studies."   The Gramophone, 50 (October 1972), pp. 729-30.

A review of the Argo recording ZRG 704, composers (including Bennett and Thea Musgrave) at the pianos. See: D7, D16

B294. Noble, Jeremy. "The Mines of Sulphur." Music and Musicians, 13 (April 1965), pp. 18-19.

"From the very first orchestral gesture of The Mines of Sulphur two things are obvious - that Richard Rodney Bennett is in absolute technical control of his medium, and that he has a real flair for creating atmosphere." See: W2a

B295. Noble, Jeremy. "Shakespeare Concert." The Financial Times, 25 April 1972, p. 3.

"Richard Rodney Bennett contributed exquisitely sensuous settings of a linked pair of sonnets for tenor and strings...." See: W166a

B296. Noble, Jeremy. "Winter Music." The Gramophone, 40 (March 1963), pp. 430-1.

A review of the Delta recording SDEL 18005 which includes Winter Music, played by William Bennett and Susan Bradshaw. See: W42

B297. Norris, Geoffrey. "Music in London: Orchestral." The Musical Times, 123 (November 1982), p. 769.

"In this all-English concert, the BBCSO and James Loughran gave the first performance of Richard Rodney Bennett's new piece d'occasion, Anniversaries vigorously orchestrated (sometimes with recourse to gamelan effects)...." See: W8a

B298. Northcott, Bayan. "Bennett's Spells." Tempo, no. 115 (December 1975), pp. 48-9.

An account and personal view of Bennett's cantata Spells. See: W139

B299. Northcott, Bayan. "Composers of the Sixties." Music and Musicians, 18 (January 1970), pp. 32-36 + 40.

Evaluation of certain English composers including Bennett and Thea Musgrave.

B300. Oakes, Meredith. "Bennett guitar concerto." Music and Musicians, 19 (January 1971), p. 66.

"Richard Rodney Bennett's Concerto for Guitar and Chamber Ensemble...is a finely calculated piece demanding finely controlled performances. As well, it abounds in technical difficulties for the soloist." See: W12a.

B301. O'Loughlin, Niall. "Crosstalk." The Musical Times, 120 (January 1979), pp. 44-5.

A review of the Chantry/Discourses recording ABM 24 which includes "Bennett's delightful Crosstalk (which) is given in the original version for two basset horns instead of the published version...for clarinets." See: D11

B302. Oliver, Michael. "Bennett in Maryland." Music and Musicians, 19 (January 1971), pp. 18-19.

An interview with Richard Rodney Bennett who ...is doing Earle Brown's job for a year, as composer-in-residence at the Peabody Institute, Baltimore."

B303. Osborne, Charles. "The Mines of Sulphur." London Magazine, May 1965, pp. 75-81.

An edited transcript of a recorded conversation, broadcast on the BBC Third Programme, about the opera with its composer, its librettist and Colin Graham who produced the work at Sadler's Wells. See: W2

B304. Palmer, Christopher. "Lady Caroline Lamb." The Gramophone, 50 (January 1973), pp. 1388-9.

A review of the HMV recording CSD 3728, music from the film Lady Caroline Lamb, in which"...Bennett stands out as the superbly-equipped professional." See: D23

B305. Palmer, Christopher. "Murder on the Orient Express." Gramophone, 52 (May 1975), p. 2045.

A review of the EMI recording EMC 3054, music for the soundtrack of the film. "Most celebrated is the music which accompanies the Express as it pulls out of the station, an exhilarating pastiche of Ravel's 'La Valse', most beautifully and expertly done...." See: D25

B306. Palmer, Christopher. "Nicholas and Alexandra." The musical Times, 113 (June 1972), p.568.

A review of the recording Bell 202 of Bennett's music for the film Nicholas and Alexandra. "The NPO play his clear-limbed music warmly and with precision, and the recording is full-bodied." See: D26

B307. Palmer, Christopher and Foreman, Lewis. "Richard Rodney Bennett" in British Music Now, London, Elek, 1975, pp. 108-119.

A fascinating and detailed account of Bennett's life, career and music.

B308.Palmer, Christopher, "The versatility of Richard Rodney
      Bennett." Crecendo International, 13 (November
      1974), pp. 14-15.

         An interview with the composer about his life and
         music, particularly that for films.

B309.Payne, Anthony. "Birthday Reflections." Music and
      Musicians, 12 (December 1963), p.36.

         "Of the various groups who have honoured Benjamin
         Britten's 50th birthday, the Macnaghten Concerts
         have so far shown the most enterprise. For their
         celebration... they commissioned Reflections on a
         Theme of Britten, three movements contributed by
         Richard Rodney Bennett, Nicholas Maw and Malcolm
         Williamson...." See: W84a

B310.Payne Anthony, "Cheltenham" The Musical Times, 108
      (September 1967), pp.826-7.

         "Canon... for string trio by Richard Rodney Bennett
         [was]... typical of [his] view of delicate
         romanticism." See: W47a

B311.Payne, Anthony. "English evening." Music and Musicians,
      13 (November 1964), pp.34-5.

         "Aubade ... was a lovely piece, largely in the
         style of last year's Nocturnes, and is possibly the
         most technically perfect work he has yet given us,
         being beautifully made in form and texture." See:
         W9a

B312.Payne, Anthony. "First performances." Tempo, No. 66-67
      (Autumn/Winter 1963), p.39.

         An analysis of Bennett's contribution to
         Reflections on a Theme of Benjamin Britten. See:
         W84

B313.Payne, Anthony. "Songs without words." Music and
      Musicians, 11 (May 1963), p.20.

         A survey of the Bishopsgate Institute's 'Composer
         at the Piano' series at which Bennett was
         represented.

B314.Percival, John. "Cool." Dance and Dancers, 19 (February
      1968), pp.14-16.

         An account of Jazz Calendar, movement by movement.
         See: W66b

B315.Pettitt, Stephen. "Pegasus/Crossland." The Times, 29
      October 1984, p.8.

         A review of the first performance in London of Sea
         Change, performed by Pegasus. See: W137b

B316.Pirie Peter J. "The Bermudas." Music Review, 37 (1976),
     pp.244-5.

     A review of the music of The Bermudas in which "...
     he writes beautiful if limited music that raises no
     problems; it is a perfect thing in itself. The
     words are hauntingly lovely, and Bennett has
     matched them with characteristic and beautiful
     music." See: W177

B317.Pirie, Peter J. "Symphony No.1" The Musical Times, 109
     (April 1968), p.344.

     A review of the RCA recording SB 6730. "The
     Bennett symphony is simply a spendid abstract
     symphony, bursting with promise and high in
     achievement. Bennett is slowly emerging, for me,
     as the composer of his generation of whom we can
     hope most." See: D35

B318.Plaistow, Stephen. "Cheltenham." The Musical Times, 102
     (September 1961), p.570.

     "... Richard Rodney Bennett's Journal ... shows a
     striking ability to match sound with idea: an
     ability to calculate orchestral textures to a
     nicety and to bewitch the ear with colour." See:
     W26a

B319.Plaistow, Stephen. "A week of birthdays." The
     Gramophone 40 (December 1962), p.296.

     A review of the jupiter recording JEP OC26, music
     played by Bennett and Susan Bradshaw. "Richard
     Rodney Bennett wrote his suite A Week of Birthdays
     with the aim of introducing children to the sounds
     of modern music; he gives it here a persuasive
     performance...." See:D41

B320.Porter, Andrew, "Aubade." The Financial Times, 12
     September 1964, p.7.

     A review of Aubade which is described as "... an
     attractive work, with agreeable and diverse
     incident, scored with an imaginative and sensitive
     ear." See: W9a

B321.Porter, Andrew. "Jazz Calendar." The Financial Times,
     11 January 1968, p.22.

     "A new work by Sir Frederick Ashton is always an
     event, and the newest of them, Jazz Calendar, was
     received on Tuesday evening with warm prolonged
     enthusiasm. the score is Richard Rodney Bennett's
     Jazz Calendar, composed for 12 jazz players." See:
     W66b. Also printed in About the House 1968 (2),
     pp.43-45.

B322.Porter, Andrew. "The Mines of Sulphur." The Financial
     Times, 25 February 1965, p.24.

    "...Mines of Sulphur is surely one of the most
     professionally adept and successful first full
     operas ever produced.
     "His scoring is masterly (and the words come
     through with exceptional clarity). And his sense
     of the theatre is brilliant. At first hearing The
     Mines of Sulphur is impressive. At second it
     proved engrossing." See: W2a

B323.Porter, Andrew. "Music in London." The Musical Times,
     110 (April 1969), pp.390-1.

    "Richard Rodney Bennett's Second Symphony... is
     skilfully, fluently, elegantly crafted; it made an
     agreeable but not very deep impression. See: W38b

B324.Potter, Keith. "Boulez and Stockhausen, Bennett and
     Cardew." The Musical Times, 122 (March 1981),
     pp.170-1.

    An article about Bennett's and Cardew's gradual
     involvment with the European avant garde including
     Pierre Boulez.

B325.Potter, Keith. "Richard Rodney Bennett." Classical
     Music, 30 May 1981, p.12.

    An interview with Bennett "... about his more
     'avant garde' days in the 1950s when first as a
     student at the Royal Academy and later at first
     hand in Paris he got to know the music of the young
     and radical Pierre Boulez and decided, apparently
     upon an avant garde future: 'this is the thing for
     me', as he wrote at the time in a letter to Susan
     Bradshaw, who soon followed him to Paris to inbibe
     the New Music at first hand."

B326.Pryce-Jones, David. "A child in the forest." The
     Listener, 96 (9 December 1976), p.764.

    A review of Abide with Me and brief mention of the
     music: "Richard Rodney Bennett's theme music was
     Chopin without tears." See: W240a

B327.R.,H.S. "Opera and Ballet in London." Musical Opinion,
     85 (October 1961), pp.9+11.

    A review of The Ledge, Bennett's first opera which
     "... within its strictly limited scope, made an
     exceedingly good first impression." See: W1a

B328.R.,H.S. "Sadler's Wells Opera." Musical Opinion, 88
     (April 1965), p.393.

    "...The Mines of Sulphur duly came to production
     (and) justified at once the commission....... it is

the composer who has set the seal of distinction on the opera, and he has done so without resorting to any shock-producing orchestral slight of hand." See: W2a

B329. R.,H.S. "Sadler's Wells Opera." Musical Opinion, 97 (November 1973), p.65.

A review of the revival of The Mines of Sulphur at the Coliseum in September 1973. See: W2f

B330. Rees, C.B. "Richard Rodney Bennett." Musical Events, August 1965, pp.9-10.

A thumbnail sketch and impressions of the composer.

B331. Reynolds, Gordon. "English Choral Music." Gramophone, 59 (October 1981), p.596.

A review of the Cabaletta recording CDN 5001 which contains one of Bennett's five carols: Out of your sleep. See:D29

B332. Richards, Denby. "Actaeon man." Radio Times, 6-12 August 1977, p.12.

An interview with Bennett at home in London who is described as "... an essentially quiet man, working in a comfortable home in an Islington Square."

B333. Richards, Denby, "Double-basses." Music and Musicians, 27 (March 1979), p.60.

"Sadly Richard Rodney Bennett's Double Bass Concerto ... was a disappointment. Bennett ... seemed ill at ease when writing for the double-bass." See:W11a

B334. Richards, Denby. "Lancaster." Music and Musicians, 22 (July 1974), pp.52-3.

Details about the 1974 BBC Piano Competition. "The exception was the set-piece specially commissioned for the occasion from Richard Rodney Bennett, a seven-minute work aptly titled Scena. Bennett... provided a fascinating composition which was interpreted in a wide variety of ways. Some contestants obviously regarded it as an exercise in rhythms and dynamics, while others seemed frightened by the jazz elements, and consciously tried to underplay them with a strictly conventional reading." See: W85a

B335. Roberts, Peter. "Isolation." Plays and Players, 12 (September 1965), pp.34-5.

A review of Times of Athens, directed at Stratford-on-Avon by John Schlesinger, but with no mention of Bennett's music. See: W265a

B336.S., P.H. "The last horn." The Times (London), 28 April
     1969, p.8.

          The composer's views on writing a new signature
          tune for the BBC1 current affairs programme Twenty
          Four Hours, a commission which he found "rather
          frightening." See: W267

B337.Sadie, Stanley. "Carols for a church choir." The Times
     (London), 25 September 1967, p.6.

          "Bennett's new pieces are five settings of old or
          traditional texts. Being designed for a church
          choir, they are reasonably straightforward music.
          And they are laid out with consummate craftsmanship
          ." See: W123b

B338.Sadie, Stanley. "London Music:Concerts." The Musical
     Times, 106 (March 1965), p.202.

          "The Macnaghten concert on 29 January introduced
          Richard Rodney Bennett's second solo Violin Sonata.
          Harmonic sweetness is a salient characteristic of
          Bennett's music and, although dealing mainly with a
          single   line...   this   harmonic   flavour   is
          ever-present in the sonata, with its soaring
          phrases and easily followed melodic intervals.
          It's a violinistic piece in the best sense...."
          See:W98a

B339.Sadie, Stanley. "Lucid and elegant symphony score." The
     Times (London), 21 February 1969, p.11.

          "Richard Rodney Bennett is the most professional,
          the   most   polished   English   composer   of   his
          generation. The (second) symphony is lucidly, even
          elegantly,   scored;   its   ideas   are   argued
          interestingly, developed in a way that is easy to
          follow; and the timing of events makes good sense.
          An impressive piece, in fact...." See: W38b

B340.Sadie, Stanley. "(The) Mines of Sulphur." Tempo 73
     (Summer 1965), p.24.

          A review of the opera. "Not many composers came to
          the writing of their first full-length opera with
          as prodigious a fund of technical skill as Richard
          Rodney Bennett. The Mines of Sulphur... benefits
          enormously from Bennett's capacity to handle his
          orchestral   forces   with   precision,   for   this
          precision is used to great effect in the evocation
          of atmosphere and character." See: W2

B341.Sadie, Stanley. "New London Ensemble." The Times
     (London), 9 January 1975, p.12.

          "Richard Rodney Bennett's Sonnet Sequence is a
          superbly professional piece...."

The music has confidence and expressive
urgency...." <u>See</u>: W166c

B342.Saez, Jose, L. "Richard Rodney Bennett." <u>Cinestudio</u>,
111 (July 1972), pp.24-5.

An article (in Spanish) about Bennett's music,
especially his film music.

B343.Samsa, Gregor. "Who could ask for anything more?" <u>Night
and Day</u>, 4-10 August 1986, p.69.

An interesting account about J's restaurant in New
York at which Bennett entertains by singing and
playing the piano. "... but never obrusive, his
music transformed our dining experience into a
special occasion."

B344.Sanders, Rick. "Blowing the horn at the Proms." <u>Sunday
Times</u> (Supplement), 6 August 1977, p.13.

A report on a notable musical collaboration
(<u>Actaeon</u>) which had its world premiere on 12 August
1977 at the Promenade Concerts in London. <u>See</u>: W7

B345.Sartori, Claudio. "Italy." <u>Opera</u>, 17 (May 1966), p.391.

A review of <u>The Mines of Sulphur</u> at La Scala Milan.
"... it can be said that his score is thoughtful
and technically accomplished." <u>See</u>: W2b

B346.Schiffer, Brigitte. "The new generation follows
traditional paths." <u>Melos</u>, 41 (no.3) 1975, pp.214-6.

A review (in German) of and background to <u>Sonnet
Sequence</u>. "He (Bennett) understands all the
orchestra's secrets, and the subtleties of
instrumentation, and yet this song-cycle, whose
theme is time, comes closer to Henze's "ideal of
sound" (Klangideal) than to Boulez's pointillist
structures and it has a great deal in common with
Benjamin Britten's 'Les Illuminations," yet this
does not diminish either its impact or its
success." <u>See</u>: W166c

B347.Schiffer, Brigitte. "Victory at Covent Garden." <u>Melos</u>,
37 (June 1970). pp. 251-2.

A review (in German) of Bennett's opera which "...
had great success with the audience. Throughout
one could see the hand of an experienced technician
...." <u>See</u>: W4a

B348.Schlotel, Brian. "Richard Rodney Bennett's music for
young people." <u>Music Teacher</u>, 51 (May 1972),
pp.12-13.

A survey of and useful introduction for teachers to Bennett's compositions for children and young people.

B349. Schmidt-Garre, Helmut. "A Penny for a Song at the National Theatre" Neue ZFM, 129 (March 1968), pp.95-6.

A review (in German) of the first performance in Germany of "Napoleon Kommt" (A Penny for a Song). The music is described as "pretty" and "presented by Christoph von Dohnanyi with great delicacy." See:W3b

B350. Schonberg, Harold C. "Music: The Mines of Sulphur Sung at Juilliard." The New York Times, 18 January 1968, p.48.

"The writing is secure throughout. Mr. Bennett is a fine, confident technician.
As for the production itself, it was superb, quite the best that Juilliard has presented in a long time." See: W2e

B351. Schwinger, Wolfram. "Bennett's new opera 'Victory'." Musica, 24, no.3 (1970), pp. 257-9.

A review (in German) of Victory which is described as "... very favourable...." See:W4a

B352. Scott-Maddocks, Daniel. "Triple Bill." Music and Musicians, 10 (October 1961), p.31.

"Having already heard a number of Bennett's works that particularly impressed by their freshness and imagination, I found The Ledge deeply disappointing. Its score was eclectic, drawing upon the lushest and most neurotic aspects of Berg and Schoenberg, and the vocal writing was at best functional." See: W1a

B353. Seckerson, Edward. "Four Piece Suite." Gramophone, 66 (November 1988), p.799.

A review of the EMI recording EL 749116-1. "...these occasional dance pieces – the affectionate tribute of an Englishman adapted by America's first city – are pleasing enough." See: D17

B354. Sensier, P. "Guitar and Lute Concertos." Gramophone, 53 (February 1976), p.1350.

A review of the RCA recording ARL3 0997 which includes Bennett's Guitar Concerto. See:D9

B355. Shaw, A.T. "Pershore recital showed organist's great versatility." Evening News (Worcester), 29 August 1975, p.3.

"The evening concert in the cathedral was unquestionably a great triumph for the chorus, for the superb soloist, Jane Manning, for Richard Rodney Bennett, composer of Spells, for Donald Hunt, who pulled off the first performance brilliantly, and for the RPO.
The glitter and sheen which is characteristic of Bennett's handling of the orchestra is turned to expressive use in five of the movements. The fourth... Spell of Sleep is... unaccompanied."
See: W139a

B356.Shawe-Taylor, Desmond. "The optimism wasn't unfounded." The Sunday Times, 28 February 1965, p.46.

"The Mines of Sulphur is a compelling piece of musical theatre which grips our attention from the first bars and the rise of the curtain. The professional touch is constantly and blessedly in evidence...." See: W2a

B357.Shawe-Taylor, Desmond. "The passions of Provence." The Sunday Times, 14 August 1977, p.31.

A review of the first performance of Actaeon which is described as "... brilliantly accomplished ... (and) offers ample scope both to the soloist, whose brilliant feats included a prestissimo three-octave downward run, and to the orchestra. It is a piece of concert drama, in line with several of Bennett's recent works, notable rather for skilful treatment than for boldness of invention." See:W7a

B358.Shawe-Taylor, Desmond. "Young man's symphony." The Sunday Times, 13 February 1966, p.38.

"Facility has been Bennett's problem as well as his greatest asset; he can do anything required, and almost (it seems) in any style.
...Bennett's symphony is an attractive and shapely work which not only promises well for the future, but should stand up to repeated hearings on its own merits." See: W37a

B359.Shuttleworth, Martin. "Dreams at the Piano." The Listener, 68 (23 August 1962), pp.295-6.

"The Long-Distance Piano-Player ... was a very remarkable piece of work.
The music for the piano, which was composed and played by Richard Rodney Bennett, ran well in harness and, towards the middle, when it was free to do so, ran out to where the play was." See: W255a

B360.Simmons, David. "London Music." Musical Opinion, 92 (April 1069) pp.342-3.

"A greater admire of Henze is our own Richard Rodney Bennett, whose second symphony was given its British premiere by the LSO.... This extremely terse piece... is far less stark and noisey than its predecessor. It is beautifully formed in its proportions, and the whole has an enviable symmetry which has evaded many recent British symphonists." See:W38b

B361. Smith, Steven M. "The Piano Concerto after Bartok." Doctor of Musical Arts Dissertation, Eastern School of Music, Rochester, New York, 1978, 509 pp.

A comprehensive investigation into the modern piano concerto, with emphasis on the postwar, post-Bartok era. Part III treats, in detail, eight recent concertos, Bennett's among them. See: W18

B362. Stadlen, Peter. "Assertive Bennett Symphony." The Daily Telegraph, 21 February 1969, p.21.

"Of its three continuous movements, the first seems to me an unqualified success. Distinctly original and well-contrasted ideas are put together with a remarkable sense of proportion, the form is unmistakable, the meaning self-assertive. Very striking, too, is a slow theme that hesitates between five-eight and three-four in a bar." See: W38b

B363. Steen, T.M.F. "The Sound Track." Films in Review, 13 (August-September 1962), pp.435-6.

A sketch of Bennett's career and music, with emphasis on some of his film scores.

B364. Steptoe, Roger. "Richard Rodney Bennett." Music and Musicians, March 1986, pp.10-11.

An article (written to mark Bennett's 50th birthday) about his music with reference to the Royal Academy of Music's own commemorative concert series.

B365. Stevens, Denis. "New York." Musical Times, 109 (June 1968), p.562.

"The following week happily brought to Philharmonic Hall a young Englishman. Richard Rodney Bennett's Second Symphony, through a resounding interpretation by Leonard Bernstein, reflected an active and questioning mind, a masterly technique in construction and scoring, and a musical message both logical and precise...." See: W38a

B366. Stoker, Richard. "Bennett in Baltimore." Composer, no.41 (Autumn 1971), pp.1-7.

An interview with Bennett about his year spent as visiting professor of composition at the Peabody Institute, Baltimore.

B367.Sutcliffe, Tom. "The Third Stream." Music and Musicians, 18 (June 1970), pp.34-6.

A discussion with Bennett, Don Banks and David Atherton about music played at the Queen Elizabeth Hall on 15 June 1970.

B368.Sutton, David. "Prom premieres." Music and Musicians, 26 (October 1977), pp.49-50.

A review of the first performing of Actaeon at a Prom concert. See: W7a

B369.Sutton, Wadham. "Sonata for Piano." Music Teacher, 45 (March 1966), p.112.

An analysis of the Piano Sonata, movement by movement. See: W95

B370.Taylor, Peter. "Opera and Ballet in London." Musical Opinion, 104 (July 1981), pp.389-392.

A detailed account of the world premiere at Covent Garden of Isadora. "Richard Rodney Bennett's score was very easy to the ear and both his many movements of pastiche and the more personal music he composed to illustrate Isadora's erotic life, impressed with their appropriateness." See:W5a

B371.Thompson, K.L. "Radio in Retrospect." Musical Opinion, 87 (July 1964), p.607.

A review of the original, radio version of A Jazz Calendar. "The happy melodic invention maintains a high level throughout, the scoring is deft, harmonic and rhythmic subleties above, and... it is freshly original...." See: W66a

B372.Thorpe, Edward. "Creating a ballet : MacMillan's Isadora." Evans Brothers, London, 1981, 80 pp.

A book about Isadora, with a chapter devoted to the score. See:W5

B373.Thorpe, Edward. "Kenneth Macmillan: the man and the ballets." Hamish Hamilton, London, 1985, 226 pp.

Chapter 24 is partly devoted to Isadora and details of its conception and subsequent production. See:W5

B374.Tomkins, Les. "Music gives the meaning to a film says Richard Rodney Bennett." Crescendo International, 20 (June 1982), pp.16-17.

An interview and discussion with Bennett about "the film music side of his work."

B375.Tracey, Edmund. "Piling on the agony." The Observer (Weekend Review), 28 February 1965, p.25.

"...Bennett and ... Cross have achieved pretty well exactly what they projected.
... Sadler's Wells have taken the commission very seriously indeed, not pinched on costs and allowed the opera to be carefully prepared and lavishly presented." See: W2a

B376.Tracey, Edmund. "Richard Rodney Bennett talks." Sadler's Wells Magazine, Autumn 1967, pp.3-5.

A conversation with the composer mainly about his operas.

B377.Vaughan, David. "Frederick Ashton and his ballets." Adam & Charles Black, London, 1977, 522 pp.

Detailed information about all of Ashton's ballets and in particular Jazz Calendar (pp.352-6). See: W66b

B378.W.,E.M. "Cheltenham: the dangers of fragmentation." Musical Opinion, 86 (August 1963), p.654.

"Richard Rodney Bennett's Nocturnes... was much more closely integrated and controlled than any new work so far.
The three pieces are scored for wind quintet, harp and string orchestra, and have a closely-woven texture of changing sonorities, some of them of extreme beauty, which form an ever-changing accompaniment to his strong melodic line." See: W30b

B379.Walsh, Stephen. "Behind Tippett's Mask." Observer (Review), 29 July 1984, p.17.

"A new work of very much more contained mastery (was) Richard Rodney Bennett's Five Sonnets of Louise Labe. Bennett captures (the) qualities in music that is darker, and certainly more physical, than we are used to from him." See:W149a

B380.Walsh, Stephen. "Music last week." The Listener, 127 (20 April 1967), pp.537-8.

A review of Epithalamion from the 1967 Leeds Festival. "Bennett, one can say without disparagement, has become the people's serialist, and an expert at clothing his technical accomplishment in terms that go straight to the most unprepared heart." See: W121a

B381.Walsh, Stephen. "New Music." The Musical Times, 113
     (April 1973), pp.381-2.

          "Bennett's concerto, written for Holliger, uses...
          the whole garment of technical resources which have
          made the Swiss oboist's playing the eight wonder of
          the world...." See: W16b

B382.Walsh, Stephen. "Richard Rodney Bennett's Symphony."
     Tempo no.76 (Spring 1966), pp.21-22.

          A review of the First Symphony, "...his first
          important piece of absolute music for more than
          five years...." See:W37a

B383.Warrack, John. "Phantoms of the Opera." The Sunday
     Telegraph, 28 February 1965, p.11.

          A review of The Mines of Sulphur which "... remains
          a real achievement and not the least encouraging
          aspect is the confidence with which it was
          mounted." See: W2a

B384.Warrack, John. "Twentieth Century Songs." Gramophone,
     51 (March 1974), p.1734.

          A review of the Unicorn recording RHS 316 which
          includes The Fly and Clock-a-Clay. See:D21

B385.Webb,S. "Church Music from Vista." Gramophone, 54
     (March 1977), p.1444.

          A review of the Vista recording VPS 1034 which
          includes Alba.
          "Bennett is the master of any form to which he
          turns his exceptional gifts and Alba exploits a
          wide range of pitch and dynamics." See:D1

B386.Webb,S. "Heare us, O heare us." Gramophone 55
     (November 1977), p.880.

          A review of the Abbey recording LPB 783 which
          includes Heare us, O heare us, one of the Verses.
          See: D18.

B387.Webber, N. "Farnham." Music and Musicians, 19 (August
     1971), p.67.

          "The penultimate work in the concert... was...
          Bennett's Party Piece for piano orchestra, which
          jogged along amiably enough." See: W185a

B388.Webster, E. "Cheltenham Festival." Music and Musicians
     International, 36 (December 1987), pp.32-3.

          "... Bennett produced two new works... After
          Ariadne... turned out to be a sumptuous, richly
          lyrical piece.... Ophelia... is instantly
          attractive and evocative...." See: W41a,W161a

B389.Webster, E. "Three Choirs Festival." Music & Musicians
     International, 36 (November 1987), p.38.

        "The 1987 Elgar Commission was Richard Rodney
        Bennett's Symphony No.3....
        The result is a work of profound and un-showy
        reflection, lyrical, inturned, serene and ecstatic,
        and filled with moments of curious repose."
        See:W39a

B390.Webster, E.M. "Cheltenham Festival." Musical Opinion,
     90 (September 1967), p.681.

        A paragraph about the Stravinsky Tempo Concert.
        "All these little works had been aired in... Tempo,
        but none of them had been played.
        Richard Rodney Bennett's Canon for Violin, Viola
        and Cello was absurdly elegant string writing...."
        See: 47a

B391.Weissmann, J.S. "Civic Junketings." Musical Events, 17
     (September 1962), p.14.

        "...Bennett's London Pastoral was commissioned by
        the Lord Mayor.... Intriguing, noble, adventurous
        in its organisation of sound but more careful in
        the organisation of its thematic ideas, the work is
        a valuable addition to the genre which Britten and
        Tippett had raised to eminence...." See:W127a

B392.White, M.J. "Atherton/London Sinfonietta." The Guardian,
     29 May 1986, p.10.

        A review of one of Bennett's 50th birthday concerts
        in which the first performance of Dream Dancing was
        given "... a deliciously atmospheric treatment of
        instrumental groupings chosen to reflect the sound
        pictures Debussy might have given us if he had
        lived to complete his planned sonata series." See:
        W57a

B393.Whithall, A. "Spells/Aubade" Gramophone, 57 (January
     1980), p.1182.
        A review of the Argo recording ZRG 907 which is
        devoted to Spells and Aubade. See:D3,D34

B394.Widdicombe, Gillian. "Coventry." The Musical Times, 110
     (May 1969), p.513.

        "...All the King's Men... is a delightfully
        engaging piece. A first rate text by Beverley
        Cross.... There are also some racy tunes, and a
        plaintive ending where the drummer-boy, wise to his
        Wozzeck perhaps, sadly decides that battle is a
        bore and wanders away." See:W175a

B395.Williams, Peter. "Jazz Calendar." Dance and Dancers, 19
     (February 1968), pp.12-14.

A detailed examination of <u>Jazz Calendar</u>, movement
by movement.
"...Richard Rodney Bennett's suite... suits (it)
most admirably...." <u>See</u>:W66b

B396.Wiltshire, Christopher. "Richard Rodney Bennett - a
study, with particular reference to his work in the
fields of jazz, film and light music." Master of
Music Degree (partial fulfilment), University of
Sheffield, September 1983, 2 volumes.

A detailed survey of Bennett's achievements in
these particular fields, with music examples.

Appendix I:
Alphabetical List of
Main Compositions

Numbers following each title, e.g. W133, refer to the "Works and Performances" section of this volume.

Concerto for guitar and chamber ensemble, W12
Concerto for harpsichord and orchestra, W13
Concerto for horn and orchestra, W14
Concerto for marimba and chamber orchestra, W15
Concerto for oboe and string orchestra, W16
Concerto for Orchestra, W17
Concerto for piano and orchestra, W18
Concerto No.2 for piano and orchestra, W19
Concerto for alto saxophone and string orchestra, W20
Concerto for 10 brass players, W270
Concerto for viola and chamber orchestra, W21
Concerto for violin and orchestra, W22
Concerto for Wind Quintet, W53
Conversations for two flutes, W178
Crazy Jane, W146
Crosstalk, W179
Curtmantle, W245
Cycle of pieces for piano: 1-1X, W54
Cycle II for Paul Jacobs: for piano, W55

The Devil never sleeps, W199
The Devil's Disciple, W200
The Diary of Nijinsky, W246
Dismissal leading to lustfulness, W247
Diversions for piano, W180
Duo Concertante, W56
Dream Dancing, W57
Dream-songs, W147

The Ebony Tower, W248
The Engineers, W201
The Entertainers, W249
Epithalamion, W121
Equus, W202
European Tapestry, W203
Eustace and Hilda, W250

A Face in the Night, W204
Fanfare for brass quintet, W58
Fantasy for piano, W59
Far from the madding crowd, W205
Farewell to Arms, W122
Farnham Festival Overture, W181
Figures in a Landscape, W206
First thing about me, W148
Five Carols, W123
Five Pieces for Orchestra, W23
Five Sonnets of Louise Labe, W149
Five Studies for piano, W60
The Flowers of the Forest, W271
Four Devotions, W124
Four Improvisations for solo violin, W61
Four-Piece Suite, W62
Freda's Fandango, W24
Funny Thing, W150

A Garland for Marjory Fleming, W151

Hamlet at Elsinore, W251

Soliloquy, W165
Sonata after Syrinx, W90
Sonata for cello, W91
Sonata for guitar, W92
Sonata for horn and piano, W93
Sonata for oboe and piano, W94
Sonata for piano, W95
Sonata for soprano saxophone and piano, W96
Sonata for viola, W274
Sonata No.1 for violin, W97
Sonata No.2 for violin, W98
Sonata for violin and piano, W99
Sonata for wind quintet and piano, W100
Sonatina for solo clarinet, W101
Sonatina for solo flute, W102
Song of the clouds, W233
Sonnet Sequence, W166
Sonnets to Orpheus, W33
The Sorrows of Mary, W138
Sounds and Sweet Aires, W103
Spells, W139
Stanzas for flute, W104
Stanzas for orchestra, W34
Stanzas for organ, W105
Stephen D, W259
Strange Interlude, W260
Studies for five instruments and percussion, W106
Study for trumpet and piano, W107
Suite for Skip and Sadie, W108
Suite for small orchestra, W35
Suite Francaise for small orchestra, W36
Summer Music, W187
Survival, W261
Symphony No.1, W37
Symphony No.2, W38
Symphony No.3, W39

Talking Pictures, W262
Tango after Syrinx, W109
Tea jingles, W263
Telegram for piano, W110
Tender is the Night, W264
Tenebrae, W167
Theme and Variations for violin and viola, W111
They took us to the sea, W234
this is the garden, W168
This World's Joie, W169
Three Elegies, W140
Three Madrigals, W141
Three Romantic Pieces for piano, W112
Three Songs for solo tenor, W170
The Tillaquils, W142
Time's Whiter Series, W171
Timon of Athens, W265
Tom O'Bedlam's Song, W172
The Tourelle Skull, W266
Travel Notes, Book 1, W113
Travel Notes, Book 2, W114
Trio for flute, oboe and clarinet, W115

Appendix II:
Chronological List of
Main Compositions

Numbers following each title, e.g. W137, refer to the "Works and Performances" section of this volume.

1951   Quartet No.1 for strings, W75

1952   Put away the flutes, W135
        Theme and Variations for violin and viola, W111

1953   Quartet No.2 for stings, W76
        Quartet No.3 for strings, W77
        Variations for oboe, W117

1954   Nocturnall upon St. Lucie's Day, W130
        Sonata for piano, W95
        Sonatina for flute, W102

1955   Four improvisations for violin, W61
        Parallels for trumpet and piano, W273
        Sonata for cello, W91
        Sonata for viola, W274
        Sonata No.1 for violin, W97
        Three Songs for tenor, W170
        The Tillaquils, W142

1955-56 Concerto for horn and orchestra, W14

1956   A Face in the Night, W204
        Five Pieces for Orchestra, W23
        Interpol, W210
        Ricercar, W136
        Song of the clouds, W233
        The World Assured, W237

1956-57 Cycle of pieces for piano:1-1X, W54

1957   Quintet for flute, oboe, clarinet, horn and
        bassoon, W80
        The Safecracker, W230
        Studies for five instruments and percussion, W106

Study for trumpet and piano, W107

1957-58   Cycle II for Paul Jacobs: for piano, W55
           Music for two pianos: I-IV, W73

1958   The Angry Hills, W192
           The Devil's Disciple, W200
           Indiscreet, W209
           The Man Inside, W212

1959   Blind Date, W195
           Farewell to Arms, W122
           The Man who could cheat death, W213
           Music for an Occasion, W28
           Stanzas for flute, W104
           Stanzas for orchestra, W34

1959-60   The Approaches of Sleep, W120

1960   Calendar for Chamber Ensemble, W46
           Journal for Orchestra, W26
           Lament for tenor and guitar, W154
           Out of Harmony, W222
           A Question of Springing, W227
           Stanzas for organ, W105
           This World's Joie, W169
           Winter Music, W118

1960s   Tea jingles, W263

1960-61   The Ledge, W1

1961   Childe Rolande to the Dark Tower came, W174
           The Devil never sleeps, W199
           The Mark, W214
           Only Two can Play, W221
           The Purple Stream, W225
           Sonata for oboe and piano, W94
           Suite Francaise for small orchestra, W36
           They took us to the sea, W234
           Three Madrigals, W141
           Tom O'Bedlam's Song, W172
           Week of Birthdays, W190

1961-62   Quintet for clarinet, string trio and piano, W79

1962   African Awakening, W191
           Circus Drawings, W198
           Curtmantle, W245
           Fanfare for brass quintet, W58
           Fantasy for piano, W59
           Judith, W253
           London Pastoral, W127
           The Long Distance Piano Player, W255
           Nowell, Nowell Tidings True, W133
           The Quest for Perfection, W226
           Seven days a week, W186
           Three elegies, W140

The Wrong Arm of the law, W238

1962-63   Nocturnes for chamber orchestra, W30

1962/64   Five studies for piano, W60

1962-64   A Jazz Calendar, W66

1963   Billy Liar, W194
          Hamlet at Elsinore, W251
          Heavens Above, W207
          The Midnight Thief, W183
          The Mines of Sulphur, W2
          Oxford Nursery Song Book: arrangements, W184
          Rondo: Reflections on a theme of Benjamin Britten,
            W84
          Stephen D, W259
          The Tourelle Skull, W266
          Two Lullabies, W144

1964   Aubade for orchestra, W9
          The Aztecs, W269
          Conversations for two flutes, W178
          Diversions for piano, W180
          Farnham Festival Overture, W181
          Malatesta, W256
          One way pendulum, W220
          Quartet No.4 for strings, W78
          Sonata No.2 for violin, W98
          The Sorrows of Mary, W138
          Trio for three violins or two violins and viola,
            W116
          Verses, W145

1964-65   Trio for flute, oboe and clarinet, W115

1965   The Aviary, W176
          The Diary of Nijinsky, W246
          The Engineers, W201
          European Tapestry, W203
          Hereward the Wake, W252
          The Insect World, W182
          The Nanny, W217
          One Evening, W160
          The R-and-B Man, W228
          Suite for small orchestra, W35
          Symphony No.1, W37
          Timon of Athens, W265

1966   Crosstalk, W179
          Epithalamion, W121
          Iphigenia in Taurus, W272
          The Order, W257
          A Penny for a Song, W3
          A Penny for your thoughts, W223
          The Witches, W236

1966-67   Soliloquy, W165

1967   Billion dollar brain, W193
            A Canon for Stravinsky, W47
            Dismissal leading to lustfulness, W247
            Far from the madding crowd, W205
            Five carols, W123
            The Music that her echo is, W158
            Symphony No.2, W38

1967-68   Quintet for flute, oboe, clarinet, horn and
            bassoon, W8

1968   All the King's Men, W175
            Capriccio, W48
            Concerto for piano and orchestra, W18
            Crazy Jane, W146
            Impromptus for guitar, W65
            Secret Ceremony, W231
            Two Carols, W143

1968-69   Victory, W4

1969   A Garland for Marjory Fleming, W151
            Impromptu for solo flute, W63
            Jazz Pastoral, W153
            Twenty-four hours, W267

1969-70   Concerto for oboe and string orchestra, W16

1970   The Buttercup Chain, W197
            Concerto for guitar and chamber ensemble, W12
            Figures in a Landscape, W206
            Intrada for orchestra, W25
            Partypiece, W185

1970s   First thing about me, W148
            Funny Thing, W150
            Our own kind of dancing, W162
            She reminds me of you, W164

1970-71   Anagram, W45
            Madrigals, W69

1971   The Bermudas, W177
            Four devotions, W124
            The House of Sleepe, W125
            Nicholas and Alexandra, W218
            Tenebrae, W167

1972   Commedia I, W49
            Commedia II, W50
            Lady Caroline Lamb, W211
            Nightpiece, W159
            Quietly with bright eyes, W163
            Sonnet Sequence, W166

1973   Alba, W44
            Commedia III, W51
            Commedia IV, W52
            Concerto for Orchestra, W17

Concerto for viola and chamber orchestra, W21
Of Jewels and Gold, W219
Scena I for piano, W85
Scena II for cello, W86
Voices, W235

1974   Four-piece suite, W62
            Murder on the Orient Express, W215
            Time's Whiter Series, W171

1974-75   Quartet for oboe and string trio, W74
            Spells, W139

1975   Concerto for violin and orchestra, W22
            Permission to Kill, W224
            Travel Notes, Book 1, W113

1975-76   Zodiac, W40

1976   Abide with me, W240
            Concerto No.2 for piano and chamber orchestra, W19
            The little ghost who died for love, W156
            Serenade, W31
            Sherlock Holmes in New York, W232
            Survival, W261
            Telegram, W110
            Travel Notes, Book 2, W114

1976-77   Actaeon, W7

1977   The Christians, W244
            Equus, W202
            Eustace and Hilda, W250
            L'Imprecateur, W208
            Kandinsky Variations, W67
            Music for Strings, W29
            Scena III for clarinet, W87

1978   The Brink's Job, W196
            Concerto for double -bass and chamber orchestra,
              W11
            Let's go and live in the country, W155
            Sonata for horn and piano, W93
            Sonata for violin and piano, W99

1978-79   Sonnets to Orpheus, W33

1979   Arena: La Dame aux Gladiolas, W241
            Nonsense, W131
            Up Bow, Down Bow, Book 1, W188
            Up Bow, Down Bow, Book 2, W189
            Yanks, W239

1979-80   Isadora, W5

1980   Concerto for harpsichord and orchestra, W13
            Metamorphoses, W71
            Puer Nobis, W134

1980s   I never went away, W152

1981   Impromptu on the name of Haydn, W64
          Letters to Lindbergh, W126
          Music for String Quartet, W72
          Noctuary, W6
          Six tunes for the instruction of singing-birds, W89
          Sonatina for solo clarinet, W101
          Vocalese, W173

1982   After Syrinx I, W42
          Anniversaries, W8
          Freda's Fandango, W24
          Poor little rich girl, W258
          Return of the soldier, W229
          Summer music, W187

1982-84   Lovesongs, W157

1983   Concerto for wind quintet, W53
          Memento, W70
          Seachange, W137
          Sonata for guitar, W92

1984   After Syrinx II, W43
          The Ebony Tower, W248
          Five Sonnets of Louise Labé, W149
          Knockback, W254
          Lullay mine liking, W129
          Moving into Aquarius, W27
          Serenade No.2 for ondes martenot and piano, W88
          Sinfonietta, W32
          this is the garden, W168

1985   Duo concertante, W56
          Murder with mirrors, W216
          Reflections on a theme of William Walton, W82
          Romances for horn and piano, W83
          Sonata after Syrinx, W90
          Sounds and Sweet Aires, W103
          Tango after Syrinx, W109
          Tender is the night, W264

1985-86   Dream Dancing, W57

1986   After Ariadne, W41
          And death shall have no dominion, W119
          The Charmer, W243
          Dream-songs, W147
          The Entertainers, W249
          Lamento d'Arianna, W68
          Lullaby Baby, W128
          Morning Music, W268
          Nowell, W132
          Sonata for soprano saxophone and piano, W96
          Suite for Skip and Sadie, W108

1986-87   Sonata for Wind Quintet and Piano, W100

1987   The Attic: The Hiding of Anne Frank, W242
            Concerto for clarinet and string orchestra, W10
            Ophelia, W161
            Strange Interlude, W260
            Symphony No.3, W39
            Talking Pictures, W262

1987-88   Concerto for marimba and chamber orchestra, W15

1988   Concerto for alto saxophone and string orchestra,
              W20
            Three Romantic Pieces for solo piano, W112

1988-89   Concerto for 10 brass players, W270

1989   The Flowers of the Forest, W271

Index

Page number references refer to pages in the "Bibliography";
other entries refer to individual items in the "Works and
Performances" list (W), the "Discography" (D) and the
"Bibliography" (B).
Since the Bibliography is alphabetical by author, index
entries for these items have not been included under the
author's name (although, of course, other references to those
authors are indexed).

Abrams, Sasha, W151, W151a
Academy of St. Martin-in-the-Fields, W29, W29a, W71, W71a,
    W71b
Adams, Peter, W254
Adams, Phyllis, W5
Addison, John, W160
Adeney, Richard, W115, W115a
Aeberli, Hans, B5
Aldeburgh Festival, p.5; W107; B239
Aldrich, Robert, W192
Alexander, Patrick, W257
Alexander, Peter, W151, W151a
Alexander, Sasha, W147
Allbutt, Graham, W175a
Alldis, John, W123b, W138a
Allegri String Quartet, W78a
Allen, Alexander, W101a
Altman, Elizabeth, W85a
Amis, Kingsley, W221
Andrewes, John, D4, D21
Andrews, David, W177a
Anglia TV, W261
Archambault, Jonnie, W266
Arlen, Harold, p.5; W96; D48, D50
Armstrong, John, W227, W233
Armstrong, John Gates, W201
Armstrong, Moira, W240
Arnold, Malcolm, W25, W195
Aronowitz, Cecil, W74a
Arts Council of Great Britain, W27, W29, W32, W33, W44, W49,
    W51, W70, W125, W268
Ashby, Arnold, W76a, W77a

About the Compiler

STEWART R. CRAGGS is Reader Services Librarian at the Polytechnic Library in Sunderland, U.K. He is the author of *Arthur Bliss: A Bio-Bibliography, William Alwyn: A Catalogue of His Music,* and *Sir William Walton: A Thematic Catalogue.* He has also published articles in *Perspectives in Music* and *Musical Times.*